Corporate Manslaughter and Corporate Homicide

Corporate Manslaughter and Corporate Homicide

Scope for a New Legislation In India

Shivam Goel

PARTRIDGE

ISBN: Softcover 978-1-4828-4683-6
eBook 978-1-4828-4682-9

Print information available on the last page.

To order additional copies of this book, contact
Partridge India
000 800 10062 62
orders.india@partridgepublishing.com

www.partridgepublishing.com/india

Contents

Acknowledgement

> "Finite bodies have an end, but that which possesses and uses the body is infinite, illimitable, eternal and indestructible. Therefore fight, O Bharata."
>
> - Chapter 2, Verse 18, *Srimad Bhagavad Gita.*

Aristotelians believe, "*law is a reason free from passion*", while Realists believe, "*law is a good reason of a bad man*". Based on these, to best of my knowledge and belief, there are two schools of thoughts, "*law according to justice*" and "*justice in accordance with law*". This piece of work is a dedication to the former school of thought, for it believes that, every saint has a past and every sinner has a future, and law is but the means, justice is the end.

I offer my highest regards to Dr. Sandeepa Bhat B., without whose guidance and mentorship, not even an iota of this work would have met its completion. Sir, working under you has been a great learning experience, and I shall cherish the same throughout my life.

I offer my deepest gratitude to Dr. P. Ishwara Bhat (Vice- Chancellor, WBNUJS), for keeping me inspired and motivated throughout my term at WBNUJS.

I am grateful to my mom, dad and sister; Dad, you are an epitome of excellence; Mom, you are my conscience; Sister, you have inspired me beyond measures.

Chapter 1

Introduction

1.1. Introduction:

'Company' is an artificial legal person; a juristic person- having perpetual succession and common seal; lexically speaking, it is an association of persons as distinguished from an association of individuals. A company can own property in its name and can dispose of the same. The liabilities of the company are of its own and not of its directors, members or shareholders. Speaking jurisprudentially, though, 'company' is not a "living individual" having flesh and blood; but never the less, it works through individuals having 'head and brain'. Behind the corporate veil lies an army of individuals managing the affairs of the company; not only in regards to how a company should function that is, from what sources capital is to be generated; in what form it is to be raised (debt capital as distinguished from equity capital); who all are the stakeholders in the business carried on by the company; and how can wealth of all the shareholders be maximised, insuring that the welfare of all stakeholders is kept in sight; what business a company should cater to; how to expand the business, how to tap the potential market, what products and business diversifications- need to be brought in; who are the potential business competitors of the company and how strategically they need to be tackled; but also chalking out policies of all sorts- capital structure policies; market related policies; competition related policies and policies relating to the nuances of consumerism.

During the course of its operation (in the dynamic business environment), a company incurs liabilities and so also losses; principally and fundamentally, company in capacity of an 'artificial legal person' is responsible for it 'absolutely'; but when the array of liabilities to tortuous liabilities and claims is furthered, we enter a field of legal exclamations, governed by a host of doctrines such as: vicarious liability, strict liability and absolute liability. We tend to come across some principles of ever-growing jurisprudence that is, the identification principle and the principle of determining the "mind and will" of the company (also known as the alter ego approach). Now from this standpoint the Researcher/ author saw the growth of a new field of jurisprudence- dealing in with the comprehensive crimes of corporate manslaughter and corporate homicide (as part and parcel of the theory of corporate criminal liability).

For a corporation to be held criminally liable, the employee committing the crime must act within the scope of his employment and must have actual or apparent authority to engage in the act (particular) in question. Actual authority occurs when a corporation knowingly gives authority to an employee and the apparent authority occurs if a third party, like a customer, reasonably believes that the agent has the authority to perform the act in question. Courts have ruled that actual authority may occur even when the illegal behaviour is not condoned by the corporation but is nonetheless within the scope of the employee's authority.

Corporate manslaughter and corporate homicide refer to the decisions undertaken by a company that went wrong either in regards to their execution (owing to negligence) or due to existence of some inherent fault or loophole in the decision making and its subsequent execution, resulting in or causing death of a person or persons. A company exists only in the contemplation of law and thus cannot be put behind bars in lieu of punishment hence, what can be imposed on to the company is not imprisonment but fine only.

In furtherance of his research, the researcher has tried to explore- jurisprudential development from *the Bhopal gas tragedy* to *the Uphaar Cinema Tragedy* and thereafter the decisions so rendered in the case of the *Standard Chartered Bank* and *Iridium- Motorola*. The researcher firmly believes that, India should enact a statute in the nature of the Corporate Manslaughter and Corporate Homicide Act of 2007[1], as is holding ground in the U.K. Moreover the researcher has looked into the fundamentals of law, punishing corporations for

1 In nutshell: Under the Corporate Manslaughter and Corporate Homicide Act 2007 an offence will be committed where failings by an organisation's senior management are a substantial element in any gross breach of the duty of care owed to the organisation's

the crime of manslaughter and homicide, as such prevailing in the common-law countries of **U.S.**, **U.K.**, **New Zealand**, **Canada** and **Australia** and thereafter has compared the standards prevailing in these countries with the standards prevalent in India. In regards to the concept of corporate liability, the Researcher has done an explorative study, analysing the principles of *strict liability*, *absolute liability* and the *deep-pocket theory*. The Researcher has reviewed logically, the applicability of the principles of *vicarious liability* (applicable in U.K.), *respondeat superior* (applicable in U.S.), *identification doctrine* (applicable in New Zealand), *aggregation doctrine* (applicable in U.S.), *reactive- corporate fault* (given by Fisse and Braithwaite of the Cambridge University), *management failure model* (applicable in U.K.) and *corporate mens-rea* (applicable in Australia), along with the innovative test of the recent time- the *senior management test-* specifically provided for in Section 4(c) (i) & (ii) of the Corporate Manslaughter and Corporate Homicide Act of 2007. "Senior Management", in relation to an organisation, means the persons who play significant role in - (i) - The making of decisions about how the whole or substantial part of the organisation's activities are to be managed or organised, or (ii) - The actual managing or organising of the whole or substantial part of those activities.

1.2. Statement of Problems:

Eighteenth- century courts and legal thinkers approached corporate liability with an obsessive focus on theories of corporate personality; a more pragmatic approach was not developed until the twentieth century. In the common law jurisdiction, historically speaking, companies have been open to manslaughter proceedings since 1965. Inspiration has been taken time and again from the following words of an English jurist- "Companies have a soul to damn, but no body to kick."

Traditionally, in the cases of corporate killings- the prosecution had to prove two things: first, that a single individual in the company was guilty of gross negligence manslaughter; second, that this individual was the 'controlling mind'

employees or members of the public, which results in death. The maximum penalty is an unlimited fine and the court can additionally make a publicity order requiring the organisation to publish details of its conviction and fine.

of the company. If there was not enough evidence to convict an individual, there could be no prosecution of the company. But now this position is fast a change, laws relating to conviction of corporations have now been taken to a different level altogether.

Corporate criminal liability and corporate civil liability share two important characteristics. Both impose liability on the corporation and further the goal of deterring corporate misconduct. The researcher has made note of four characteristics that differentiate- corporate criminal liability from corporate civil liability, these are, the corporate criminal liability has stronger procedural protections; more powerful enforcement devices; more severe and arguably, unique sanctions (such as stigma); and a greater message-sending role than corporate civil liability which usually is in the nature of: cash fines, loss of license and equity fines.[2]

So far as corporate criminal liability is concerned the focus has always been on the following theories, the *identification principle*, *aggregation principle*, *management-failure model*, *reactive corporate fault* and the *principle of corporate mens rea* (*single actor mens rea* and *collective mens rea standard*).

The researcher has placed necessary focus on the *identification principle*, for it is the most recognised corporate criminal liability standard in New Zealand, U.K. and Canada. To reflect upon it, in detail, the researcher discusses that, the identification principle was a major obstacle to the securing of a conviction under the common law offence of gross negligence manslaughter, particularly with a company of any size or with any complexity in its management structure. It requires there to be an individual holding a sufficiently senior position in the company, who could be identified with the company as its *directing mind and will* and who individually fulfils the elements of the gross negligence offence, fatality following a gross breach of duty of care which posed the risk of death. The only successful prosecutions against corporate entities for gross negligence were in relation to small companies, where there was more likely, a single person directly and immediately responsible for the death and who was senior enough to be regarded as the *directing mind and will* of a company.

---

2 See: V.S. Khanna, *Corporate Criminal Liability: What Purpose Does It Serve?;* The Harvard Law Review, May 1996, Volume 109, Number 7, Pg. 1492

It is necessary to keep in mind the definition of manslaughter that is, someone causing the unintentional death of another person(s). The controversy surrounding 'Corporate Manslaughter' laws in the U.K. is that, if a corporation is found guilty, no one is actually sent to jail, instead the company is fined. There is no limit on the fine levied and company (accused) is ordered to change its policies and practices to avoid further instances. In U.K. so far as the offence of corporate manslaughter is concerned, it is of a nascent creation- historically speaking, hundreds of people have died in disasters like the **Kings Cross fire of 1987**, the **Piper Alpha oil rig fire of 1988**, the **sinking of the 'Marchioness' in 1989** and various train crashes like the **Clapham Rail Disaster**. There were no prosecutions for manslaughter in any of these incidents, although there were (unsuccessful) prosecutions in the '**Herald of Free Enterprise**' disaster and the '**Southall Rail Crash of 1997**'.[3] The legislative intent behind the Corporate Manslaughter and Corporate Homicide Act of 2007, fails to take into account the fact that deaths are just the tip of the iceberg, of dangerous practices leading to thousands of serious injuries each year. Legislation targeting these injuries, rather than deaths would have been far more useful. All these factors lead commentators to suggest that the Act will have far more 'symbolic' than 'instrumental' value.[4]However what cannot be ignored is the fact that- U.K. has set a precedent, internationally, by enacting a legislation that takes account for corporate killings and imposes sanctions for the same.

The Researcher, advancing his area of research to the U.S. jurisdiction found that the prevalent standard of corporate criminal liability in U.S. is the *principle of respondeat superior*. In regards to this, the researcher has taken due note of the fact that- under this doctrine, three requirements must be fulfilled for the purpose of imposition of liability on a corporation. First, a corporate agent must have committed an illegal act (*actus reus*) with the requisite state of mind (*mens rea*); Second, the agent must have acted within the scope of his employment; Third, the agent must have intended to benefit the corporation.

3 See: Sanders, Young & Burton, *Criminal Justice,* Oxford University Press, Fourth Edition, Chapter 7.5.2- Corporate Manslaughter, p.416

4 See: Gobert, *The Corporate Manslaughter And Corporate Homicide Act 2007,* (2008) 71 MLR 413; Also see: Ormerod and Taylor, *The Corporate Manslaughter and Corporate Homicide Act 2007,* (2008) Crim. LR 589, and Celia Wells, *Corporate Manslaughter: Why Does Reform Matter?,* (2006) 122 South African LJ 646.

The Researcher has taken note of the fact that corporate manslaughter is more in the nature of gross negligence manslaughter by companies, which in turn requires establishment of- criminal intent; reasonable conduct; negligence and, individual and corporate liability.

The premise of law in regards to corporate killings is weak in India, however, many researchers counter-argue by saying that the doctrine of absolute liability took birth in India. In the garb the Bhopal Gas Tragedy, the researcher puts forth the following argument:

Although the development of laws post the Bhopal Gas Tragedy is impressive but is not substantial, as the Acts enacted post the Bhopal Gas Tragedy and the Oleum Gas Leakage Case, that is the Environment Protection Act of 1986 and the Public Liability Insurance Act of 1991, have failed at all pedestals to give a comprehensive definition of the term "hazardous substances" and the absolute liability principle when read with the deep-pocket theory, makes the absolute liability principle a weak principle. Bhopal Gas Tragedy is not just a story of corporate gross negligence but is also a saga of failed virtues, corporate killings and corrupt corporate-political nexus. Research and analysis undertaken post the incident show that many factors that led to the tragedy could have been avoided. The location of a poisonous pesticide factory too proximate to the city, ill maintained tools and equipments, cutting corners on safety checks, ignoring previous warnings rendered qua plant safety, labour issues; all these factors have been identified by studies, post the incident. There are two guilty parties upon whom the blame can be impinged, they are- the company (Union Carbide) that owned the plant and the various government (administrative and quasi-administrative) authorities that gave approvals for the plant to run. More disturbing was the post-incident handling of the affairs by the Government of India. It is reported that the Government of India actually (willingly and consciously) assisted Warren Anderson (CEO of Union Carbide India Limited) in leaving the country. The seven other accused were punished after 25 years, getting a maximum of two years sentence, and as expected, they were let out on bail after furnishing a bail bond of merely Rs. 25,000 each.

The attitude India has adopted post the Bhopal Gas Tragedy is more shocking than sorry. On one hand, nearly all the developed and developing countries in the world are working towards enacting novel legislative strategies to bring the corporate criminals to book; to tear apart the corporate veil that is keeping the identity of the guilty in anonymity (so that real perpetrators can be punished for their criminal deeds in their individual capacity); India still, more often than less, relies upon the traditional theories of *vicarious liability*, *respondeat superior* and the theory of *lifting up of the corporate veil*, with few added novelties of recent times, *principles of absolute liability* and *deep pocket theory.*

It is motivating to see, the rising consciousness world over in regards to *coinciding* the corporate crimes in the nature of corporate killings with 'individuals' as such and not with the 'legal personality of the company'. New principles are fast emerging on the domain of corporate criminal liability and are rendering the lexical-terminology of corporate manslaughter and corporate homicide- new and expansive meaning. These principles are- *single actor mens rea*, *collective mens rea standard*, *aggregation principle*, *management failure model* and *senior management test.*

As already stated, U.K. has equipped itself with the Corporate Manslaughter and Corporate Homicide Act, 2007[5], and U.S. and Australia are fast working in this direction. New Zealand too has drafted in 2013, a statute that punishes 'corporate killings'; however the same is pending for official notification. In spate of these circumstances if we search for laws in India that would stand as guard against corporate killings, it will be disheartening to find that the phenomena of corporate criminal liability itself is very nascent in India.

Post the Bhopal Gas tragedy, India has equipped itself with the *absolute liability principle*, the *deep pocket theory*, the Environment Protection Act of 1986, the Public Liability Insurance Act of 1991 and the Protection of Human Rights Act of 1993; these measures over the period of time have proved not much effective. What is surprising to note is the new Act, the Companies Act of

5 The Government at the time of enacting the legislation stated its belief that- the creation of a new offence of corporate killing would give useful emphasis to the seriousness of health and safety offences and would give force to the need to consider health and safety as a management issue. See: David Ormerod, *Smith and Hogan's Criminal Law*, Oxford University Press, 13th Edition- 2011, Chapter 15- Manslaughter, p. 563

2013, makes no mention of the terms- 'corporate manslaughter' or 'corporate homicide', not even in-directly.

The Researcher to show how weak the laws in India are- has made a comparative analysis between the Bhopal Gas disaster and the 2010- Gulf of Mexico- oil spill, which took place nearly 65 kilometres away from the U.S. shoreline. To state briefly- the spill started in the April of 2010, due to an explosion on board deepwater horizon, an offshore drilling rig leased by BP (world's leading oil exploration company). About 11 people died in the explosion and not less than 17 were injured. The spill also caused significant damage to marine life and ecology.

The Government of U.S. left no stone unturned to bring BP to books, despite the fact that the consciousness in regards to corporate killings is still on a rise and has not fully mushroomed in the U.S. In a short span (post the incident), Courts in the U.S. were flooded with lawsuits, challenging the deploring acts of BP. Barack Obama (President, U.S.) went on record making several heated statements grilling BP for its gross negligence and promising to do 'what it takes' to bring BP to books. Such was the fear of the resolve of the Government of U.S., to teach the accused-company a lesson that the shares of the company doomed, touching an all time low with BP loosing close to $ 105 billion since the spill actually happened. BP was pressurised to create a $ 20 billion trust to compensate claims and was forced to pay about $ 8 billion as damages. (Ironically, the accused in Bhopal were let out on bail for a fraction of amount, that is, Rs. 25,000). BP was forced to cut its dividend to a meagre sum of money, in an attempt to plug the leak.

In India, awakening is still to happen. Equipping the nation with necessary laws is one end of the stream, to see that the laws enacted are successfully implemented is the other end of the stream. In India, necessary laws are *still* to be enacted, implementation is secondary. Bhopal Gas Tragedy is now three decades old but wounds are still fresh and the problem is still there.

Newspapers have been reporting since long about the kids in several villages of Punjab, developing neurological problems and deformities due to injection of uranium in the lakes and rivers by the plants and factories operating nearby these villages. Though, the Supreme Court of India has given due recognition to the five timeless principles of law relating to environment protection: the polluter pays principle; precautionary principle; principle of sustainable development; inter-generational and intra-generational equity principle; and the doctrine of public trust, but these are of no avail. In *M.C. Mehta* v. *Kamal Nath and Others*[6], Justice Kuldeep, speaking for majority said that international customary law which is not in conflict with the domestic law of the country can be regarded as the municipal law of the country, thus the Supreme Court through this judgement gave recognition to the international environment law principles, emphasising their applicability in India. Thus, the situation in India seems very peculiar to the Researcher, as most of the times in India we don't have adequate laws and if so we have adequate laws then their implementation is very cynical.

More-over, the Civil Liability for Nuclear Damage Act of 2010 seems to be nothing but a paper-tiger, as far as the aspects of retribution and deterrence are concerned. The Act caps the liability of nuclear plant operators for nuclear accidents to 1500 crore rupees that is roughly 325 million dollars. This amount is lower than the 470-million-dollar compensation awarded in the *Bhopal* case, which in itself was grossly inadequate.

Over the course of research, the belief of the researcher became more firm as to the premise that, the risk of liability should be substantial, only then the corporations will deter from bad behaviour. When a corporation does not have sufficient net assets to pay the optimal cash fine, other penalties, such as **loss of license**, **probation**, and **debarment**, should supplement the fine. The preferable supplemental sanction should depend on the operations and the history of the corporation, the desired severity of the penalty, and the nature of the firm's misconduct- for example, debarring the corporation from access to government tenders and contracts would be most effective when the firm's primary customer or supplier is the government. When the government is not the primary supplier or customer of the corporation, and still there is desire for a huge penalty, loss of license can be used as a measure to prevent the corporation from dealing with all of its customers in the applicable market.

6 (1997) 1 SCC 388

Probation may be desirable that is, courts may place corporations on probation and restrict their activities.

India is growing but growth for the sake of growth is nothing but, merely a property of a cancerous cell. A lot of distance is still to be covered, within the constrained time; for the lacking is ours and so is the fault.

1.3. Research Questions:

- What is the meaning and what are the ingredients of the crimes in the nature of corporate manslaughter and corporate homicide?
- What are the dimensions that exist in regards to the crimes of corporate manslaughter and corporate homicide?
- What are the standards that exist in certain major jurisdictions of the U.K., New Zealand, U.S., Canada and Australia, to punish the corporations for the crimes of manslaughter and homicide?
- How far has the consciousness risen in India to punish the corporations for the crimes of manslaughter and homicide, post the Bhopal Gas Tragedy and, what measures can be suggested to encounter these crimes?

1.4. Hypothesis:

India needs a comprehensive piece of legislation that punishes corporations for the crimes in the nature of manslaughter and homicide in light of the fact that India has already witnessed tragedies in the nature of *Bhopal Gas Disaster* (1984), the *Oleum Gas Leakage Case* (1985) and the *Uphaar Cinema Tragedy* (1997) and in view of the fact that the statutes enacted post the Bhopal Gas Tragedy, that is the Environment Protection Act of 1986, the Public Liability Insurance Act of 1991 and the Protection of Human Rights Act of 1993, have delivered much less than expected. India needs a corporate manslaughter legislation that punishes the faulting corporations with innovative sentencing regime in the nature of, **unlimited fines**, **publicity orders**, **equity fines**, **loss of license** and **loss of statutory and non-statutory benefits**.

1.5. Objective of the study:

The objective of the research is to emphasise that it is high time for India to become part of the global rising consciousness in regards to enacting legislation for punishing corporations for the crimes of manslaughter and homicide. Despite the *Bhopal Gas Tragedy*, the *Oleum Gas Leakage Case* and the *Uphaar Cinema Tragedy*, India still awaits enactment of legislation that may punish corporations for the crimes of manslaughter and homicide. The objective of the research is to bring to light the examples of other common law countries such as U.S., U.K., New Zealand, Canada and Australia, which have enacted legislations to punish corporations for the crimes of manslaughter and homicide. The objective of the research is to stress on the fact that it is time for India to enact a legislation that punishes corporations for crimes of manslaughter and homicide with innovative sentencing regimes in the nature of **unlimited fines**, **equity fines**, **loss of license**, and **publicity orders**.

1.6. Scope of the study:

The research undertaken attempts to propose enactment of a legislation that may prosecute and punish corporations for the crimes of manslaughter and homicide in India, with innovative sentencing regimes in the nature of **unlimited fines**, **publicity orders**, **loss of license** and **loss of statutory and non-statutory benefits.** The research undertaken proposes that India should take inspiration from the "senior management test" as is applicable in the U.K. post the enactment of the Corporate Manslaughter and Corporate Homicide Act of 2007; in the light of the fact that, absolute liability principle when read with the deep-pocket theory, makes the absolute liability principle a weak principle.

1.7. Research Methodology:

Researcher has primarily used the doctrinal method of legal research, thereby exposing himself to exhaustive literature (books, journals, case- laws and commentaries) written on the subject of corporate manslaughter and corporate homicide. As a matter of observation made by the researcher, not much literature has been written on the subject as the concept is still nascent in India. Hence, the researcher has mostly relied on and has taken inspiration from the foreign literature; primarily that of the U.K. and the U.S. So far as the sources in regards to the doctrinal method of legal research are concerned, the researcher has made a classification in terms of primary and secondary sources. Primary sources- consist of the various statutes enacted in various jurisdictions targeting the crime of corporate killings. Secondary sources- consist of journals, commentaries, articles and books written on the subject qualifying the present research.

The researcher has also made use of the historical method of legal research, tracing the historical development of the concept of corporate criminal liability, corporate manslaughter and corporate homicide. A high degree of emphasis was placed on critical analysis of the legislation enacted in the U.K. i.e. the *Corporate Manslaughter and Corporate Homicide Act, 2007*, which (broadly speaking) is in the nature of a legislative breakthrough in the field of corporate manslaughter and corporate homicide.

For the purpose of jurisdictional analysis of the problem pertaining to corporate killings the researcher has made use of the *comparative method of legal research*, whereby he carried out comparative analysis of the law relating to corporate killings as so existing in the jurisdictions of the U.K., U.S., New Zealand and Australia. The purpose of such comparison is to see where India stands among various nations so far as targeting the problem of corporate killings is concerned. The researcher has specifically picked on these nations (U.K., U.S., New Zealand and Australia) for two reasons. Firstly, these nations have natured over a period of time the *rise in consciousness* as against corporate killings on a global platform and secondly, these nations are *common law countries* and hence, a clear line of association can be witnessed in regards to laws enacted there-under with respect to India. The researcher shall undertake *case law based legal research* for the purpose of conceptual clarity on the subject. The researcher will undertake a relatively detailed study of the following case-laws of the U.K.: The *Herald of Free Enterprise Case* (1987); the *Clapham Rail Disaster Case* (1988); the *Lyme Bay Canoeing Tragedy* (1993); the *Transco Case* (1999) and the *Hatfield Disaster Case* (2000). These cases led to the formation of law against corporate killings as it stands in U.K., today. In regards to U.S., the researcher has laid specific stress on the following cases- *Gimbel* v. *Signal Co., Inc.*; *Imperial Food Products, Inc. Case* and the *SabreTech Case.*

So far as New Zealand is concerned, the researcher has analysed as to how the law against corporate killings solidified post the *Canterbury Earthquake* (2011) and the *Pike River Mine Disaster* (2010) and what position existed prior to these cases, through the case of *Murray Wright Ltd.* [(1970) NZLR 476].

Lastly as to India, the researcher has laid down necessary stress on the following case-laws: the *Bhopal Gas Tragedy*, the *Oleum Gas Leakage Case*, the *Standard Chartered Bank Case* and the *Iridium- Motorola Case.*

1.8. Chapterisation:

Chapter 1: Introduction

This chapter deals with the introduction, the statement of problems, the research questions formulated, the hypothesis, the objective of the study, the scope of the study, the research methodology used by the researcher and the chapterisation.

Chapter 2: Corporate Manslaughter and Corporate Homicide- Meaning and Ingredients

This chapter looks into the various theories of corporate personality (the *Fiction Theory*, the *Realist Theory*, the *Purpose Theory*, the *Bracket Theory* and the *Concession Theory*). This chapter further deals with the jurisprudential analysis of the *doctrine of separate legal entity* and the *doctrine of lifting up of the corporate veil.* The Researcher discusses in this chapter, the various doctrines and principles formulated over a period of time to impute civil and criminal liability over the corporations, that is, the *vicarious liability principle*, the *identification doctrine*, the *aggregation doctrine*, the *principle of reactive corporate fault* and the *doctrine of corporate mens rea.* This chapter discusses how the imputation of liability over corporations in India takes place, by discussing in detail the principle of *absolute liability* and the *deep-pocket theory*. This chapter points out towards the debate that, can a corporation in its capacity of an artificial legal person, existing only in the contemplation of law be punished for crimes of manslaughter and homicide.

Chapter 3: Analysis of the existing dimensions of the crimes of corporate manslaughter and corporate homicide

This chapter discusses the essential ingredients that must be fulfilled to impute charges of manslaughter and homicide over a flouting corporation. The chapter further discusses the *four* dimensions that exist to punish corporations for the crimes of manslaughter and homicide, these are: the death of a worker owing to the unhealthy and hazardous work conditions; or the tools, equipments and machinery employed by the body corporate being obsolete and un-standardised; deaths due to gross negligence employed in regards to the nature of work carried by a corporation; deaths owing to the environment disasters triggered by the activities undertaken by the body corporate; deaths due to the use of "products" manufactured by the corporations being either unsafe for human consumption, or otherwise being adulterated and un-standardised. This chapter also discusses as to how India is turning into the world's leading toxic waste "garbage can" with all toxic waste (without any exception) been imported from Jeddah, Malaysia and Barcelona, to India for treatment and disposal.

Chapter 4: Corporate Manslaughter and Corporate Homicide: Comparative analysis of the standards prevailing in the major jurisdictions

This chapter analyses the laws and the standards prevailing in the major jurisdictions of U.K., U.S., New Zealand, Canada and Australia, for punishing corporations for the crimes in the nature of corporate manslaughter and corporate homicide. The standards prevailing in these major jurisdictions are not only compared with each other inter-se but are also compared with the standards prevailing in India. This chapter also reflects upon the reasons for the selection of these major jurisdictions.

Chapter 5: Corporate Manslaughter and Corporate Homicide in India: The-Rising-Jurisprudence

This chapter deals with the prospective rise in the corporate criminal jurisprudence in India, post the *Bhopal Gas Tragedy*, the *Oleum Gas Leakage Case* and the *Uphaar Cinema Tragedy*; and how the *principle of corporate criminal liability* got judicial recognition in India before it got the legislative recognition through the Companies (Amendment) Act of 2013. This chapter also reflects upon the application of principles of *vicarious liability*, *strict liability*, *absolute liability* and the *deep-pocket theory* in India.

Chapter 6: Conclusion and Suggestions

The *first part* of this chapter deals with the conclusion, the researcher reached in regards to, why India should have a comprehensive corporate manslaughter and corporate homicide legislation with innovative sentencing regimes. The *second part* of this chapter deals with the suggestions given by the researcher in regards to, how the proposed legislation can be made a comprehensive code imputing punishments on flouting corporations accused of the crimes of manslaughter and homicide. The *third part* of this chapter deals with the remarks given by the researcher in regards to how India can improve its corporate criminal sentencing regimes by taking examples from some of the major jurisdictions of U.K., U.S., New Zealand, Canada and Australia.

Chapter 2

Corporate Manslaughter and Corporate Homicide- Meaning and Ingredients

2.1. Introduction:

Justice Lindley has described the jurisprudential essence of the term *company* as follows: "A company is an association of persons; these persons contribute *money or money's worth* to a common stock. The common stock so contributed is denoted in money and is called as *capital* of the company. The persons who contribute the capital are called as *members* of the company. The capital is employed in some *trade or business.* The members *share the profits and losses* arising from such business. The proportion of capital to which each member is entitled is called as his *share.* The shares are always transferable although the right to transfer is often more or less restricted."

2.2. Theories of Corporate Personality:

The theories of 'corporate personality' formulated by scholars over the period of time creates a room for an interesting discussion as to how the operations of the companies are perceived by law and as to how the crimes committed by the companies make them legally liable.

2.2.1. Fiction Theory: The Fiction Theory[7] primarily developed by Savigny and Salmond, states that the juristic persons should be treated as if they are individuals, that is human beings. This theory states that the concept of

[7] This theory appears to have originated during the Holy Roman Empire and at the height of Papal authority. It is thought that Sinibald Fieschi, who became Pope Innocent IV in 1243, was the first to employ the idea of *persona ficta; 'cum collegium in causa universitatis fingatur una persona'.*

"corporate personality" must coincide with the idea of man. The fiction theory emphasises that some groups and institutions regard themselves as persons and do not find it necessary to answer why. Fiction theory offers flexibility to enable the courts to accommodate cases in English law where the mask is lifted to determine the *mind and will* of an association or a group or an institution, which are treated as "person" for some purposes and not so for other purposes. This theory is particularly popular among the English writers due to the very flexibility it offers and partly because of its non-political character.[8] The *doctrine of the lifting up of the corporate veil* has been derived from this theory.

<u>2.2.2. Realist Theory</u>: The Realist Theory[9], of which Gierke is the principal exponent and Maitland a sympathiser, asserts that 'juristic persons' enjoy a real or actual existence either in the form of a group or an association or an institution. A group, comprising of individuals becomes a unit and thereafter functions as such. The 'organism theory', with which the realist theory is closely associated, asserts that 'groups' comprising of individuals are in fact 'persons', corresponding biologically to human beings. This justifies the special use of the term 'organism' and the implications in regards to the biological comparison cannot therefore lead to absurdity. It is said that they (groups/institutions/associations) have a real life. Professor Wolff however has critical contentions as he points out that, if there is a contract between two companies whereby one company owing to the contentions as such agreed in the contract, is to undergo voluntary liquidation, would it then amount to a void agreement, as an agreement to commit suicide is void *ab initio*. Professor Wolff further contends that, a group, an institution or an association is said to have a 'group will' which is independent of the will of its component members. Professor Wolff points out that the 'group will' is only the result of mutually influenced will or concerted will, which even a staunch supporter of the fictionist theory would admit or agree. Gray, quoting Windscheid has said that, "to get rid of

8 See: Kamala Sankaran, Mahavir Singh, Anju Vali Tikoo, Alok Sharma & Vageshwari Deswal, *JurisprudenceII: Concepts*, Case Material, Faculty of Law, University of Delhi, January 2013, p.165

9 This theory is of German origin. Until the time of Bismarck, Germany consisted of a large number of separate states. Unification was their ideal, and the movement towards it assumed almost the character of a crusade. The very idea of unity and of collective working has never ceased to be something of a marvel, which may be one reason for the aura of mysticism and emotion which is seldom far from this theory.

the fiction of an attributed will, by saying that a corporation has a real general will, is to drive out one fiction by another".[10] Associated with the realist theory is the 'institutional theory' which is more or less symbolic of a shift in emphasis from an individualist to a collectivist outlook. Individuals when are integrated into an institution, to signify the potential existence of the individuals as such (behind the veil of institution), the realist theory is applied.[11]

2.2.3. Purpose Theory: The Purpose Theory[12] was primarily formulated by Brinz, and was later developed by Barker in England. This theory assumes that the term 'person' is applicable only to individuals that is, human beings and they alone can be the subjects of "jural relations". The so-called 'juristic' persons are not always 'artificial legal persons', speaking in terms of human individuality. Since the 'juristic' persons are treated distinct from their human sub-stratum, jural relations cannot be presumed to subsist always among human beings. Juristic persons are generally regarded as 'subject-less properties' designed for certain purposes. This theory is not applicable to the English law. Judges have repeatedly asserted that corporations are 'persons', and it is this use of the word 'persons' that needs explanation, that is if they say that corporations are 'persons', then to challenge the usage of this word as to be applicable only in regards to human beings is dichotomous.[13]

2.2.4. Bracket Theory: The Bracket Theory[14], formulated by Ihering states that, the members of a corporation and the beneficiaries of a foundation are the only 'persons', speaking specifically in terms of their human individuality. 'Juristic Person' is nothing but a symbol or a label, to help effectuating the purpose of a group. This theory believes in putting a bracket on the members

---

10 This theory asserts that group entities are 'real' in a different sense from human beings. The 'reality' is physical, namely the unity of spirit, purpose, interests, and organisation. Even so, it fails to explain the inconsistencies of the law with regards to corporations.

11 See: Kamala Sankaran, Mahavir Singh, Anju Vali Tikoo, Alok Sharma & Vageshwari Deswal, *Jurisprudence II: Concepts*, Case Material, Faculty of Law, University of Delhi, January 2013, p.165-166

12 This theory was designed mainly to explain the vacant inheritance, the *hereditas jacens*, of the Roman law.

13 See: R.W.M. Dias, *Jurisprudence*, Fifth Edition, 1994, p.265-270

14 This theory is commonly known as the 'symbolist theory'.

(individuals as such) in order to treat them as a unit. This theory assumes that the use of the word 'person' is confined to individuals, that is, human beings only. This theory takes no account of the policy that the courts follow, in regards to the varying ways in which the phrase, such as, X & Co. or XYZ Ltd. is used, to create an artificial legal entity as separate and distinct from individuals of which a group, institution or an association comprises. It is for the courts to decide whether or not to and in which all cases the corporate veil needs to be lifted or the bracket needs to be removed.

2.2.5. Concession Theory: The Concession Theory[15] emphasises that it is for the State to decide whether or not to give the conferment of "separate legal entity" to a group of individuals composing an association or an institution. The 'State' is identified in parlance with the 'law', so far as this theory is concerned. The identification of 'law' with 'State' is necessary for the concession theory, however it is not so, so far as the fiction theory is concerned. The concession theory has been used for political purposes, mainly to strengthen the State and to suppress autonomous bodies that are subject to the "will" of the State.

These theories discussing the jurisprudential aspects of 'legal personality' with the prime focus on the corporations carrying out their business activities behind the veil of corporate juristic personality need necessary focus because dissection in terms of a company being legally represented on paper under law as a separate legal person and, a company being viewed as a group of individuals in the last filtered analysis, would make things simpler and viably understandable as regards the fact that it's the individual decisions operating behind the corporate veil, forming the mind and the will of the company that are responsible for all actions of the company and hence when a company commits crimes in the nature of 'homicide' or 'manslaughter', in no way can they be allowed to go scot free.

15 This theory is allied to the fiction theory and, in fact, supporters of the one tend also to support the other. The conferment of title as to 'juristic person' is within the discretion of the State. This theory is a product of the era of power of the national state, which superseded the Holy Roman Empire and in which the supremacy of the State was emphasised.

2.3. Limited liability characteristic of a Company:

One of the chief characteristics of the company is 'limited liability'. Before we discuss the notion of corporate criminal liability and by virtue of that, target the comprehensive meaning of the terms 'corporate manslaughter' and 'corporate homicide', we shall attempt to understand the meaning of the characteristic feature of 'limited liability' of the company. By the chief characteristic feature of limited liability of a company, we mean, the members of a company cannot be held liable for the debts incurred by the company. In case of a limited company, liability of members is limited. The members are liable to pay only such amount as is due from them to the company (as per the relevant provisions of the Act and memorandum), which can be explained below:

Nature of Company	**Extent of liability of members**
Company limited by shares	Amount unpaid on the shares held by every member
Company limited by guarantee	Amount guaranteed by every member
Company limited by guarantee and having share capital	Aggregate of amount unpaid on the shares held by a member and the amount guaranteed by him
Unlimited Company	Liable to contribute to the assets of the company until all the debts of the company are paid in full

Now, separate from the notion of the limited liability characteristic of the company is the theory of corporate criminal liability. Before, we begin our analysis of corporate criminal liability and there-after of, corporate manslaughter and homicide; it is necessary for us to supply due emphasis on the principle of separate legal entity and lifting or piercing of corporate veil.

2.4. Doctrine of Separate Legal Entity:

The principle of separate legal entity states that, a company is a legal entity separate from its owners (i.e. members). It is a person distinct from the persons who form it.[16] It is known by its own name, has rights and liabilities of its own. Thus, a company is a body corporate.

Implications of the rule of separate legal entity are as follows- there can be a transfer of property from a member to the company and vice versa; a person can be a member, director, employee and creditor of the company at the same time[17]; a member can enter into a contract with the company in the same manner as any

---

16 See: *Salomon* v. *Salomon & Co. Ltd.*, [1897] AC 22. In this case Mr. Salomon was carrying on the business of boot manufacturing as a sole proprietor. He incorporated a company named Salomon & Co. Ltd. for the purpose of taking over this business. Payment of purchase consideration by the company was of £ 39000 (cash paid- £ 9000, fully paid shares of £ 1 issued to Salomon- £ 20000 and secured debentures issued to Salomon- £ 10000). Other members of the company were the family members of Salomon (the six members of the family of Mr. Salomon were issued one share each). Salomon & Co. was a 'one man company' since Salomon was the leading shareholder and all other shareholders were nominees of Salomon. Hence, Salomon held virtually the entire share capital of the company and he was also the managing director of the company.

In the course of business, the company borrowed from creditors to the extent of £ 7000. Due to trade depression, the company ran into financial difficulties and eventually went into liquidation. The assets realised only £ 6000.

Contention of the unsecured creditors was that 'one man cannot owe to himself'. Salomon was carrying on business in the name of Salomon & Co. Ltd. Thus, Salomon & Co. Ltd. was a mere agent of Salomon.

Court held- Salomon & Co. was a real company fulfilling all legal requirements. It had an identity different from its members, and therefore the secured debentures even though held by Salomon, were to be paid in priority to unsecured creditors.

17 See: *Lee* v. *Lee's Air Farming Ltd.*, [1961] UKPC 33. In this case, Lee was a qualified pilot. He virtually owned all the shares and he was the sole governing director of the company. He was also receiving salary from the company for being a chief pilot under the company. He was eventually killed in an air accident while working for the company. It was held that Lee was a separate person from the company he had formed. Therefore, he could be legitimately employed under the company. As he was killed in the course of employment under the company, his widow was entitled to compensation.

See also: *Bacha F. Guzdar* v. *Commissioner of Income Tax*, [1955] 27 ITR 1 (SC). In this case, a shareholder received dividend income from a company carrying on agricultural business. The income from agriculture business was exempt from tax. The shareholder contended that her dividend income should be treated as agricultural income and therefore exempt from tax. The Court held that the company was a separate person from its members, having its own business, and its own income. The income received by the shareholders was not the same income as earned by the company.

other person can; a company has the rights and duties of its own, which are different from the rights and duties of its members; a company shall have a separate legal entity even if virtually entire share capital of the company is held by one person.

2.5. Lifting or Piercing of Corporate Veil:

By fiction of law a company is seen as a distinct entity, yet in reality it is an association of persons who are in fact the beneficial owners of all the corporate property. This fiction is created by a fictional veil, i.e. the corporate veil.

2.5.1. Effect of Corporate Veil: The business is carried on by the company and not by the directors or the members of the company. Only a company is responsible for the acts and defaults done in the name of the company, even though members, directors, or any officer or employee of the company had acted on behalf of the company. No member shall be held liable for the acts of the company even if he holds virtually the entire share capital of the company.

2.5.2. Meaning of Lifting or Piercing of Corporate Veil: Lifting of the corporate veil means ignoring the separate legal identity of a company. Lifting of the corporate veil means; disregarding the corporate personality and looking behind the real persons who are in the control of the company.

2.5.3. Lifting of corporate veil is permissible only in exceptional cases: Lifting up of corporate veil is allowed only if it is permitted by the Statute or if there is clear evidence that the device of incorporation was abused. The Court has the discretion whether or not to lift the corporate veil. It is not possible to lay down a specific set of circumstances in which corporate veil may be lifted.

2.5.3.1. Lifting of corporate veil under statutory provisions:

The corporate veil may be lifted in instances of reduction of membership *below* the statutory minimum.[18] Where the number of members has reduced *below* the statutory minimum, the remaining members shall be held personally liable for the debts of the company.

---

18 See: Section 45 of the Indian Companies Act of 1956

Corporate veil may be lifted under statutory provisions when there is wrong description on name.[19] Where an officer or employee of a company enters into a contract on behalf of the company but fails to mention the name of the company in such contract or, where an officer or employee enters into a contract in the name of the company but mentions the name of the company incorrectly in such contract. Then, the officer at fault shall be held personally liable on such instrument and shall be punishable with fine. Hence, the corporate veil shall be lifted.

Corporate veil may be lifted in due compliance with the statutory provisions (the Companies Act of 1956 as amended in 2013) particularly in instances of "group accounts". Section 212 of the Companies Act of 1956 required that a holding company is to furnish the annual accounts of the subsidiary along with the annual accounts of the holding company. However, Section 212 does not require presentation of consolidated accounts by a holding company. The effect of Section 212 is that, ordinarily, a company is a legal person distinct from its members. However, Section 212 makes a subsidiary company an agent of the holding company as far as furnishing of annual accounts of the subsidiary company are concerned.

Instances of fraudulent trading call for statutory piercing of the corporate veil.[20] If in a winding up, it appears to the Court that the business of the company has been carried on with the intent to defraud its creditors or any other person or for any fraudulent purpose, the court may declare that any of the directors or officers who are 'knowingly' the parties to the fraud shall be held personally liable, without any limitation of liability, for all or any of the debts of the company.

Arrears of tax, forms another area where by in due compliance with the statutory provisions corporate veil may be lifted. Ordinarily, only a company is liable for the debts incurred by it. However, as per Section 179 of the Income Tax Act of 1961, all the directors of the company shall also be liable for the

19 See: Section 147 of the Indian Companies Act of 1956 (which forms Section 12 of the Companies Act of 2013)

20 See: Section 542 of the Indian Companies Act of 1956 (which forms Section 339 of the Companies Act of 2013)

payment of taxes payable by the company. Similarly, Section 18 of the Central Sales Tax Act provides that all the directors of the company shall also be liable for the payment of taxes payable by the company. However, these sections apply only to a private company and that too at the time of winding up.

Ultra vires acts by the individuals forming the "determining mind and will" of the company calls for statutory lifting up of the corporate veil. The directors of a company are held personally liable for all the *ultra vires* acts done by them on behalf of the company.

2.5.3.2. Lifting of Corporate Veil under Judicial Decisions:

There have been instances where in regards for the protection of revenue, sham companies are created. Over the period of time 'judicial notice' of the same led to piercing of the corporate veil in such matters. See for example, the case of *Re, Sir Dinshaw Maneckjee Pettit*[21]. In this case, an assessee was receiving huge dividend and interest income on certain investments. He formed four private companies. The whole of the investments were transferred to these private companies. The interest and dividend received by these companies were within the exempted limits under the Income Tax Act of that time. These companies did not have any business or asset except these investments. The income received on investments by these companies was diverted to the assessee in the form of pretended loans, which were never paid back. The Court held that the only purpose of incorporating these private companies was to evade taxes. Each of these companies was a sham. Therefore, income earned by all these private companies was treated as the income of the assessee.

For the purpose of prevention of fraud and improper conduct, courts have been lifting the corporate veil to shatter the fictional veil and to catch the real perpetrators. The corporate veil may be lifted if the company is formed to defeat the law; defraud creditors; and avoid legal obligations. In the case of *Gilford Motor Co. Ltd.* v. *Horne*[22], an employee entered into a contract with his employer, that he will not solicit the customers of the employer after leaving the employment. After leaving the employment, the employee incorporated a

21 (1927) 29 BOMLR 447

22 (1933) Ch. 935

company. He, his wife and one other person were the only members of this company. The company started soliciting the customers of the employer. The Court held that, the purpose of formation of the company was to avoid the legal obligation arising from the contract, which was not permissible. Therefore the company was restrained from soliciting the customers of the employer.

For the determination of the character of the company, whether an enemy company, the corporate veil may be lifted. In the case of *Daimler Co. Ltd.* v. *Continental Tyre & Rubber Co. Ltd*[23], a company was formed in England for the purpose of selling tyres made by a German company. The German company virtually held the entire share capital of the English company. All the directors were German residents. During the First World War, the English company commenced an action to recover a trade debt from another English company. It was held that the corporate personality of the company should be ignored and the individuals ultimately controlling the company should be considered. Since the persons controlling the company were enemies, the suit was held to be 'not maintainable'.

There have been instances where by sham companies are being created for the purpose of avoidance of obligations arising from welfare legislations. See for example in the case of, *Workmen employed in Associated Rubber Industries Ltd.* v. *Associated Rubber Industries Ltd*[24]. A company was earning huge profits. As per the Bonus Act, the bonus was paid to the workers as a proportion of profits of the company. The company incorporated a subsidiary company and transferred some valuable investments to it. The subsidiary company did no business, and had no assets except the investments transferred to it. Looking at the purpose of formation of the subsidiary, the Court lifted the corporate veil. It was held that the subsidiary was formed merely for the purpose of reducing the liability of bonus payable under the Bonus Act. It amounted to avoiding the obligations arising qua welfare legislation by escaping the liability to pay bonus. Such an action was held to be impermissible, and therefore the profits earned by the subsidiary company were held to be the profits of the holding company.

---

23 (1916) 2 AC 307

24 AIR 1986 SC 1

Corporate veil may be lifted to give effect to obligations arising in regards to a company as a matter of public policy. The Court lifts the corporate veil for the purpose of protecting the public policy and to prevent the transaction contrary to public policy.

Having discussed the theories of *corporate personality*, *separate legal entity* and the *doctrine of lifting up of the corporate veil*, we have premised ourselves with a strong foundation to introduce ourselves to the theories of corporate liabilities, in the nature of *strict liability principle* and *absolute liability principle.*

2.6. Strict Liability Principle and Absolute Liability Principle:

The rule laid down in *Ryland* v. *Fletcher*[25] is generally known as the 'Rule of Strict Liability', because of the various exceptions to the applicability of this rule. It would be preferable to call it the rule of strict liability, rather than the rule of absolute liability. While formulating the rule in *M.C. Mehta* v. *U.O.I*[26], the Supreme Court of India termed the liability recognised in this case as absolute liability, stating that such a liability will not be subject to 'such exceptions' as have been recognised in the *Ryland* v. *Fletcher*[27] case.

Enunciating the *doctrine of strict liability* in the case of *Ryland* v. *Fletcher*[28], Justice Blackburn[29] held as follows-

---

25 (1868) L.R. 3 H.L. 330

26 AIR 1987 SC 1086

27 See: R.K. Bangia, *Law of Torts,* Allahabad Law Agency, Nineteenth Edition, 2006, Chapter 16: Rules of Strict and Absolute Liability, p.379-380

28 In *Ryland* v. *Fletcher*, the defendant got a reservoir constructed through independent contractors over his land for provisioning water to his mill. There were old disused shafts under the site of the reservoir, which the contractors failed to observe and so did not block them. When the water was filled in the reservoir, it burst through the shafts and flooded the plaintiff's coal-mines on the adjoining land. The defendant did not know of the shafts and had not been negligent although the independent contractors had been. Even though the defendant had not been negligent, he was held liable.

29 The rule was formulated by Blackburn J. in Exchequer Chamber in *Fletcher* v. *Ryland,* [(1866) L.R. 1 Ex. 265] and the same was approved by the House of Lords in *Ryland* v. *Fletcher*, [(1868) L.R. 3 H.L. 330].

"We think that the rule of law is, that the person who for his own purposes brings on his land and keeps there anything likely to do mischief if it escapes, must keep it in at his peril, and if he does not do so, is prima facie answerable for all the damage which is the natural consequence of its escape. He can excuse himself by showing that the escape was owing to the plaintiff's default; or perhaps that the escape was the consequence of *Vis Major,* or the act of God; but as nothing of this sort exists here, it is unnecessary to inquire what excuse would be sufficient."

To the above rule laid down by Blackburn, J. in the Court of Exchequer Chamber, another important qualification was made by the House of Lords when the case came before it. It was held that for the liability under the rule, the use of land should be "non- natural" as was the position in *Ryland* v. *Fletcher* itself.

For the application of the rule, therefore, the following three essentials should be there. **Firstly**, some dangerous thing must have been brought by a person on his land. According to this rule the liability for the escape of a thing from one's land arises provided the thing collected was a dangerous thing, that is, a thing likely to do mischief if it escapes. In *Ryland* v. *Fletcher*, the thing so collected was a large body of water. The rule has further been applied to gas[30], electricity[31], vibrations[32], yew trees[33], sewage[34], flag pole[35], rusty wire[36], noxious fumes[37] and explosives[38]. **Secondly**, the thing brought or kept by a

30 See: *Batcheller* v. *Tunbrige Wells Gas Co.* [(190) 84 L.T. 765], *North Western Utilities Ltd.* v. *London Guarantee and Accident Co.* [(1936) A.C. 108]

31 See: *National Telephone Co.* v. *Baker* [(1893) 2 Ch. 186], *Eastern and South African Telephone Co.* v. *Cape Town Tramways Co.* [(1936) A.C. 381]

32 See: *Hoare & Co.* v. *Mc. Alpine* [(1893) 1 Ch. 167]

33 See: *Crowhurst* v. *Amersham Burial Board* [(1878) 4 Ex. D. 5], *Ponting* v. *Noakes* [(1894) 2 Q.B. 281]

34 See: *Tenant* v. *Goldwin* [(1704) 1 Salk, 360], *Foster* v. *Warblington Urban Council* [(1906) 1 K.B. 648], *Jones* v. *Llanrwst U.D.C.* [(1911) 1 Ch. 393]

35 See: *Shiffman* v. *Graud Priory* [(1936) 1 All. E.R. 557]

36 See: *Firth* v. *Bowling Iron Co.* [(1878) C.P.D. 254]

37 See: *West* v. *Bristol Tramways Co.* [(1908) 2 K.B. 14]

38 See: *T.C. Balakrishnan* v. *T.R. Subramanian* [AIR 1968 Kerala 151], *Ratnham Chemical Works* v. *Belvedere Fish Gauno Co.* [(1921) 2 A.C. 465], *Read* v. *Lyons* [(1947) A.C. 156]

person on his land must escape. For the rule in *Ryland* v. *Fletcher* to apply, it is essential that the thing causing the damage must escape to the area outside the occupation and control of the defendant. As for example in the case of, *Read* v. *Lyons & Co.*[39], the plaintiff was an employee in the defendant's ammunition factory, while she was performing her duties inside the defendant's premises, a shell, which was being manufactured there exploded, hence she was injured. There was no evidence of negligence on the part of the defendants. Even though the shell which had exploded was a dangerous thing, it was held that the defendants were not liable because there was no escape of the thing outside the defendant's premises and, therefore, the rule in *Ryland* v. *Fletcher* did not apply to this case.[40] **Thirdly**, there must be non-natural use of land. Water collected in the reservoir in such a huge quantity in *Ryland* v. *Fletcher* was held to be non-natural use of land. Keeping water for ordinary domestic purposes is 'natural use'.[41] It is important to note that electric wiring in a house or a shop[42], supply of gas in gas pipes in a dwelling house[43], water installation in a house; are few examples of natural use of land.

Also, in the case of *T.C. Balakrishnan Menon* v. *T.C. Subramanian*[44], it was held that the use of explosives in an open ground even on a day of festival is a "non-natural" use of land because under the Indian Explosives Act, for making and storing explosive substances even on such places and at such occasions, licenses have to be taken from the prescribed authorities.

2.6.1. The following exceptions to the strict liability principle have been recognised by the *Ryland* v. *Fletcher* Rule:

2.6.1.1. Plaintiff the wrongdoer: Damage caused by escape of a dangerous thing due to plaintiff's own fault was considered to be a good defence in *Ryland* v. *Fletcher*. When the damage to the plaintiff's property is caused not

---

39 (1947) A.C. 156; (1946) 2 All E.R. 471

40 It is interesting to note that, had this case been decided with the intelligentsia of the absolute liability principle, the defendant would have been held liable. The absolute liability principle is in doctrinal terms is known as the 'no-fault liability' principle.

41 See: *Richards* v. *Lothian* [(1913) A.C. 263]

42 See: *Collingwood* v. *Home and Colonial Stores Ltd.* [(1936) All. E.R. 200]

43 See: *Miller* v. *Addie & Sons Collieries* [1934 S.C. 150]

44 AIR 1968 Kerala 151

so much by the 'escape' of the dangerous thing collected by the defendant as by the unusual sensitiveness of the plaintiff's property itself, the plaintiff cannot recover anything.[45]

2.6.1.2. Act of God: Act of God or *Vis Major* was considered as a defence to an action under the rule of *Ryland* v. *Fletcher* by Justice Blackburn. An "Act of God" has been defined as, "Circumstances which no human foresight can provide against, and of which human prudence or pragmatism is not reasonably bound to recognise the possibility of."[46]

2.6.1.3. Consent of the plaintiff: In case of *volenti non fit injuria,* that is, where the plaintiff has consented to the accumulation of the dangerous thing on the defendant's land, the liability under the '*Ryland* v. *Fletcher* Rule' does not arise. Such consent is implied where the source of danger is for the "common benefit" of both the plaintiff and the defendant.

2.6.1.4. Act of third party: If the harm has been caused due to the act of a stranger who is neither, the defendant's servant or employee, nor the defendant has any control over him; the defendant will not be liable under the 'Rule of *Ryland* v. *Fletcher*'.[47] To understand this point comprehensively, it is necessary to take note of the following case, *M.P. Electricity Board* v. *Shail Kumar*[48]. In this case, one Joginder Singh, aged 37 years, was riding on his bicycle on the night of 23rd September, 1997 while returning from his factory. A snapped live electric wire was lying on the road. There was rain and the road was partially inundated with water. The cyclist could not notice the electric wire and as he

---

45 For example: In the case of *Eastern and South African Telegraph Co. Ltd.* v. *Cape Town Tramways Co.* [(1902) A.C. 381], the plaintiff's submarine cable transmissions were disturbed by escape of electric current from defendant's tramways. It was found that the damage was due to unusual sensitiveness of the plaintiff's apparatus and such damage would not occur to a person carrying on ordinary business, the defendant was held not liable for the escape.

46 See: *Tennent* v. *Earl of Glasgow* [(1864) 2 M (H.L.) 22, 26-27]

47 For example: In the case of *Box* v. *Jubb* [(1879) 4 Ex. D. 76], the overflow from the defendant's reservoir was caused by the blocking of a drain by strangers, the defendant was held not liable for that.

48 AIR 2002 SC 551; In this case, the rule of strict liability was applied by the Supreme Court and the defect of the dangerous thing being an 'act of stranger' was not allowed because the same could have been foreseen.

came in contact with the same, he died instantaneously due to electrocution. An action was brought against the M.P. Electricity Board by the widow and minor son of Joginder Singh. The 'Rule of Strict Liability' was applied and it was held that the Board had statutory duty to supply electricity in the area. If the energy so transmitted causes injury or death of a human being, who gets unknowingly trapped into it, the electric supplier shall be liable for the same. If the electric wire was snapped the current should have been automatically cut off. Authorities manning such dangerous commodities have extra duty to chalk out measures to prevent such mishaps. The defence that the snapping of wire was due to the act of the stranger who might have tried to pilfer the electricity was rejected. Such act should have been foreseen by the Electricity Board and at any rate; the consequences of the stranger's act should have been prevented by the appellant Board.

2.6.1.5. Statutory Authority: An act done under the authority of a statute is a defence to an action for tort. The defence is also available when the action is under the rule in *Ryland* v. *Fletcher*.[49] 'Statutory Authority', however, cannot be pleaded as a defence when there is negligence.[50] As for example, in the case of *Green* v. *Chelsea Waterworks Co.*[51]; the defendant Co. had a statutory duty to maintain continuous supply of water. A main belonging to the company burst without any negligence on its part, as a consequence of which the plaintiff's premises were flooded with water. It was held that the company was not liable as the company was engaged in performing a statutory duty.

The jurisprudence behind the philosophy of corporate manslaughter and corporate homicide, points towards the notion of corporate killings, which in turn draws existence from the theory of corporate criminal liability. Corporate criminal liability in its simplest form can be understood by way of the doctrinal analysis of 'strict liability' principle and 'absolute liability' principle. Having discussed the strict liability principle, having its origin in U.K.; now we shall be discussing the absolute liability principle, having its origin in India.

---

49 See: *Green* v. *Chelsea Waterworks Co.* [(1894) 70 L.T. 547], *Charing Cross Electricity Co.* v. *Hydraulic Power Co.* [(1914) 3 K.B. 772]

50 See: *Manchester Corporation* v. *Farnworth* [(1930) A.C. 171], *North Western Utilities Ltd.* v. *London Guarantee & Accident Co.* [(1936) A.C. 138]

51 (1894) 70 L.T. 547

2.6.2. Jurisprudence advanced post the "*Ryland* v. *Fletcher* Rule": In *M.C. Mehta* v. *U.O.I*[52], the Supreme Court of India was dealing with claims arising from the leakage of oleum gas on the 4th and 6th of December, 1985 from one of the units of Shriram Foods and Fertilisers Industries, in the city of Delhi, belonging to the Delhi Cloth Mills Ltd. As a consequence of this leakage, it was alleged that one advocate practicing in the Tis Hazari Court (Delhi) had died and several others were affected by the same. The action was brought through a writ petition under Article 32[53] of the Constitution of India, by way of public interest litigation. The Court had in mind that within a period of one year, this was a second case of large scale leakage of deadly gas in India, as a year earlier due to the leakage of MIC gas from the Union Carbide plant in Bhopal, more than 3000 persons had died and lakhs of others were subjected to serious diseases of various kinds. If the rule of Strict Liability as laid down in *Ryland* v. *Fletcher* was applied to such situations, then those who had established industries dealing in the production and manufacturing of hazardous substances in and around the thickly populated areas could escape the liability for the havoc caused thereby, by pleading some exception to the rule of strict liability as stated in the *Ryland* v. *Fletcher* case. For example, when the escape of the substance causing damage was due to the act of a stranger or due to sabotage, there was no liability under that rule.

The Supreme Court took a bold decision holding that it was not bound to follow the 19th century rule of the English Law, and it could evolve a rule suitable to the socio-economic conditions prevailing in India at the present day and hence came about the principle of 'no-fault liability'.[54]

---

52 AIR 1987 SC 1086;

This case was decided by a Bench consisting of 7 Judges on a reference made by a Bench of three Judges. That Bench had earlier decided whether the working of the Shri Ram Food and Fertilizer Industries should be re-started, and if so, with what conditions.

53 Article 32 forms part of the Constitution of India, Part III, which expressly deals with the fundamental rights. Article 32 provides for the right to constitutional remedies.

54 Bhagwati, C.J., observed:

"This rule of strict liability evolved in the 19th century at a time when all these developments of science and technology had not taken place cannot afford any guidance in evolving any standard of liability consistent with the constitutional norms and the needs of the present day economy and social structure. Law cannot allow our judicial thinking to be constrained by reference to the law as it prevails in England or for the matter of that in any other foreign legal order. We, in India cannot hold our hands back and I

The Supreme Court of India evolved a new rule creating 'absolute liability' for harm caused by dangerous substances as was hitherto not there. Chief Justice Bhagwati, enunciating the 'no-fault liability' principle held that, an enterprise engaged in manufacturing of hazardous substances, inherently dangerous to the health and safety of the individuals working in the enterprise and to those residing in the surrounding areas, owes an 'absolute' and 'non-derogable' duty to the community as such, to ensure that no harm results to anyone on account of its hazardous and inherently dangerous activities which are undertaken by it. The enterprise is under an obligation to provide that the hazardous or inherently dangerous activity, in which it is engaged, should be conducted with the highest of standards of safety and if in case any harm results, the enterprise is absolutely liable to compensate. The enterprise will not be allowed to say that it had exercised reasonable care and caution, and that the harm occurred without any negligence on its part.[55]

The Court thus asserted that, the rule of absolute liability shall not be subjected to the exceptions as available to the rule of strict liability. The Court held that, in instances such as the escape of toxic gas, the enterprise is 'strictly' and 'absolutely' liable to compensate all those who are affected by the accident and such liability is not subjected to any of the exceptions which operate vis-à-vis the tortuous principle of strict liability operating under the aegis of the rule enunciated in *Ryland* v. *Flectcher.*[56]

The Court opined that:

"If the enterprise is permitted to carry on any hazardous or inherently dangerous activity for its profit, the law must presume that such permission is conditional on the enterprise absorbing the cost of any accident arising on

---

venture to evolve a new principle of liability which English Courts have not done." See: [AIR 1987 SC 1086] at p.1098-1099

55 AIR 1987 SC 1086

56 The Court gave two reasons justifying the rule:

a. That the enterprise carrying on such hazardous and inherently dangerous activity for private profit has a social obligation to compensate those suffering there from, and it should absorb such loss as an item of overheads.

b. That the enterprise alone has the resources to discover and guard against such hazards and dangers.

account of such hazardous or inherently dangerous activity as an appropriate item of its overheads. Such hazardous or inherently dangerous activity for private profit can be tolerated only on condition that the enterprise engaged in such hazardous or inherently dangerous activity indemnifies all those who suffer on account of the carrying on of such hazardous or inherently dangerous activity regardless of whether it is carried on carefully or not. This principle is also sustainable on the ground that the enterprise also has the resource to discover and guard against hazards or dangers and to provide warning against potential hazard."

The Court showcasing the necessary judicial activism; came up with the 'deep-pocket theory'[57], there by stating that the measure of compensation payable should be correlated to or should be directly proportional with the magnitude and capacity of the enterprise, so that the same can have a deterrent effect.

Broadly speaking, 'corporate liability' can arise in terms of 'corporate tortuous liability' and 'corporate criminal liability'. When we speak of corporate manslaughter and corporate homicide, we necessarily focus on the 'corporate criminal liability' and to see the same in terms of environment legal jurisprudence can be a tedious exercise, but none the less, a fruitful effort. The environment law in post–independent India may hold corporations liable if their activities do not conform to the standards laid down as such by environment law legislations holding the ground in India, but liabilities arising as such under these statutes, is more in the nature of 'tortuous liability', however the scenario has greatly changed after the verdict of the Supreme Court in the Oleum Gas Leakage Case.[58] Now, as the trend shows, high- level of awareness is visible in India

---

57 The deep-pocket theory, as defined by the Supreme Court is thus:
"The larger and more prosperous the enterprise, greater must be the amount of compensation payable by it for the harm caused on account of an accident in the carrying on of the hazardous or inherently dangerous activity by the enterprise."

58 Post-Independence India was quite late in undertaking to create a legal framework for environment pollution. It was not until 1970s that the government started enacting environment laws, such as the Wild Life (Protection) Act of 1972; the Water (Prevention and Control of Pollution) Act of 1974; the Forest (Conservation) Act of 1980; the Air (Prevention and Control of Pollution) Act of 1981. Even still, it was the Bhopal Gas Disaster of December 1984 that changed the landscape, triggering the enactment of the Environment (Protection) Act in 1986 and other laws, and also

post the coming into being of the 'absolute liability principle'. Bhopal Gas Tragedy, of late has been termed as a case of corporate manslaughter, claiming thousands of lives, owing to the negligence of a corporate giant.[59] Hence, waste disposal by companies into the water bodies, there by claiming lives of people who consume such water as such is no-more just an environment tort; it's a case of corporate homicide; as it will be believed that the companies dodged the necessary environment protection laws and convened the lethal practice of discharging life-claiming industrial effluents into the water bodies, thus contaminating the water which when consumed claimed lives of the people.

More-over, the difficulties experienced by victims in securing some form of immediate compensation following an industrial disaster such as Bhopal led to the enactment of the Public Liability Insurance Act (PLIA) in 1991. The PLIA aims to provide "immediate relief" to "persons affected by accident(s) occurring while handling any hazardous substance and for matters connected therewith or incidental thereto".[60] Accordingly, it introduces a provision for no-fault compensation to victims of not all industrial accidents but only to those involving hazardous substances.[61] Section 3(1) of the PLIA provides that where death or injury to any person (other than a workman) or damage to any property has resulted from an accident, the owner shall be liable to give the specified compensation. Claimants under this provision are not "required to plead and establish that the death, injury or damage was due to any wrongful act, neglect or default of any person".[62]

Justice Kuldeep, while delivering the judgement in the case of *M.C. Mehta* v. *Kamal Nath*[63], held that, pollution is a tort (civil wrong). Pollution by its very nature is a wrong committed against the community as a whole. A person (including an artificial legal person such as a company) who is guilty of causing

---

raising awareness amongst a range of stakeholders as to the seriousness of handling environmental issues.

59 See: *Bhopal Case: A Corporate Manslaughter*, http://www.ndtv.com/article/india/bhopal-case-a-corporate-manslaughter-sushma-swaraj-43679, Visited on: 09-06-2014

60 See: The Public Liability Insurance Act of 1991

61 'Hazardous substance' means any substance or preparation which is defined to be a hazardous substance under the Environment (Protection) Act, 1986, Section 2(d).

62 Section 3(1) read with Section 3(2) of the PLIA of 1991

63 1996 1 SCC 38

pollution has to pay damages (in form of compensation) for restoration of the environment. Also, it is a settled proposition of law that, international customary law, which is not in conflict with the 'municipal law' of the country, becomes the 'domestic law' of the country and hence is enforceable like any other legislation enacted by the Parliament. Thus, 'polluter-pays principle', 'precautionary principle', 'doctrine of public trust', 'inter-generational & intra-generational equity principle' and the 'principle of sustainable development' are very much applicable in India, forming a vital part of the Indian environment law jurisprudence. No person, including corporations, can be allowed to degrade the environment, infringing the basic right to life of the citizens of the country. Seriousness of offences in regards to environmental degradation, have culled out such offences from the realm of 'tort', placing the same in the league of 'crime', as the very 'life' of people in general is at risk and corporations having known the ills of the harmful effluents, released the same 'un-treated', despite having the knowledge of the harmful effects of the same on plants, animals and humans beings.

In *Vellore Citizen Welfare Forum* v. *U.O.I*[64], the Supreme Court emphasised on the application of the "polluter pays" principle. More importantly, the Court held that this principle and the precautionary principle are integral parts of the principle of sustainable development and the public trust doctrine. In the instant case, public-interest litigation was filed regarding pollution caused by enormous discharge of untreated effluents by tanneries and other industrial corporations in the State of Tamil Nadu. The untreated effluents had been discharged in a river that was the main source of water supply to the residents of the area. The Court observed that, although the leather industry is of vital importance to the country, generating foreign exchange and providing employment, it has no right to destroy the ecology (flora and fauna), degrade the environment, pose health hazards and claim human lives. Referring to international environment law jurisprudence, the Court held that the "precautionary principle" and the "polluter pays principle" are essential features of sustainable development. The Court thus ordered the tanneries and the industrial corporations to either close down or treat all the

64 AIR 1996 SC 2715

waste they dispose off, before disposing of the same into the river bodies or open areas.[65]

Also, the Supreme Court of India in *Indian Council for Enviro-Legal Action* v. *U.O.I*[66] followed its earlier decision, *M.C. Mehta* v. *U.O.I*[67], imposing absolute liability on enterprises carrying on hazardous and inherently dangerous activity. In this case, there was environment pollution caused in the Bichhri village and other adjacent villages, on account of production of 'H' acid and the discharges from sulphuric acid qua the industrial-plant of the respondents. A writ petition was filed before the Supreme Court under Article 32 of the Constitution of India, by way of 'social action litigation' on behalf of the villagers affected by the pollution resulting in infringement on their right to life, enshrined in Article 21 of the Constitution of India. The writ petition was directed against Central and State Governments and State Pollution Control Board to compel them to perform their statutory duties.

It was held by the Supreme Court that the writ petition was maintainable as the Supreme Court had the power and duty to intervene and protect the 'right to life' of the citizens and also hold the industrial corporations responsible in case of deaths of citizens as such. Also, it was held that the Supreme Court could direct the Central Government to recover costs of remedial measures from the private companies. The Central Government was to determine the amount required for carrying out the remedial measures including the removal of sludge and muck lying in and around the complex of the respondent industries.

The factories, plant, machinery and all other immovable assets of respondent companies were ordered to be attached and the amount so determined to be recovered and utilised by the Ministry of Environment and Forests, Government of India (MoEF) for carrying out all the remedial measures to restore soil fertility, water resources and the environment in general of the affected area to its former state. On account of their continuous, persistent

---

65 See: *Access to Justice: Human Rights Abuses Involving Corporations*, A Project of the International Commission of Jurists, India, International Commission of Jurists, Chapter 1: Legal Liability for Corporations Under Indian Law, p.23

66 AIR 1996 SC 1446

67 AIR 1987 SC 1086

and insolent violations of law, the respondent industries, being characterised as "rogue industries", which had inflicted untold misery upon the poor unsuspecting villagers, despoiling their land, their water sources, and their entire environment, were ordered to be closed down. The liability of these "rogue industries" was held to be based on the principle of 'polluter pays', apart from the principle of 'absolute liability' as was recognised in the Oleum Gas Leakage Case.[68]

When we talk about 'manslaughter', we mean 'the crime of killing a person without intending to do so', so also 'homicide' means 'the act of killing another person'. When corporations indulge in the exercise of manslaughter and homicide, it is termed as 'corporate manslaughter' and 'corporate homicide' respectively.

When corporate giants, guided with the motive of profit maximisation, act with bilk by disposing the waste into the water bodies or by releasing harmful effluents in the open air without prior treating the same, there-by causing loss of human life and environment degradation, then they can be prosecuted for crimes in the nature of manslaughter and homicide.[69]

Few examples of corporate manslaughter owing to environment degradation by corporate giants, apart from the 'Bhopal Gas Tragedy' are:

First: The '2006 Ivory Coast toxic waste dump' led to health crisis in the Ivory Coast in which a ship registered in Panama, the "Probo Koala", chartered by the Swiss-based oil and commodity shipping company Trafigura Beheer BV, offloaded toxic waste at the Ivorian port of Abidjan. The waste was dumped by a local contractor at as many as 12 sites in and around the City of Abidjan in August 2006. The gas caused by the release of these chemicals, is blamed by

---

68 See: R.K. Bangia, *Law of Torts,* Allahabad Law Agency, Nineteenth Edition, 2006, Chapter 16: Rules of Strict and Absolute Liability, p.393-394

69 Environment crimes often result in death, disease and injury. In 1998, a Tampa, Florida company and the company's plant manger were found guilty of violating a federal hazardous waste law. Those illegal acts resulted in the deaths of two 9-year-old-boys who were playing in a dumpster at the company's facility. The company was held guilty of the following deaths. See: The Corporate Crime Reporter, http://www.corporatecrimereporter.com/top100.html, Visited on: 09-06-2014

the United Nations and the Government of the Ivory Coast, for the deaths of 17 and the injury to over 30,000 Ivorians with injuries that ranged from mild headaches to severe burns of skin and lungs. Almost 100,000 Ivorians sought medical attention for the effects of these chemicals. In 2007, the company paid US $198 million for "cleaning-up operations" to the Ivorian government without admitting wrongdoing, and the Ivorian government pledged not to prosecute the company. A series of protests and resignations of Ivorian Government officials followed this deal.[70]

Second: The Ajkai Timfoldgyar disaster- On 5th of October, 2010, about 600,000-700,000 cubic metres of sludge escaped from a reservoir at the Ajkai Timfoldgyar plant (the plant made alumina, a synthetically produced aluminium oxide) in the town of Ajkai, about 160-km from the capital, Budapest, affecting an area of 40 sq. km. With 7,000 people affected directly by the disaster, a state of emergency was declared in the county of Veszprem where the spill occurred, and Gyor-Moson-Sopron and Vas, where the sludge appeared to be heading. In this corporate-environment disaster about four people died, seven went missing and about 120 were seriously injured. This disaster has been termed as one of the worst 'chemical disasters' ever faced by Hungary. MAL Rt, the Hungarian company which owns the plant, defended itself by saying that, by EU standards the sludge had not been considered hazardous. A series of charges and prosecution has been levelled against the company for one of the most horrendous 'chemical disaster' of its kind, with lately the managing director of MAL been arrested with charges of 'criminal negligence resulting in public catastrophe'.[71]

Third: The B.P. oil spill disaster, off the coast of New Orleans in 2010 brought the issue to fore in the United States of America qua corporate criminal negligence. Oil flowed from the Deepwater Horizon oil rig for three months in 2010 and the spill is said to be one of the most hazardous marine oil spill

---

[70] See: The Environment Green Crimes, http://www.historylearningsite.co.uk/environmental_green_crimes.htm, Visited on: 05-06-2014

[71] See: The Ajkia Timfoldgyar Plant, *The BBC*, http://www.bbc.com/news/world-europe-11481740, Visited on: 03-06-2014; Also see: Ajkia Timfoldgyar Disaster, *The New York Times*, http://www.nytimes.com/2010/10/12/world/europe/12hungary.html?_r=2&pagewanted=all&, Visited on: 03-06-2014

accident in the history of the fuel industry. The spill stemmed from the sea-floor oil gusher, resulting from the 20th April, 2010 explosion. The explosion killed 11 men working on the platform and injured 17 others. On 15th July, 2010 the leak was stopped by capping the gushing wellhead, after it had released approximately 205.8 million gallons of crude oil. It was estimated that 53,000 barrels of crude oil per day was escaping from the well just before it was capped. Once the spill had been fixed, the much anticipated 'blame game' took off, for attributing of liability for ascertaining as to who was responsible. This even included President Obama who came out to blame and bash the B.P., raising the stakes even higher by making it clear that, it was the British company that was to be held responsible for this American disaster. The final report on the spill was released in January 2011. It blamed B.P., Halliburton and Transocean for making a series of cost-cutting decisions. The report also highlighted the lack of a system to ensure the necessary safety.[72] The fear of the U.S. Government's resolve to teach B.P. a lesson, resulted in shares of B.P. losing close to $105 billion, since the spill, also B.P. was forced to create a $20 billion trust to compensate claims and pay $8 billion in damages.[73]

After witnessing the cases in regards to 'corporate manslaughter' in environment law jurisprudence, we shall be moving a step further to witness the rise in consciousness in U.K. in regards to corporate criminal liability, to see how 'corporate manslaughter' and 'corporate homicide' theories came up to hold the ground, expanding the realm of corporate criminal liability jurisprudence further.

It has been asserted time and again that, when persons are injured or are killed by corporate activities it may be possible for State to initiate a criminal prosecution. The most serious charge would be that of manslaughter. However, a criminal prosecution for corporate manslaughter will only succeed if it can be proved that the action undertaken by the organisation was deliberately fashioned to cause such a result, and, additionally, that a senior executive within the company could be pinpointed for having been responsible for

---

72 See: The B.P. Oil Spill, *The Guardian*, http://www.theguardian.com/environment/bp-oil-spill, Visited on: 02-06-2014

73 See: Chetan Bhagat, *What Young India Wants*, Rupa Publications, 2012, p.40-41

the incident.[74] In U.K., the public unease about episodes which included the sinking of the ferry the 'Herald of Free Enterprise' (in which 192 died) and the 'King's Cross Underground Fire' (which killed 31 people) in 1987, the fire on the 'Piper Alpha Oil Rig' and the 'Clapham Rail Crash' in 1998 (in which 167 and 37 individuals died), and the 'Marchioness River Boat Sinking' in 1989 (in which 51 people perished when the ship collided with the dredger, the *Bowbelle*) prompted a review of the existing law in U.K. by the Law Commission. Placed forward was a proposal to replace the existing offence of corporate manslaughter with a new offence of corporate killing in which a jury would be asked to decide whether there had been a management failure, whether this was one of the causes of the individual's death and whether this management failure 'fell far below from what could reasonably be expected of the corporation in the circumstances'[75].[76]

The Government (U.K.) published a response to this and although no action was immediately forthcoming, further tragedies such as the 1999 'Paddington Rail Disaster' (in which 32 people died) and the 2000 'Hatfield Disaster' (where an unrepaired broken rail caused the deaths of 4 people) re-ignited the debate. In the latter case, charges against the former chief executive of rail-track and two other managers were dropped before the main trial, when a High Court judge ruled that there was insufficient evidence confirming that the accident was due to profit making having been put before safety.[77]

---

74 The Corporate Manslaughter and Corporate Homicide Act of 2007 (a U.K. legislation), Section 4(c)(i) & (ii), specifically speak of the 'senior management test', in relation to an organisation, it means the persons who play significant role in-

a. The making decisions about how the whole or substantial part of its activities are to be managed or organised or,

b. The actual managing or organising of the whole or a substantial part of those activities.

75 Management Failure Model is one of the principles to impute liability on corporations in cases of manslaughter and homicide. The principle says that, if it is established that a corporation did not employ reasonable care and caution in carrying out its business activities and if any mishap happens, there-by claiming human life, then in that case, the management of the corporation will be held legally liable. The U.K. legislation i.e. the Corporate Manslaughter and Corporate Homicide Act of 2007 employs this theory of 'management failure model'.

76 See: The U.K. Law Commission Report of 1996

77 See: Peter Joyce, *Criminal Justice: An Introduction to Crime and the Criminal Justice System*, William Publishing, Chapter 2: Crime and Crime Prevention, p.78-79

In 2004, the U.K. Prime Minister promised to bring forward legislation to provide for the offence of corporate manslaughter whereby company directors would be held responsible for deaths due to management failure. In 2007, U.K. came up with the legislation in the name of the Corporate Manslaughter and Corporate Homicide Act of 2007, to punish corporate perpetrators for crimes of manslaughter and homicide.

It is pitiful that, in India despite the 'Bhopal Gas Tragedy' and the 'Oleum Gas Leakage Case', no legislation has been brought to force, to punish the corporations for the crimes in the nature of manslaughter and homicide. Although, Environment Protection Act of 1986; the Public Liability Insurance Act of 1991 and the Protection of Human Rights Act of 1993, have been enacted, their enforcement have been less than effective and also, the results desired have not been achieved as such.[78]

Many principles have been employed world-over for imputation of liability in regards to crimes of corporate manslaughter and corporate homicide. The principles employed in the legislation enacted in the U.K. (*The Corporate Manslaughter and Corporate Homicide Act of 2007*) are in the nature of the 'senior management test' and 'management failure model'.

---

78 There have been cases in the nature of *U.P. Pollution Control Board* v. *Modi Distillery* [(1987) 3 SCR 798], where the Supreme Court considered the question in a case involving discharge of noxious effluents from a factory into a river, which constituted a case in the nature of environment degradation. The Court held that the managing director, directors and other persons responsible for the company's conduct be prosecuted even if, due to technicality, the company was not prosecuted. The Court reasoned that it would be a travesty of justice if a big business entity were "allowed to defeat the prosecution launched and avoid facing the trial on a technical flaw which is incurable". But still there have been cases of corporate manslaughter (despite the rising awareness in regards to the same) in the nature of Uphaar Cinema Tragedy which happened on 13th June, 1997, where-by due to lack of reasonable care employed by the owners of the cinema hall, the fire as so which had broken into the cinema hall could not be controlled and it claimed about 59 lives and more than 103 got seriously injured. On 5th March 2014 the Supreme Court gave its verdict holding the Ansal brothers responsible for the mishap. The Court imposed a liability of Rs. 100 crores over the Ansal brothers for been negligent and giving priority to profits over and above the safety of the customers generally.

2.7. Other Principles:

The other principles are- the *identification doctrine*, the *aggregation doctrine*, the *reactive corporate fault principle*, the *vicarious liability principle* and the *principle of corporate mens rea.*

2.7.1. The Identification Doctrine: This doctrine came into existence in the 1940s, institutionalising a mechanism to impute criminal liability on to the corporations. During the 1940s in a variety of cases it was observed that a company is capable of being malicious[79], could intend to deceive[80], and could conspire[81]. This seemed a significant development as because prior to 1940s, the courts firmly believed that it was inappropriate to prosecute a company for common law offence requiring proof of a subjective mental element.[82] A glimpse of this doctrine can be found in the case of *Lennard's Carrying Co.* v. *Asiatic Petroleum Co.*[83], where Lord Viscount Haldane observed that the corporation is an 'abstraction', and that its 'active and directing will' must be sought in a person who is the very ego and centre of its personality, which is an agent or the board of directors. And so, Morris L.J., in *H.L. Bolton Engineering* v. *T.J. Graham*[84] identified the 'active and directing will' of the respondent company as the directors, having regard to their standing in the control of the business. In *Tesco* v. *Nattrass*[85], it was held that only those who control or manage the affairs of the company were to be regarded as embodying or acting as the company for these purposes (the case concerned a charge against the company under the Trade Descriptions Act of 1968). This over a period of time came to be known as the 'directing mind' theory of corporate liability.[86]

---

79 See: *Triplex Glass Safety* v. *Lancegay Safety Glass* [(1939) 2 K.B. 395]

80 See: *DPP* v. *Kent and Sussex Contractors* [(1944) K.B. 146]; *Moore* v. *Bresler* [(1944) 2 All E.R. 515]

81 See: *R* v. *ICR Haulage Ltd.* [(1944) K.B. 551]; *R* v. *Sorsky* [(1944) 2 All E.R. 333]

82 See: Celia Wells, *The Millennium Bug and Corporate Criminal Liability,* 2 J.I.L.T. (1999), http://www2.warwick.ac.uk/fac/soc/law/elj/jilt/1999_2/wells/, Visited on: 23-06-2014

83 (1915) A.C. 705, 713

84 (1957) 1 Q.B. 159

85 (1972) A.C. 153

86 In the words of Lord Reid: "The person who acts is acting as the company and his mind which directs his acts is the mind of the company. If it is a guilty mind then that is the guilt of the company."

This theory however, has an inherent failure as it states that a company could be held liable for serious offences only if its senior-most officers had acted with fault.[87] In brief, this principle states that, an offence of corporate manslaughter will be made out when all the individual elements, which necessarily need to be present for making out the offence of manslaughter are present in an offence committed. Hence, for this principle to apply there must be corporate killings and these killings must be owing to corporate negligence i.e. non-employment of duty of reasonable care. This principle in nature prosecutes the determining mind and will of the company i.e. individuals holding senior positions in the management (corporate hierarchy).[88]

2.7.2. The Aggregation Doctrine: This doctrine is also known as the collective knowledge doctrine. Here, all acts of all the employees of a company along with the decision making activities of the managerial heads of the company are looked into, to see the sequence of events resulting in the crime of corporate manslaughter and corporate homicide. This doctrine had its origin in the U.S. Once the sequence of events as looked into indicate the existence of all elements constituting the crime of manslaughter or homicide by the corporation, the corporation is held liable and accountable.

2.7.3. Reactive Corporate Fault: Under this principle, attachment of liability in regards to offences in the nature of manslaughter or homicide is done on individual basis, but after supplying due emphasis on the fact as to for which corporation/enterprise/organisation the individual had been working and on whose instructions, the individual acted. If the individual had committed the crime of manslaughter, during the course of his employment, the corporation is as such held liable and will be prosecuted. But if an individual has committed the crime of manslaughter during the course of his employment but acting outside the course of authority expressly conferred to him, owing to his own negligence; the corporation shall be expected to take severe action against the

87 See: Ananthi Bharadwaj, NALSAR University, Hyderabad, *Corporate Manslaughter and Corporate Homicide Act, 2007,* National Law School of India Review, Volume 21(1), 2009, p.203-204

88 This principle was employed by the Courts in U.K. before enacting the legislation in the nature of the Corporate Manslaughter and Corporate Homicide Act of 2007.

delinquent employee, and in absence of the same, company can be made to undergo the necessary prosecution.

2.7.4. Vicarious Liability Principle: This principle simply states that, a servant shall be responsible for the acts of his master provided such acts have been done or else performed, within the authority duly conferred qua such acts, having been done during the course of the servant's employment. This principle was employed by the Courts in the U.K. to charge the corporations and to attribute liability onto them for their illegal and unlawful acts. This same principle in U.S. is known as the principle of *respondeat superior*. The key elements that need to be established for holding a corporation liable under this principle are as follows: a corporate agent must have committed an illegal act (*actus reus*) with the requisite state of mind (*mens rea*); the agent must have acted within his scope of employment; the agent must have intended to benefit the corporation. *Mousell Bros.* v. *London and North Western Railway*[89] was the first case in which a corporation was held vicariously liable for the *mens rea* offence, beyond the confines of strict liability and nuisance.[90] Though this case was expected to serve as a basis for developing further judicial dicta in the direction of imposing criminal liability on corporations, it stood out as an exception amongst cases decided during that period in which courts expressed their inability to impute criminal liability onto corporations.[91]

2.7.5. Principle of Corporate *Mens Rea*: For attribution of a crime, two ingredients must be present: firstly, *actus reus* and secondly, *mens rea*. The complexity arises when corporate criminal liability is to be established. In

---

89 (1917) 2 K.B. 836, 845

90 The Court punished the corporation for the act of its manager in giving a false account with the intent to avoid payment of tolls, which was contrary to the Railway Clauses Consolidation Act of 1845. Here, Atkin J. laid down a test for establishing vicarious liability under a statute:

"Whether a particular provision imposes vicarious liability on an employer (whether natural or corporate) is a matter of construction depending upon the object of the statute, the words used, the nature of the duty laid down, the person upon whom it is imposed, the person by whom it would in ordinary circumstances be performed, and the person upon whom the penalty is imposed."

91 See: Ananthi Bharadwaj, NALSAR University, Hyderabad, *Corporate Manslaughter and Corporate Homicide Act of 2007,* National Law School of India Review, Volume 21(1), 2009, p.203

corporate crimes, under this principle, what is to be seen is that, 'who' in a corporation can be imputed with the necessary *mens rea* so that the corporation as such, in its capacity of an artificial legal person can be held accountable. So what is to be seen is, who are the individuals forming the 'determining mind and will of the company' and to see whether these individuals were working within the authority expressly conferred to them, within the course of their respective employment. This question is not difficult when the corporation is small and the owner of the corporation is also its manager, but with modern corporations having complex managerial structures, the problem becomes manifold. This principle has been hugely advocated in U.S. and this principle was introduced in Australia in 1995.

2.8. Chapter Conclusion:

Despite the Bhopal Gas Tragedy and the Oleum Gas Leakage disaster followed by cases in the nature of Uphaar Cinema Tragedy and atrocities inflicted by corporate monsters such as Vedanta Corporation carrying out bauxite mining in Niyamgiri Hills, which is responsible for killing thousands of 'adivasi people' (indigenous people) in accidents, injuries, illness and forced displacement[92]; there has hardly been any rise in consciousness in India in regards to having a legislation enacted which can come down strongly against corporations indulging in crimes of corporate manslaughter and homicide. Indian courts have always relied on the principles of *vicarious liability*; the *absolute liability* principle (rooting out from the *strict liability* principle), the *deep-pocket theory* and to some extent the *multipliers method*[93] for computing compensation that needs to be given to victims suffering from ills of corporate activities. India is fast realising that the *absolute liability* principle, qua the dicta in the Oleum Gas Leakage case, needs to be read necessarily in consonance with the *deep-pocket theory*, this in reality makes the absolute liability principle a weak principle; if a tragedy in the nature of Bhopal Gas happens, owing to the gross

92 See: *Stop Vedanta, The Killer Corporate*; http://www.southasiasolidarity.org/2011/08/04/foil-vedanta-stop-the-killer-corporate/, Visited on: 18-05-2014

93 The multiplier method calculates compensation based on the estimated future income of the deceased. It depends on the age of the deceased at the time of death, since it multiplies the estimated figure of annual income by the estimated number of years the deceased would have been earning for. This principle has been provided for under the Indian legislation, the Motor Vehicles Act of 1988.

negligence of a corporation which is operating on a small scale, having shallow pockets (ability to compensate), then in that case, although the corporation will be accused following the principle of *no-fault* but at the same time, the amount of compensation that can be ordered against it will be hardly satisfactory.

In this Chapter, after discussing the various theories of corporate personality, the author has reached the conclusion that each theory of corporate personality in its last logical analysis, directly or indirectly, points that a company (or a corporation) is an 'artificial legal person' existing only in the 'contemplation of law', having a 'common seal' and 'perpetual succession'. The company does not run on its own for it is devoid of head and brain vis-à-vis flesh and blood. It is the individuals working behind the legal fiction, lexically termed as "company", forms the 'determining mind' and 'intending will' of the artificial juridical person. The doctrine of separate legal entity has done more harm than good, *dehors* anything else, based on this doctrine of artificial legal person- a delinquent company is saved from serious crimes such as homicide and manslaughter. The doctrine of lifting up of the corporate veil has been of little help, as the corporate veil is usually lifted only in the cases of corporate fraud and misrepresentation. Deaths taking place, whether of workers or of consumers or of other individuals forming part of the general public, owing to the gross negligence of the corporation is punished in India by reading progressively the provisions of the Indian Penal Code of 1860. The punishment provided for death taking place owing to the gross negligence is fine and imprisonment, as per the provisions of the Indian Penal Code of 1860. A corporation being a legal person existing only in the contemplation of law is punished only with fines, no imprisonment is imposed upon it, as an artificial legal person cannot be incarcerated.

India is presently witnessing absence of necessary statute such as the U.K.'s, Corporate Manslaughter and Corporate Homicide Act of 2007, which employs the "senior management test" to put the individuals forming the "determining mind and intending will" of the corporation to trial in cases of corporate-gross-negligence-manslaughter. India can no longer ignore the fact that crimes in the nature of "corporate killings" need to be dealt with an iron fist to make the corporations realise that whatever the case may be, it is the corporations that will be forced to bear the burden of their own insensitivity.

Chapter 3

Analysis of the existing dimensions of the crimes of corporate manslaughter and corporate homicide.

3.1. Introduction:

The principle of corporate criminal liability has over the period of time, shed much light on the terms "corporate manslaughter" and "corporate homicide". Crimes in the nature of corporate manslaughter and corporate homicide are not nascent; these crimes have always existed but due to the inherent limitation of corporations, as artificial legal persons which cannot be incarcerated, legal focus on these crimes became blurred. But, the rise in consciousness among the people generally with the media playing an activist role, these crimes of corporate killings were lexically defined in terms of crimes of 'corporate manslaughter and homicide'. In this chapter we shall explore the varied dimensions in regards to these crimes as so presently existing.

3.2. Can corporations be held criminally liable?:

Corporate criminality and related concepts are not of nascent origin. Explorative study of legal history in this regard would suggest that right from the early 16th century, there was a common belief that corporations could not be held criminally liable. The very early criminal law legislation faced **four fundamental problems** in punishing corporations for their alleged criminal activities, these were:

3.2.1. The problem of 'attribution of criminal liability' over a non-natural or an artificial legal person i.e. corporation.

3.2.2. The issue in regards to the belief that an artificial legal person cannot possess a 'blameworthy state of mind', that is *mens rea.*

3.2.3. Even after the development of some theoretical arguments in this behalf, the third and the most pragmatic problem was that of the 'doctrine of *ultra vires*', where courts failed to hold a corporation liable for an act committed by its employee when such an act was not covered under its charter (that is, the Memorandum of Association).

3.2.4. The last and the most fundamental obstacle, was the literal understanding of criminal procedures by jurists and law officers of the court. Here they thought that for all criminal prosecutions, the accused must be brought to the court in person, that is in their respective "human individuality" and the accusations must be framed against them after giving personal hearing which was nothing but impossible when someone wants to prosecute a company (as companies exist only in the contemplation of law).

Cumulatively, these *four* fundamental obstacles never allowed traditional penal statutes to prosecute corporations for their crimes.[94] It was the incremental development in the penal laws, such as environmental law, anti-trust law and the securities law that a new wave of demand for prosecuting corporations started. Initially, corporations were punished for their omissions resulting in environmental nuisance, as in such type of cases neither act was required to be 'attributed' nor was there any requirement of proving *mens rea.* In the later developments, courts started punishing corporations for acts requiring 'criminal intent' either by attributing *mens rea* or by strictly reading (literal interpretation) the penal statutes, where *mens rea* seemed to be excluded by necessary implications. The deterrence theory of punishment played a 'pilot role' in this regard. Various theories have been developed and acts of employees have been 'attributed' against corporations if, knowledge, convenience or even connivance is proved on part of the persons in-charge, in the corporation.

---

94 See: Dr. Girjesh Shukla, *Criminology: Crime Causation, Sentencing and Rehabilitation of Victims,* Lexis Nexis Publication, 2013, Chapter 8: Sentencing and Penal Policy, p.188

3.3. Criminal sanction that can be imposed on corporations accused of the crimes of manslaughter and homicide:

Law Commission of India has over the period of time suggested new type of criminal sanctions devised for tackling corporate crimes; these sanctions are in the nature of: *imposing exemplary fine*; *loss of license*; and, *loss of fiscal benefits*. However, the most obvious challenge was in regards to punishing the corporations for those offences where by mandatory imprisonment sentences were to be casted.[95] This question, of late has been resolved by the Apex Court in India, not satisfactorily but vide progressive judicial thought so far as criminal jurisprudence in India is concerned, through the judgement rendered in the case of *Standard Chartered Bank* v. *Directorate of Enforcement*[96]. In this case the Supreme Court held that, when a corporation is to be mandatorily punished for an offence under the criminal law with fine and imprisonment then, the accused corporations must be prosecuted and punished, at least with fines. However, the Court did not develop its reasoning far enough so as to specifically hold that a corporation is capable of forming *mens rea* and is capable of acting pursuant to it.

Corporate crimes can be a cause of injury, or even death. 'Death' does occur in the course of, and as a result of, legitimate corporate activities such as exploration, mining and machine failure. Many times, corporate activities which result in deaths and serious injuries are a result of illegitimate albeit

---

95 In *State of Maharashtra* v. *Jugamander Lal* [AIR 1966 SC 940]; *State of Maharashtra* v. *Syndicate Transport* [1963 Bom LR 197], it was held that the company cannot be prosecuted for offences which necessarily entail consequences of a corporal punishment or imprisonment and prosecuting a company for such offences would only result in the court stultifying itself by embarking on a trial in which the verdict of guilty is returned and no effective order by way of sentence can be made; In *Badsha* v. *Income Tax officer* [1987 (1) KLT 112], Justice Thomas, following the decision of the Allahabad High Court in *Modi Industries Limited* v. *B.C. Goel* [144 ITR 496 (1983)], held that: "A company registered under the Companies Act, 1956 is a juristic person and cannot be awarded the punishment of imprisonment and hence cannot be prosecuted for breach of Sections 277 and 278 of the Act" and therefore the Court held that the first accused being a firm was not liable to be prosecuted for offences under Sections 277 and 278.

96 AIR 2005 SC 1227; See also: *Anz Grindlays Bank Limited* v. *Directorate of Enforcement* [Appeal (Civil) 1748 of 1999]

wanton disregard for the health and safety of employees or customers. Corporations often disregard the interests of society as a whole, in pursuit of their corporate goals, so they dump toxic waste, emit dangerous fumes into the atmosphere, fit faulty equipment to products such as cars, and expose employees or others to dangers.[97]

3.4. Dimensions of the crime of corporate manslaughter:

So far as the existing dimensions of the crime in the nature of corporate manslaughter and corporate homicide is concerned, it can take place in either of the ways:

3.4.1. Corporate Workplace Deaths: Crime of corporate manslaughter can be made out against a corporation for having dealt with culpable criminal negligence, owing to either unhealthy or hazardous work conditions under which the workers of the corporation are forced to work in; or owing to accidents, claiming lives of workmen (during the course of their employment) as a result of machinery employed to carry out the work necessary being obsolete or un-standardised; or the workers made to work overtime, without giving due consideration to their normal work ability[98].

It shall be thoughtful for us to take into consideration the successful corporate manslaughter prosecution, as so took place in the case of, *Cotswold Geotechnical (Holdings) Ltd. (U.K.)* in 2011 owing to the enactment of the Corporate Manslaughter and Corporate Homicide Act of 2007. In this case, on 8th of September, 2008, Alex Wright, a 27-years old junior geologist employed by Cotswold, was left working alone in a 3.5 metre deep trench, taking soil samples.

---

97 See: Katherine S. Williams, *Textbook on Criminology,* Oxford University Press, Fifth Edition, Chapter 3: Public conceptions and misconceptions of crime, p.59

98 As for example, see the case of: *R* v. *Bowles* (1999), in this case, two directors (a brother and sister) of a haulage company were found guilty of corporate manslaughter, after ignoring the excessive work hours of one of their drivers, who caused a fatal crash after falling asleep at the wheel of his lorry. Stephen and Julie Bowles were convicted when the jury decided that they knew, or that they should have known; that their driver, Andrew Cox, was in a "dangerously exhausted state". Cox who often worked more than 60 hours without taking proper breaks killed two motorists on the M25 in October 1997.

When the unsupported soil wall of the trench collapsed and smothered him, he died of traumatic asphyxiation. The well-established industry guidelines as so operational in the U.K. stated that, for excavations in deep pits or trenches; the excavations should be allowed to a maximum depth of 1.2 metres. Cotswold Geotechnical (Holdings) Ltd. was accordingly convicted for gross negligence manslaughter and was fined for £385,000, payable over 10 years owing to the poor financial state of affairs of the company. The decision rendered in this case is criticised on the grounds of compensation offered being not appropriate, as the Sentencing Guidelines Council recommends that the appropriate fine for corporate manslaughter convictions should seldom be less than £500,000.

A plethora of statutes have been enacted to protect the interests of workers in India, for example, the Workmen's Compensation Act of 1923, the Trade Unions Act of 1926, the Payment of Wages Act of 1936, the Industrial Disputes Act of 1947, the Factories Act of 1948, the Employees State Insurance Act of 1948, the Employees Provident Fund and Miscellaneous Provisions Act of 1952, the Mines Act of 1952, the Maternity Benefits Act of 1961, the Contract Labour (Abolition and Regulation) Act of 1970, the Payment of Gratuity Act of 1972, the Equal Remuneration Act of 1972, the Bonded Labour System (Abolition) Act of 1976 and the Child Labour (Prohibition and Regulation) Act of 1986.[99] A more recent addition to the listed is the Unorganised Workers' Social Security Act of 2008, which seeks to provide for the social security and welfare of the unorganised workers such as those who work from home or are self employed.

These Acts are nothing, but a means to protect the workers of an organisation from human rights abuses involving corporations. But none of these legislations hold corporations accountable for crimes in the nature of corporate homicide. The pity is that, these legislations provide measures to ensure that workers in an organisation work under safe conditions and are not exploited; that they are paid amounts legitimately accruable to them (taking due note of extra compensation payable in case the workers are made to work 'overtime') but once a corporate mishap happens, claiming the lives of the workmen, these statutes fall silent; at best providing only just means for compensating the

---

[99] See: Mohan R. Pillay, Paul R. Sandosham & Nandakumar Ponniya, *Doing Business in India,* Sweet & Maxwell- Singapore, 2004, p. 197-214

families of the deceased workmen. None of these statutes sheds a light of concern, looking into the fact as to how the criminal liability can be made attributable to the corporations and how can the 'determining mind and intending will' of the corporation be put to severe punishment, for lacking was theirs and hence, they must be made to 'make good the loss'.

No amount of compensation can be equated with the remedying of the loss of human life. Author agrees, that punishing the 'determining mind and will' of the corporation cannot remedy the loss suffered, but necessary detrimental consequences that faulting corporations shall face qua the offence must be put under the lamp-post with necessary highlights. Prime inspiration can be taken from the consequences following the incident which happened on the 3rd of September, 1991 where by fire broke-out at the Imperial Food Products, Inc., a North Carolina chicken processing plant. The fire, which claimed 25 lives, was devastatingly deadly, more because the plant had no sprinkler system, windows, or escape routes. Adding to the tragedy, the company executives locked the exit doors to prevent employee pilferage. Emmett Roe, the firm's owner, was convicted of involuntary manslaughter and received a 19-year prison sentence. In this case, a clear initiative was taken to prosecute corporate executive as a violent criminal.[100]

The international standard for prosecuting corporations for the crime of manslaughter, owing to the death of workmen has been laid down in the following words, in the case of, *R* v. *Northern Strip Mining Construction Co. Ltd.*[101]:

"It is for the prosecution to show that the defendant company, in person of the managing director or other individuals forming the 'determining mind and will of the company', was guilty to such a degree of negligence that amounted to a reckless disregard for the life and limb of the workmen".

---

100 See: Larry Siegel, *Criminology,* Wadsworth Publishers, Seventh Edition, Chapter 13: White Collar and Organised Crime, p.410

101 See: *The Times*, 2, 4 & 5 February 1965. This case was decided by the Courts in the U.K. on 1st February, 1965 but was not reported. This case marked the first judicial recognition as to for the crime of corporate manslaughter on a global pedestal.

According to the law stated in *R* v. *Northern Strip Mining Construction Co. Ltd.* (1965) and the preliminary ruling given by Mr. Justice Turner in *R* v. *P & O European Ferries (Dover) Ltd.* (1990), it is possible for a company to be convicted for the crime of manslaughter, if it can be proved beyond reasonable doubt that: the victim who died had been subjected to an "obvious and serious risk" of some physical injury prior to death; that a senior manager or director of the company who was the "controlling mind" of the company was responsible for the act or omission which led to the death; and that when the relevant directors committed the *actus reus*, having appropriate *mens rea*, they gave no thought to the possibility that, the worker would be put in danger of physical injury, or having recognised that there was such a risk, still allowed him to continue. It is also necessary to prove that the relevant conduct of the directors of the company was at least a "substantial cause" for the death of the workmen, that is, they "contributed significantly" to the death.

Professor Gary Slapper estimates that, between 1969 to 1993, more than 18,151 people got killed at work in U.K. and so far as U.S. is concerned, in 1972 alone more than 114,000 people died owing to occupational hazards, diseases and accidents.[102] Also, Professor Slapper estimates that, in 20% of workplace deaths, globally speaking, there is a prima facie case of manslaughter as in many cases foremen; managers and/or directors are responsible for these deaths.[103] Moving a step further, Professor Slapper states that hundreds of people have died in disasters like the **Kings Cross Fire of 1987**, the **Piper Alpha Oil Rig Fire of 1988**, the **Sinking of the Marchioness in 1989** and various train crashes in the U.K. and these incidents in turn raised a public outcry for enacting a legislation that not only defines the offence of corporate manslaughter and corporate homicide but also punishes the corporations in such a way that they are unable to take the shield of 'having existence only in the contemplation of law' or 'having no body to kick'. This led to the enactment of the Corporate Manslaughter and Corporate Homicide Act of 2007.[104]

---

102 See: Gary Slapper, *Corporate Manslaughter,* (1993) 2 Social and Legal Studies 423, http://oro.open.ac.uk/20975/2/1535A240.pdf, Visited on: 25-05-2014

103 See: Gary Slapper, *The Guardian,* 23 February 1999

104 See: Andrew Sanders, Richard Young & Mandy Burton, *Criminal Justice,* Oxford University Press, Fourth Edition, Chapter 7: Prosecutions, p.415-417

Absence of legislation in the nature of the 2007 Act (of the U.K.) is now strongly felt in India. It has been timelessly argued that in India, the **Workmen Compensation Act of 1923** provides social security to the workmen. Under this Act, if a workman dies during the course of his employment or suffers total or partial disablement, then the family of the deceased workman or he, himself shall be provided compensation, as the case may be, from the employer. However, no attempt has been made to prosecute, under the aegis of the legislation, the senior management of the industrial corporation for ignoring the safety concerns or for employing machineries of un-standardised quality. 'One stop' solution this legislation provides is compensation by virtue of Section 3(1) of the legislation. Moreover, if a worker contracts an occupational disease then what he is entitled to is, a 'just compensation', that to if he was in employment with the industrial corporation for a period of more than six months.

Although as a matter of judicial activism, the principle of *no-fault liability* has been read into the legislation[105], but the legislation does not seem pro-workmen for it explicitly states that, if due to any accident or other mishap, a worker suffers disablement for about 3 days (only), then, he is not entitled to any compensation.

The **Factories Act of 1948** is another comprehensive piece of legislation that seeks to protect the interest of labourers working in the factories. The Act contains extensive provisions aimed at safeguarding the health and safety of factory workers. There are also affirmative provisions for workers' welfare, such as those requiring first-aid facilities or immediate medical help.[106] The Factories Act of 1948 provides that no adult worker should be required or should be allowed to work in the factory for more than 48 hours in any week or more than 9 hours on any day.[107] The workers, who slough for more than these limits set under the Act, are entitled to wages at the rate of *twice* their

---

105 See: *Mar Themotheous* v. *Santosh Raj* [2001 LLR 164 (Ker HC DB)]

106 See: Chapter V, The Factories Act of 1948

107 See: Sections 51 and 54 of the Factories Act of 1948

ordinary rate of wages.[108] Also, no child below the age of 14 years should be allowed to work in any factory.[109]

Important amendments to this statute were made post the Bhopal Gas Tragedy. The 1987 amendment to this statute provided that, in case of a company, the director of the company will be deemed to be the "occupier", who in fact is "a person who has the ultimate control over the affairs of the factory".[110] The statute as amended makes directors personally responsible for the health and safety of the factory workers.[111] In a subsequent case, the Supreme Court characterised this amendment as a response to 'the escape routes which the employers have found to shift their responsibilities, accountability and liabilities on some employees to escape the punishment and the penalty'.[112]

Section 7A of the Factories Act further provides that, "Every occupier shall ensure, so far as is reasonably practicable, the health, safety and welfare of all workers, while they are at work in the factory".[113] The law requires the State Governments to appoint inspectors and vigilance officers, who may enter any factory with or without prior notice to conduct a range of health and safety-related examinations, as they may deem necessary.[114]

The newly inserted Chapter IV-A in the Factories Act of 1948, also added special provisions relating to "hazardous processes", that can be thought of as another direct response to the Bhopal Gas Tragedy. The Chapter provides for: the Constitution of Site Appraisal Committees to decide where a factory may be located; compulsory disclosure of information to the Chief Inspector of

---

108 See: Section 59(1) of the Factories Act of 1948

109 See: Section 67 of the Factories Act of 1948

110 See: Section 2(n) of the Factories Act of 1948

111 Where the occupier is able to demonstrate that it was not him, but someone else, who was the actual offender, he would have to prove to the satisfaction of the Court that he had exercised due diligence to enforce the execution of the Act and 'that the said other person committed the offence in question without his knowledge, consent or convenience. See: Section 101 of the Factories Act of 1948 as amended in 1987.

112 See: *J.K. Industries Ltd.* v. *Chief Inspector of Factories & Boilers* [(1996) 6 SCC 665]

113 This section also imposes other specific obligations (such as related to maintenance of the plant and machinery, and supervision and training of workers) on occupiers that were triggered by Bhopal.

114 See: Section 8 & Section 9 of the Factories Act of 1948

Factories, the local authority and the general public (living in the vicinity) about the potential risks and hazards; limits on permissible exposure to chemicals and toxic substances; drawing up in advance "on-site emergency plans" and "detailed disaster control measures"; and workers' right to participate in the safety management.

Recognising that concerns in regards to "industrial secrecy" may discourage companies from disclosing certain information about their factories and areas of operations, the Factories Act authorises the State Government inspectors to collect and check samples if they suspect any contravention in regards to circumvention of the provisions of the Act, or are of the opinion that bodily injury may be caused or the health of workers may be adversely affected.[115]

Moreover, the breach of the provisions of the Factories Act has been made a criminal offence, post the amendments. Section 92 prescribes that, "the occupier and the manager of the factory shall each be guilty of an offence, punishable with imprisonment for a term which may extend to two years or with fine which may extend to one lakh rupees or with both, if the contravention continued even after the conviction, with a further fine which may extend to one thousand rupees for each day qua which the contravention is so continued." There is also an enhanced penalty if a person commits an offence for which, he has been already convicted in the past.[116]

On paper it seems that, India has equipped itself with necessary precautionary measures so that industrial catastrophe in the nature of Bhopal Gas Tragedy does not happen again, but the compliance of legal provisions is another area that needs regular and consolidated focus.

Corporations in India, if are accused of manslaughter or homicide, at the most they are charged with penalty in the nature of compensation payable, which seems to have neither any deterrent effect nor retributive tendency. Inspiration needs to be drawn from the developing international jurisprudence on this issue. Corporations can be punished by prohibiting them from applying for the government contracts and also by curbing or limiting their business activities

---

115 See: Section 91(1) of the Factories Act of 1948

116 See: Section 94 of the Factories Act of 1948

to only certain areas. Moreover, awareness can be spread qua the illegitimate and lethal activities of the corporation, claiming to be injurious to human life.

3.4.2. Corporate killings owing to gross negligence exercised in regards to the nature of work carried out by a corporation: A case of corporate manslaughter and homicide can be made out against a company, owing to the nature of work carried out by a company that is, gross negligence on the part of the company claiming potential lives.[117] It shall also be interesting to take note of the **Clapham Rail Disaster** which is considered as Britain's worst rail disaster, claiming about 35 lives after three trains collided on 12th December 1998. The British Rail Board admitted liability for the accident, which was attributed to careless work by signal engineers. As the board was responsible under the "vicarious liability" principle, it paid compensation reaching £1 million in some cases, although there were no prosecutions for manslaughter. However, such a case if today is looked into under the prism of present U.K. legislation, the Corporate Manslaughter and Corporate Homicide Act of 2007, a case of corporate manslaughter can definitely be made out.[118]

To exemplify this point we can cite few examples, for example, Company X is given a tender by the Indian Railways to supply food in the railways, if the food supplied by the company is unhygienic and there by the passengers fall ill with food poisoning or die, a claim can be sustained against the company with Indian Railways being made party to the suit. This point can further be illustrated vide the words of Lord Atkin, as were stated in the case of *Donoghue*

---

117 In the MV *Sewol* case, the South Korean prosecutors have indicted Chonghaejin Marine Co. Ltd and four of its crew members of the ferry 'MV *Sewol*' that capsized in April 2014, killing more than 280 passengers for manslaughter. The prosecution also indicted all 11 other surviving crew members of the *Sewol* for negligence. The crew has been under criminal investigation after they were believed to have escaped the sinking vessel before many passengers. See: *South Korea indicts four crew members of ferry for manslaughter*, The Times of India, 15 May 2014, http://timesofindia.indiatimes.com/world/rest-of-world/South-Korea-indicts-four-crew-members-of-ferry-for-manslaughter/articleshow/35142602.cms, Visited on: 14-06-2014

118 See: Szu Ping Chan, *History of Corporate Manslaughter: Five Key Cases*, The Telegraph, 18 February 2011, http://www.telegraph.co.uk/finance/yourbusiness/8330905/History-of-corporate-manslaughter-five-key-cases.html, Visited on: 20-05-2014

v. *Stevenson*[119]: A manufacturer of products, selling the products in such a form, so as to show that he intends to reach the ultimate consumer. His supply chain functions in a form which leaves him with no reasonable possibility of intermediate examination but, he has adequate knowledge that the absence of reasonable care in the manufacturing of the products will result in an injury to consumer's life or property. Having this awareness, he owes a duty to the consumer, to take reasonable care qua manufacturing of his products.

Although the rule in *Donoghue* v. *Stevenson* is one of the most celebrated rule of the tort law but, over the period of time, necessary inspiration has been taken from this case to advance the frontiers of the criminal jurisprudence; in particular to hold persons (artificial and others) responsible for the crime of homicide and manslaughter. Hence, the ruling in this case has not remained limited only to the manufacturers of products; it has been extended to include repairers[120], assemblers[121], builders[122] and suppliers[123].

The thing that needs to be established for attribution of liability in regards to an offence of manslaughter is, 'someone causing the unintentional death of another person(s)'. Thus, an offence of manslaughter can be committed by an individual or a corporation.

---

119 (1932) A.C. 562

In this case, the plaintiff accompanied by her friend went to a restaurant. The friend, apart from some other refreshment, ordered for a bottle of ginger-beer manufactured by the defendants. The bottle of ginger-beer was sealed and of opaque glass. A part of the contents of the bottle were served to the plaintiff. After she had taken that, when the remaining ginger-beer was poured into her glass, the decomposed remains of a snail floated out. The plaintiff contended that as a result of having consumed the injurious drink, she had suffered in her health. The House of Lords held that in these circumstances, the manufacturers owed a duty of care towards the consumer.

120 See: *Malfroot* v. *Noxal* [(1935) 51 T.L.R. 551]; *Stennett* v. *Hancock* [(1939) 2 All E.R. 578]; *Herschtal* v. *Stewart & Ardern* [(1940) 1 K.B. 155]; *Haseldine* v. *Daw* [(1941) 2 K.B. 343]

121 See: *Howard* v. *Furness Houldar Ltd.* [(1936) 2 All E.R. 296]

122 See: *Sharpe* v. *E.T. Sweepings & Son Ltd.* [(1963) 1 W.L.R. 665]

123 See: *Read* v. *Croydon Corporation* [(1938) 4 All E.R. 631]; *Barnes* v. *Irwell Valley Water Board* [(1939) 1 K.B. 21]

More-so-over, there can be instances where by the Government gives a tender to a construction company to build a bridge or a dam, but due to the raw materials used, having been of poor quality or the overall engineering been poor, the bridge or the dam constructed collapses. Even in these cases, a prima facie case of manslaughter can be made out against the company with the Government being made an 'impleading party'.

There have been many instances of Delhi Metro Rail pillars collapsing, due to poor engineering and lack of solid testing; safety checks (or mechanisms) not adhered to, thus causing a complete lack of vigilance, there by precious lives of not only workers at site but also the common public getting lost. Since 12th of July, 2009, there have been countless accidents involving Delhi Metro Rail pillars collapsing and Government trying to cover up these cases by pointing out reasons that make these accidents appear falling outside the purview of exercisable due care and caution, which the Government and the respective contactors were obliged to have carried out. However, lately the CAG (Comptroller Auditor General of India) report asserts that these accidents have been happening due to sheer gross negligence on the part of DMRC (Delhi Metro Rail Corporation) and the respective contractors associated with the Delhi Metro Rail Projects. These cases are nothing but instances of corporate gross negligence manslaughter. Although the DMRC and other associated contractors have been asked to pay compensation as against or in lieu of the unfortunate-accidents that so occurred but the public sentiments as witnessed post the events show that something more is required and this highlights the need of having a separate legislation to deal with cases qua corporate manslaughter.[124]

Apart from imposing fines, all present and future potential contracts with 'accused contractors' must be withdrawn and social cost in the nature of rendering some potential social service (as the public deems fit) must be imposed upon them. Dehors, anything else, prison sentences must also be levied against the managerial heads of the corporations, once the knowledge

---

124 See: Metro Crash, *The Frontline,* Volume 26, Issue 16, August 01-14, 2009, http://www.frontline.in/static/html/fl2616/stories/20090814261604200.htm, Visited on: 05-05-2014

element even to the slightest degree is established or the gross negligence standard is fulfilled.

A more recent example is that of the Beas River Tragedy, where by close to 24 engineering students on their trip to Manali, recreating near the banks of the Beas River, enjoying the scenic beauty, were washed away in the swirling water which rose to several feet untimely. The investigating authorities conclude that the reason as to why the water rose several feet was that, unwarrantedly and without any siren or general indication, gallons of water was released out of the Pandoh Dam which comes under the Larji Hydropower Project (which in fact is under the supervision and control of the Himachal Pradesh State Electricity Board Ltd., a company constituted under the Companies Act of 1956).[125] A case under Section 336[126] and Section 304-A[127] of the IPC has been registered against the authorities of Larji Project. The Himachal Pradesh High Court has termed this case as of "gross negligence", there by the authorities of Larji Project have been held liable. A compensation of Rs. 1.5 lakhs has also been announced for the family of the victims by the Himachal Pradesh Government. This case has been illustrated as a case of 'corporate gross negligence manslaughter', also demands for bringing into force legislation that takes due note and holds corporations accountable for homicides and manslaughters have up-roused even more strongly.[128]

It shall be interesting to take note of the case of Prince Sporting Club Ltd., where by a Middlesex water-sports club was charged with corporate manslaughter in relation to an incident in which a young girl was hit and killed by a speedboat in 2010. The charges related qua the death of 11-year old Mari Simon Cronje. During a birthday celebration at the Bedfont, Middlesex Club on 11th of

---

125 See: Beas River Tragedy: 7 Key Points, *The Times of India,* 10 June 2014, http://timesofindia.indiatimes.com/india/Beas-river-tragedy-7-key-points/articleshow/36357851.cms, Visited on: 14-06-2014

126 See: Section 336 of the Indian Penal Code of 1860: Act endangering life or personal safety of others.

127 See: Section 304-A of the Indian Penal Code of 1860: Causing death by negligence.

128 See: Beas Tragedy: Case Against Dam Project Authorities, Search On, *The Times of India*, 11 June 2014, http://timesofindia.indiatimes.com/india/Beas-tragedy-Case-against-dam-project-authorities-search-on/articleshow/36387471.cms, Visited on: 14-06-2014

September, 2010, she (Mari Simon Cronje) died after falling from a banana boat ride and being hit by the boat that had been towing it. The driver of the boat was not aware that she had fallen into the water and did not see her as he continued on a tight circular route. An investigation by the Marine Accident Investigation Branch concluded that the incident was partly a direct result of Prince Sporting Club's flawed process for completing risk assessments.[129] The Prince Sporting Club Ltd. was pleaded guilty to Section 1(1) of the Corporate Manslaughter and Corporate Homicide Act of 2007 and was ordered to pay a compensation of £134,580.[130]

One of the deadliest disasters in the history of garment industry came about on 24th April 2013, when an eight storied building, housing about five factories collapsed at the outskirts of Dhaka (Bangladesh), killing about 1130 people and injuring more than 2000 people. This incident came to be known as the Rana Plaza Tragedy. It has been alleged that despite cracks appearing in the building neither the owner of the building, Sohel Rana nor the owner of factories paid any attention to the same. When workers in the factories showed their concern in regards to the building turning out to be unsafe for working, their plea was ignored. The struggle for justice is still continuing despite more than a year has passed. A 400-page-report (The Khandaker Report) tabled in May, 2014 blames the Mayor for wrongly granting construction approvals and recommends charges of 'culpable homicide' against the building-owner Sohel Rana and the owners of the five garment factories which were operational in the building. If these charges are proved both Sohel Rana and the owners of the five factories can get life sentences.[131] International media has termed this case as of corporate-gross-negligence-manslaughter and moreover since the

---

129 See: Landmark Corporate Manslaughter Cases, http://www.cqms-ltd.co.uk/news/landmark_corporate_manslaughter_case.html, Visited on: 14-06-2014

130 See: London Sports Club Sentenced For Corporate Manslaughter Over Banana Boat Ride, *The Crown Prosecution Service*, 22 November 2013, http://www.cps.gov.uk/news/latest_news/london_sports_club_sentenced_for_corporate_manslaughter/, Visited on: 14-06-2014

131 See: Jim Yardley, Report on Deadly Factory Collapse in Bangladesh Finds Widespread Blame, *The New York Times*, 22 May 2013, http://www.nytimes.com/2013/05/23/world/asia/report-on-bangladesh-building-collapse-finds-widespread-blame.html?_r=0, Visited on: 15-06-2014

incident, there have been protests in Bangladesh with public demanding death sentence for the owner of the building, Sohel Rana.

In the cases of the kind as listed above, it is necessary to establish 'gross negligence' on the part of the corporation. However, it is a legal fact that the cases of corporate manslaughter fall under the category of 'involuntary manslaughter' and hence are governed by the corporate-gross-negligence standard. A necessary inspiration can be taken, to understand this point, from Section 8 of the Corporate Manslaughter and Corporate Homicide Act, 2007.

This section states that to establish an offence in the nature of corporate-manslaughter the Jury shall see, whether it is established that an organisation owed a relevant duty of care to a person and the Jury shall consider the evidence which shows that the organisation failed to comply with any health and safety legislation that relates to the alleged breach, and if so then, how serious that failure was and how much of a risk of death it posted.[132]

The Jury may also consider the extent to which the evidence shows that there were attitudes, policies, systems or accepted practices within the organisation that were likely to have encouraged any such failure or to have produced tolerance of it.[133] The Jury shall also not be prevented from having regard to any other matter they consider relevant.[134]

In India, we rely on the Indian Penal Code of 1860 for punishing individuals and corporations alike for the deaths occurring due to gross negligence on their (respective) parts. Absence of a legislation for punishing corporations for manslaughter and homicides, increases the problems manifold because under the IPC an individual can be punished by fines or imprisonment or both, in cases necessary 'life sentences' can also be given but in the realm of IPC when the definition of 'person' is looked into with regards to a corporation committing manslaughter, the only punishment which can be imposed is that of fines, because companies have a soul to damn but no body to kick.

---

[132] See: Section 8(1) and 8(2) of the Corporate Manslaughter and Corporate Homicide Act of 2007

[133] See: Section 8(3) of the Corporate Manslaughter and Corporate Homicide Act of 2007

[134] See: Section 8(4) of the Corporate Manslaughter and Corporate Homicide Act of 2007

3.4.3. Corporate Environment Crimes: *The environment crimes dwarf all other crimes committed against individuals (concerning their life, safety and property) but the position of law as it stands in the matter of sentencing in such environmental crimes is rather comfortable. A vagrant committing a theft is punished with years of imprisonment but a billion dollar price fixing executive or a partner in a concern as such comfortably escapes the consequences of environmental crime.*[135]

Despite the Bhopal Gas Tragedy and the Oleum Gas Leakage case, that is, the cases resulting in the absolute liability principle and the deep-pocket theory coming to be read into the Indian environment law jurisprudence and with the case of *M.C. Mehta* v. *Kamal Nath*[136], international environment law principles in the nature of polluter pays and precautionary principles (although already acknowledged by the Indian Supreme Court) becoming part of the country's domestic law; these are still to be made use of in practicality qua the court sentencing.

It has been reported of late that a total of 120,000 people are killed each year in India as a direct consequence of the harmful emissions released by coal power plants operational in India. These coal power plants get away with pollution control checks by bribing away the enforcement authorities. India's breakneck pace of industrialisation is causing public health crises with 80,000 to 120,000 premature deaths and 20 million new asthma cases each year, due to air pollution from coal power plants. These cases too, form a dimension of corporate gross negligence manslaughter.[137]

The human right violations and environmental pollution caused by mining and refinery operations conducted by Vedanta Corporation in the State of Orissa is another example of corporate manslaughter and corporate homicide. A recent Amnesty International Report highlights the issues at stake:

---

135 See: *Krishna Gopal* v. *State of M.P.* [(1986) CRLJ 396 (M.P.)]

136 (1997) 1 SCC 388

137 See: John Vidal, *Indian Coal Power Plants kill 120,000 people a year, says Greenpeace,* The Guardian, 10 March 2013, http://www.theguardian.com/world/2013/mar/10/india-coal-plants-emissions-greenpeace, Visited on: 15-06-2014

"The refinery expansion and mining project have serious implications for the human rights of local communities, including their rights to water, food, health, work and an adequate standard of living. Local communities have received little or no accurate information on the refinery, its proposed expansion or the mining project. Processes to assess the impact of the projects on local communities have been wholly inadequate, and both the State and National Governments have failed to respect and protect the human rights of communities as required under international human rights law. The companies involved in the mine and refinery projects have ignored community concerns, breached state and national regulatory framework and failed to adhere to accepted international standards and principles in relation to the human rights impact of business."[138]

A judicial enquiry into the Korba Chimney Collapse of 2009 which resulted in the death of at least 40 workers, found Vedanta guilty of manifold failures particularly in regards to cutting the corners of safety concerns. Charges of culpable homicide not amounting to murder were levelled against three managers of the Vedanta Mining Group.[139] The mining operations carried out by Vedanta in the State of Orissa show a proliferation of mines in tribal areas, resulting in conflict between the rights of the indigenous people and the economic interest of the mining companies. The operations of mining companies in the tribal areas are subject to the provisions of the Forest Conservation Act of 1980, the Forest Rights Act and the Wildlife Protection Act. Vedanta has been found guilty of having committed breach of all these statues.

The Supreme Court in its order dated 23rd November, 2007 in the matter of *T.N. Godhavarman Tirumulkpad* v. *Union of India*, quoted an extract from an economic daily which, inter alia, was concerned with the Vedanta Resources having being accused of causing deaths of several tribal men and women, by

---

138 See: Amnesty International, *Don't Mine Us Out Of Existence: Bauxite Mine and Refinery Devastate Lives in India*, ASA 20/001/2010, February 2010, p.6

139 See: Richard, *Manslaughter Charges Filed in Vedanta Chimney Case*, 14 January 2010, http://londonminingnetwork.org/2010/01/manslaughter-charges-filed-in-vedanta-chimney-case/, Visited on: 16-06-2014

causing high scale environment degradation. The company was also accused of causing several human and labour rights violations.

The Supreme Court stated that, even though the Apex Court is not making any deliberations qua the correctness of the reports submitted. However, the court cannot take the risk of handling over an important utilization in the hands of a company unless, it is satisfied about its due credibility.[140]

The Mines and Minerals (Development and Regulation) Act of 1957 (as amended up to 10th May, 2012) by virtue of Section 5, restricts the entry of foreign companies in mining operations by providing that, no person shall be eligible for grant of a mineral concession unless such person is an Indian National or a Company registered in India. The purpose of this amendment is to restrict the entry of 'profit-zealous' foreign mining companies in India, which believe only in profit maximisation without giving any consideration or value to human, plant or animal life.

Another case is that of Monsanto, which is by far one of the largest producers of genetically engineered seeds in the world; dominating close to about 70% -100% of the market for crops such as soy, cotton, wheat, and corn. The company is also one of the most egregious abuser of the human rights so far as food sovereignty, access to land and health is concerned. Monsanto promotes mono-culture that is, the practice of covering large swaths of land with a single crop. This practice pushes out subsistence farms and destroys the arable land by drastically decreasing the soil and the water quality for years, draining soil of its key nutrients. The company is also accused of undercutting food prices by flooding countries like Mexico, India, and Brazil with cheap-genetically modified foods products, resulting in the displacement of millions of farm workers, who are forced to migrate to cities or else, work as landless peasants or share croppers. The entry of Monsanto in the Indian seed sector was made possible with the '1998 Seed Policy' imposed by the World Bank

140 See: *Access to Justice: Human Rights Abuses Involving Corporations*, A Project of the International Commission of Jurists, India, International Commission of Jurists, Chapter 2: Available Legal Remedies for Corporate Human Rights Abuse, p.46-47

on India, requiring the Government of India to deregulate the seed sector.[141] Monsanto is blamed for more than, 200,000 farmer suicides in India (majority of which have taken place in Vidarbha, Maharashtra). As per Scientist, Dr. Vandana Shiva, every farmer suicide in India can be linked to Monsanto. It is reported that one farmer every 30 minutes commits suicide in India.[142] The problem is far worse than can be imagined; the farmers in India are promised a healthy earning if they switch from the traditional patterns of farming to the genetically modified means of farming but these promises are sham. Crop failures in India using these scientific means of farming (genetically modified seeds) are far more than any other traditional means. All that the farmers are left with, after using these genetically engineered seeds is a huge debt and a piece of land that is no more fertile. Monsanto is committing a corporate homicide, a manslaughter that shall forever weep in the Indian agricultural history. Activities of Monsanto in India, has been termed by the international media as 'GM Genocide'.[143]

According to the Indian Committee of the Netherlands and the International Labour Rights Fund; Monsanto is accused of employing children as daily wage workers. In India, an estimated 12,375 children work in cottonseed production for farmers paid by Indian and multinational seed companies, including Monsanto. A huge number of children die, and many become seriously ill due to exposure to pesticides and insecticides, while working for Monsanto.[144]

Another case of corporate manslaughter owing to environmental degradation by foreign multinational companies is that of Coca-Cola, in Kerala. Coca-Cola

---

[141] See: Dr. Vandana Shiva, *The Seeds of Suicide: How Monsanto Destroys Farming*, Global Research, 13 March 2014, http://www.globalresearch.ca/the-seeds-of-suicide-how-monsanto-destroys-farming/5329947, Visited on: 16-06-2014

[142] See: Ethan A. Huff, *Monsanto connected to at least 200,000 suicides in India throughout past decade*, 4 January 2011, http://www.naturalnews.com/030913_Monsanto_suicides.html, Visited on: 16-06-2014

[143] See: Andrew Malone, *The GM Genocide: Thousands of Indian farmers are committing suicide after using genetically modified crops*, 3 November 2008, http://www.dailymail.co.uk/news/article-1082559/The-GM-genocide-Thousands-Indian-farmers-committing-suicide-using-genetically-modified-crops.html, Visited on: 16-06-2014

[144] See: Indian Committee of the Netherlands; *Monsanto, Unilever use child labour in India*, 14 May 2003, http://www.indianet.nl/a030514.html, Visited on: 16-06-2014

is destroying the local agriculture by privatizing the country's water resources. In Plachimada, Kerala, Coca-Cola extracted close to 1.5 million litres of deep well water, which it bottled and sold under the following names: 'Dasani' and 'BonAqua'. The groundwater in Plachimada has severely depleted there by affecting thousands of local communities with water shortages, thereby destruction is caused to their agricultural activity. Due to industrial activities carried out by Coca-Cola, the remaining water has become contaminated with high chloride and high levels of bacteria, leading to scabs, eye problems, stomach aches and even deaths.[145] The company is also guilty of reselling its plants' industrial waste to farmers as fertilizers, despite knowing the fact that the waste contains hazardous chemicals like lead and cadmium.[146]

Case qua another company accused of manslaughter is that of, Dow Chemical. Dow Chemical has been destroying lives and poisoning the planet for decades. Worldwide, Dow is involved in human rights abuses involving environmental destruction, groundwater contamination, health violations, chemical poisoning and chemical warfare. In 1988, Dow provided pesticides to Saddam Hussein despite warnings that they could be used to produce chemical weapons.[147] In 2001, Dow inherited the toxic legacy of the worst peace-time chemical disaster in history when it acquired, the Union Carbide Corporation (UCC) and its outstanding liabilities in Bhopal, India.[148] Union Carbide paid compensation of $470 million in lieu of the Bhopal Gas Tragedy. This amount was far below

---

145 See: *Case against Coca-Cola Kerala State: India*, http://www.righttowater.info/rights-in-practice/legal-approaches/legal-approach-case-studies/case-against-coca-cola-kerala-state-india/, Visited on: 16-06-2014

146 Coca-Cola has been distributing solid waste to farmers in two communities, Plachimada and Mehdiganj as "fertilizer". Tests conducted by the BBC found cadmium and lead in the waste, effectively making the waste, toxic waste. Coca-Cola stopped the practice of distributing its toxic waste only when ordered to do so by the State Government.

See: Jonathan Hills, *Coca-Cola in India: A Case Study*, CSR Asia Weekly, http://csr-asia.com/csr-asia-weekly-news-detail.php?id=4146, Visited on: 16-06-2014

147 See: Julian Borger, *Rumsfeld 'offered help to Saddam'*, The Guardian, 31 December 2002, http://www.theguardian.com/world/2002/dec/31/iraq.politics, Visited on: 16-06-2014

148 On December 3rd, 1984, thousands of people in Bhopal (India) were gassed to death after a catastrophic chemical leak at a UCC pesticide plant. More than 150,000 people were left severely disabled, of whom 22,000 have since died of their injuries in a disaster now widely acknowledged as the world's worst ever.

what many lawyers and social-action groups felt was necessary to take care of the victims of the tragedy. After the merger, advocates in Bhopal began to pressurize Dow to do more, but the company insisted that it had not assumed Union Carbide's liabilities and thus had no responsibility to help. Dow still refuses to address its liabilities or even admit its existence, in regards to the Bhopal Gas Tragedy; thereby it is carrying forward the Union Carbide's legacy of profiting from extreme corporate irresponsibility. Dow and UCC's lack of accountability in the disaster that continues to affect the lives of people in Bhopal even to this day is sorrowful.[149]

In a recent spate, Dow Chemical Co. (corporate legal successor of UCC) approached the Madras High Court seeking an 'injunction' order to restrain the 'International Campaign for Justice for Bhopal Victims', launched against the UCC, and for restraining the demonstrators from picketing and holding demonstrations outside its office in Chennai, harassing and preventing the employees from entering or leaving the office premises. The protest was reportedly against Dow's refusal to own the responsibility qua the cleaning up of the toxic contaminants that had remained in the factory premises in Bhopal, ever since the Bhopal Gas Tragedy surfaced. The toxic waste lying untreated at the Bhopal Gas Tragedy site is said to be poisoning the ground water in that area. Dow has over the period of time, sought various reliefs, including a decree for a sum of Rs. 1,000,000/- together with interest on account of loss of business suffered by them and another Rs. 1,000,000/- together with interest for defamation and loss of reputation suffered by them.[150]

Justice Chandru of the Madras High Court *rejected* Dow's request for a gag order against the named respondents, because vital constitutional rights were at stake. The Court opined as follows:

"It must be noted that the people of India empowered with constitutional rights provided in the Constitution of India, are entitled to make grievance on any issue. Their mouths cannot be gagged either by the Government using its

---

149 See: Philip Mattera, *Dow Chemical: Corporate Rap Sheet*, Corporate Research Project, http://www.corp-research.org/dowchemical, Visited on: 16-06-2014

150 See: *Dow Chemical International* v. *Nithyanandam and International Campaign for Justice in Bhopal*, OA 395-397 of 2009 in Civil Suit No. 356 of 2009 (order dated 9 July 2009, Madras High Court), Para 4.

police power or by the Courts by granting preventive injunction. Before the issuance of a prior restraint on a citizen's right to free expression guaranteed under Article 19(1)(a) or their right to hold peaceful assembly under Article 19(1)(b), there must be established a clear case of infringement of the right of an aggrieved person. Otherwise, the courts are bound to protect the rights of parties to express their protest on public issue."[151]

The High Court held that:

"The people of India have a right to protest, even against a multinational company, and that unless a situation is shown where the life and liberty of an aggrieved individual or an organisation is threatened from its very existence, or their right to carry on business is curtailed, neither the State Authorities nor the Court, will rush to prevent such actions through preventive orders or impose prior-restrains."[152]

The last instance is that of POSCO. In the quest for acquiring natural resources, the companies (indigenous as well as multinational) seem to have stopped at nothing. Violent exploitation of the indigenous people, jeopardizing their livelihoods and sometimes even killing them is what corporations have been involving themselves in the sprint race of earning huge profits. Activities carried by POSCO in the Jagatsinghpur District of Orissa, India, are atrocious. POSCO, a steel company based in South Korea, has aggressively pressurized the villagers in Orissa (India) to vacate their farm-land so that the company can go forward with the establishing of a steel plant and a private seaport over there. The repercussions, POSCO's project will create are enormous for Orissa. For one, POSCO will diminish the livelihood of thousands of villagers who have cultivated the land over there, for generations together. It is estimated that POSCO's project will potentially displace 22,000 people by seizing 4,000 acres of village land. It will consequently affect 25,000 more people in surrounding villages that work and do business in that area. The vast majority of villagers make their living by cultivating and selling rice, coconuts, cashews, and the famous betel leaves for which the region is actually known for. Also, media reports (not having much evidentiary value) have reported that, POSCO has

[151] Ibid, Para 22
[152] Ibid, Para 27

been working closely with the Indian Government to coerce the villagers into surrendering their land to the multinational corporate giant. The Government is reportedly destroying the betel leaf crops, firing rubber bullets at village protesters, and is preventing the villagers from accessing medical care and education opportunities, among other injustices.[153] Secondly, POSCO plans to create a private port nearby its prospective steel plant. This private port will deprive the fishermen from accessing the valuable coastline and thereby will cripple their industry; straying them from their only source of livelihood. The villagers have remained non-violent and have been resisting the harassment that POSCO has been inflicting onto them (with the government being party to the same). Villagers have organized peaceful marches and sit-ins among all other actions taken by them to protest against the harassment inflicted upon them by POSCO. The villagers still continue to struggle as their ability to organize and make a living from farming is made more and more difficult, each passing day due to the oppressive and coercive government policies.

The villagers have stood to their ground since 2005, but it is essential that the international community must be made aware of the grave injustice that is inflicted upon the villagers of Orissa, so that greater pressure can be pitted upon POSCO. The BBC reported on July 16, 2013 that POSCO had to scrap its steel mining plant in Karnataka due to its inability to secure lands following the strong opposition from the locals. However, the project is expected to continue in Orissa. The ills that POSCO is inflicting over the villagers in Orissa by coercing them; killing them and even depriving them of clean air and water apart from infringing their right to carry on trade and business is tyrannical. POSCO is being criticized globally for its inhuman activities in Orissa and is blamed for carrying out manslaughter, in partnership with the local police authorities.[154]

---

153 See: Prafulla Das, *POSCO Land Acquisition: Police Arrest Agitating Villagers,* The Hindu, 3 February 2013, http://www.thehindu.com/news/national/other-states/posco-land-acquisition-police-arrest-agitating-villagers/article4374896.ece, Visited on: 17-06-2014

154 See: *Impact of POSCO-India's Project on the lives of local people in Jagatsinghpur, Odisha, India,* http://www.escr-net.org/sites/default/files/briefing-note-posco-india-private-ltd.pdf, Visited on: 17-06-2014

After exploring this dimension of corporate misfeasance in the nature of corporate manslaughter and corporate homicide we shall look into the next dimension dealing with goods and commodities produced by the corporations which potentially claim human life for either of the two reasons that is, inherently dangerous nature of the goods, with the user of the goods not been informed about the same or, the goods claiming human life for the reason of their faulty manufacturing or other technical defects.

3.4.4. Product Liability: A 'product' is defined as a bundle of utilities from the perspective of a potential customer. But there are cases where by these products bought by the customers become the very reason of their deaths. Justice Traynor in the case of *Escola* v. *Coca-Cola Bottling Co.*[155] held that it is incumbent upon the manufacturing company to inspect their products before marketing them as they were in the best position to do so. In this case, the plaintiff was a waitress and one of her duties was to stock the refrigerator with bottles of Coca-Cola. On one occasion, a bottle exploded in the Plaintiff's hand as she was putting it into the refrigerator, causing her serious injury. Plaintiff sued the defendant, claiming that the defendant was negligent in selling bottles containing a beverage which on account of excessive pressure of gas or by reason of some defect in the bottle was dangerous and was likely to explode. The Court in this case asserted that the public policy demanded recovery for the plaintiff even if negligence could not be proven because the manufacturing company was in the best position to insure against the damage. This position was based on the theory that the consumer does not have the same opportunity to inspect products, the same knowledge to recognise dangers, or the ability to spread the cost of such dangers. Had the consumer died in this case owing to the injuries suffered, a clear case of homicide could have been made.[156]

Another case is that of the killer antibiotic, Elixir Sulfanilamide. In 1937, Harold Watkins, chief chemist for the Massengill Company, was attempting to produce a version of sulphanilamide- the revolutionary new antibiotic- in liquid form so that it would be more palatable for kids. The drug wouldn't

155 24 Cal. 2d 453, 150 P. 2d 436

156 See: Keith N. Hylton, *The Law and Economics of Products Liability*, Boston University School of Law, http://www.bu.edu/law/faculty/scholarship/workingpapers/documents/HyltonK072512_000.pdf, Visited on: 17-06-2014

dissolve in water or alcohol, but it was soluble in diethylene glycol, an industrial solvent. Watkins tested the solution on rats (who developed kidney failure and died), and he tested it for taste and fragrance on humans (it had a raspberry flavour). But he never tested the product- which was 24 times stronger than the version tested on rats- for safety on humans. Within four weeks of its release, Massengill's Elixir Sulfanilamide had killed 105 people, a third of which were children. The company "regretted" the error, but claimed that the manufacturing process followed standards of the time. Aside from a $26,100 fine (the largest fine ever issued by the FDA at the time), the company had no other legal liability, although it was blamed for having committed one of the first ever corporate manslaughter owing to the lack of caution exercised by the manufacturing company. The following year- as a result of the public outcry- Congress passed the Food Drug and Cosmetic Act of 1938, a landmark law that for the first time required that drug companies test drug for safety before releasing them. Eventually the drug claimed its 106th victim when Harold Watkins- the chemist who invented the elixir- killed himself. In 1986, 14 deaths in India were attributed to the use of this drug and in 1990, 40 children in Nigeria died due to the use of this drug. This drug despite all international condemnation is still marketed in the developing countries and more than 3,000 cases of poisoning due to the use of this drug are reported each year.[157]

The Ford Pinto case forms an interesting read in regards to the law on the matter under discussion. In the early 1960s, in order to compete with compact foreign imports, the Ford Motor Company rushed its compact Ford Pinto model into production without testing the technical viability of it. Since retooling the assembly line seemed to be a costly investment, the company chose to proceed with production despite the fact that the results of its own crash tests indicated that the gas tank exploded in rear-end collision. Choosing profits over human lives, the company continued to avoid the federal safety standards that would have forced the Ford Motor Company to modify the quality and the positioning of the gas tank in the Ford Pinto model manufactured by it. It is estimated that about 500 individuals were burned to death because of the "firetrap engineering" of the gas tanks.

---

157 See: Ilona Bray, Richard Stim and Nolo, *Defective Products that Changed the Law,* The Lawyers Update: Magazine for Legal Professionals & Students, Universal Book Traders, Volume XIX, Part 10, October 2013, p.38

In the May of 1978, the U.S. Department of Transportation finally called-off all the 1971 to 1976 Ford Pintos, and it was the biggest auto recall up to that time. However, the decision came too late for after about 500 individuals died, and many were maimed. The Ford Pinto case is a landmark case, as for the first time in U.S. history a corporation was indicted for murder. In 1978, Indiana prosecutors charged Ford with homicide after three people were burned alive in a Pinto owing to the firetrap engineering of its gas tanks. Even though Ford was acquitted, the trial of a corporation for murder served as a signal that the public reaction towards corporate crimes in the nature of manslaughter and homicide was changing. When asked what fate Lee Iacocca, the then President of Ford, deserved, one person sarcastically remarked that someone should buy him a Ford Pinto complete with Firestone-500 tires (yet another ill-engineered product where by the manufacturers hid the defects of the product until an unacceptable number of homicides sparked of a federal action).[158]

Another case is that of the 'Ford Explorer-Firestone Tires'. In the year 2000, the executives of the Ford Motor Company and Bridgestone Firestone Inc., appeared before the U.S. Congress to answer questions regarding possible cover-ups of defects in the Ford Explorer, a sport-utility-vehicle, particularly when it was equipped with Firestone tires. The test runs showed that the tread on Firestone ATX and Wilderness tires peeled off, forcing the Ford Explorer to roll over. By the year 2000, it became apparent that numerous accidents took place due to the defects that compounded when the two products were combined.

In the February of 2000, these tires were called off in Thailand and Malaysia. In the May of 2000, the National Highway Traffic Safety Association (NHTSA) began its study exposing the ills in the product manufacturing and engineering. Ford called off about 30,000 tires in Venezuela, Ecuador, and Colombia. In August of 2000, Firestone recalled 6.5 million tires. Ford CEO Jacques Nasser apologised on television, and Bridgestone Firestone CEO Masatoshi Ono apologised to the U.S. Congress. By the end of August 2000, NHTSA reported that 1.4 million more tires were defective contributing to an

---

158 See: Frank E. Hagan, *Introduction to Criminology: Theories, Methods, and Criminal Behaviour,* Chapter 10: White Collar Crimes, Sage Publications Inc., Seventh Edition, p.322-323

estimated 88 fatalities and 250 injuries.[159] This case of Ford Explorer-Firestone Tires too is a case of corporate-gross-negligence-manslaughter.

Another case is that of SabreTech, a company dealing in with repairs, modifications and maintenance of commercial aircrafts. SabreTech was convicted in 1999 in federal court in Miami of eight counts of causing the air transportation of hazardous materials and of one count of failing to provide training in the handling of hazardous materials. The charges resulted from the actions of company employees in improperly packaging oxygen canisters, blamed for the 1996 crash of a ValuJet airplane in the Florida Everglades. In that disaster, 110 people died. The case marked the first time when, a maintenance company faced criminal charges in connection with an air disaster in the United States. The company thereby went out of business and was also charged in state court with numerous counts of murder and manslaughter in the crash.[160] As per Florida state attorney Katherine Fernandez-Rundle, this case was the first criminal homicide prosecution involving a passenger aircraft tragedy in the United States.[161] SabreTech too is a case of corporate manslaughter; where by deaths of passengers of an aircraft happened due to faulty services provided by an aircraft-maintenance-company. Also, noteworthy is the case of A.H. Robbins Company of the United States of America. In the early 1970s another pharmaceutical corporation (A.H. Robbins Company) was held accountable for gross negligence manslaughter. This pharmaceutical company distributed an intrauterine birth control device (IUD) called the Dalkon Shield to about 2.2 million women in the United States and another 2.3 million worldwide. Sold without adequate premarket testing, the Dalkon Shield turned out to be both ineffective and harmful. A design defect in the wick used to insert and remove the IUD allowed bacteria to travel up into the uterus, where it caused infection. Thousands of women who used the device were rendered sterile, suffered miscarriages, or gave birth to stillborn

---

159 See: The Statement of Joan Claybrook on "Firestone Tire Defect & Ford Explorer Rollovers", United States Senate Committee on Commerce, Science and Transportation, Washington D.C., 12 September 2000, http://www.citizen.org/autosafety/article_redirect.cfm?ID=5414, Visited on: 17-06-2014

160 See: *SabreTech charged with murder in ValuJet crash*, 13 July 1999, http://www.cnn.com/US/9907/13/valujet.indictments.03/, Visited on: 17-06-2014

161 See: Frank Schmalleger, *Criminology: A Brief Introduction*, Pearson Education Inc. 2011, Chapter 10: White- Collar and Organised Crime, p.228-229

or premature babies with congenital birth defects. At least 18 women in the United States alone died from its use before FDA forced its withdrawal from the U.S. market in 1974. A.H. Robbins, however, continued to sell the Dalkon Shield abroad for at least another nine months. The company even persuaded the U.S. Agency for International Development (USAID) to distribute it in over forty countries overseas. One USAID official reported that the IUD was still being used in Pakistan, India, and possibly South Africa till as late as 1979. In the late 1980s, after paying millions of dollars to settle thousands of gross negligence manslaughter lawsuits, A.H. Robbins agreed to a settlement and declared bankruptcy, reorganised, and established a $2.5 billion fund to compensate victims.[162]

However, during the 1980s the Eli Lilly pharmaceutical corporation marketed Oraflex, a painkiller intended for arthritis patients. When the company asked the FDA to approve the sale of the drug in the United States, it did not inform the FDA of at least 26 deaths that had been linked to Oraflex overseas. The drug was sold in the United States for about six months, but it was withdrawn after reports of deaths began circulating in the news. The company and one executive were criminally prosecuted, entered guilty pleas, and were fined for gross negligence manslaughter. The company was fined $25,000 and the executive $15,000. It is alleged that Oraflex caused the death of about 50 people overall as well as serious liver and kidney damage in more than 900 others.[163]

The jurisprudence in regards to this dimension of the law (corporate homicide and corporate manslaughter) developed over the period of time primarily owing to these two case-laws:

Jackson v. Watson[164]: In this case, the plaintiff purchased a tin of salmon from the defendant. The contents of the tin were injurious, the plaintiff's wife died by eating some salmon from that tin. It was held that the death of the plaintiff's

---

162 See: Ronald J. Berger, Marvin D. Free Jr. & Patricia Searles, *Crime, Justice and Society: An Introduction to Criminology*, Second Edition, Viva Books Private Limited, Chapter 6: Corporate and Organized Crime, p.208

163 Ibid, p.209

164 (1909) 2 K.B. 193

wife in this case had occurred due to the breach of a contract on the part of the defendant in so far as he did not provide the goods suitable for human consumption. The plaintiff was, therefore, entitled to claim compensation in regards to the death his wife owing to the gross negligence exercised by the defendants.

Baker v. *Bolton*[165]: In this case, the defendants were the proprietors and service providers as to a stage-coach in which the plaintiff and his wife were travelling. The coach was upset due to the negligence of the defendants, the plaintiff was himself much bruised and his wife was severely hurt. The wife later died about a month later in the hospital. Rationally thought, it was felt that the plaintiff could recover compensation for injury to himself and also for the loss of wife's society & distress, from the date of accident to the date of her death, but he could not recover anything for such loss after death. This case over the period of time advanced the jurisprudence in this niche area of corporate criminal liability and came to be known as the '*Baker* v. *Bolton*' Rule.

In India, the law operational to hold corporations accountable for gross-negligence-manslaughter is contained in different statutes i.e. the Consumer Protection Act of 1986, the Prevention of Food Adulteration Act of 1954, the Drugs Control Act of 1950, the Narcotic Drugs & Psychotropic Substances Act of 1985, the Drugs & Cosmetics Act of 1940, with the Indian Penal Code of 1860 being the principal statute to hold corporations accountable for gross negligence manslaughter and homicide. To attribute liability in cases of corporate homicide, the principal practice as so adopted in India is: firstly, the nature of the organisation is seen that is, whether it is a corporation or not and secondly, attribution of liability is done for homicide under the principal legislation read in pari-materia with the Indian Penal Code of 1860. As for example, an individual dies during his travel from one place to other in the train owing to the gross negligence of the railway authorities. Now in this scenario, the status of the railways as an organisation will be seen that is, it is a corporation owing to its principal legislation, the Railways Act of 1989 and now attribution of gross-negligence liability for homicide will take place under the Indian Penal Code of 1860, to hold the railway authorities liable.

165 (1808) 1 Camp 493: 10 R.R. 734

In the case of *U.O.I* v. *Nathmal Hansaria*[166]; Kabita Hansaria, the daughter of the complainants, fell down and died while passing through inter-connecting passage in the Tinsukhia Mail going from Delhi to Guwahati. The passage was not protected by any grills, etc. The State Commission held the Railway Authorities accountable for the gross negligence homicide and awarded a compensation of Rs. 2 lakhs for the death of Kabita and Rs. 25,000/- for mental agony suffered by the parents of the deceased on account of deficiency of service of the opposite party i.e. the railways. This decision was upheld by the National Commission. The National Commission held that the death was not by railway accident but by virtue of gross negligence on account of railway authorities. The jurisdiction of the Consumer Forum was not barred under Sections 13 and 15 of the Railway Claims Tribunal Act, 1987.[167]

In another case, the National Consumer Disputes Redressal Commission (NCDRC) directed a payout of Rs. 5.90 crores as compensation to the family members of Mr. Vipin Handa, who died in a lift mishap. The NCDRC through its judgement directed OTIS Elevator Co. (India) Ltd., Research Analysis Wing (RAW) and Military Engineering Services (MES) to pay the compensation to the family members of the deceased. On 20th of March, 2003, Mr. Vipin Handa was in the lift with 12 other officers after finishing a meeting at the Research Analysis Wing (RAW) office in Delhi. The lift that he had boarded stalled between the seventh and the sixth floor. All other officers except that of Mr. Vipin Handa and one-other officer, had de-boarded at the sixth floor. The one-other officer with Mr. Vipin Handa was rescued but as Mr. Vipin Handa was about to be rescued, the stalled lift started moving downwards and eventually crashed, resulting in the death of Mr. Vipin Handa. OTIS was held responsible for installing the lift without a voltage stabilizer, RAW was held guilty for not insisting on the stabilizer, failing to ensure that the contract for maintaining the lift was being followed through and turning a blind eye to the complaints received against the manufacturer. This case is

166 (1997) C.P.J. 20 (N.C.)

167 See: R.K. Bangia, *Law of Torts,* Chapter 24: The Consumer Protection Act, Allahabad Law Agency, Sixteenth Edition, 2002, p.489-490

exceptional, as for the first-time in a case involving corporate-gross-negligence-manslaughter so heavy compensation was made payable.[168]

In the case of *Centre for Public Interest Litigation* v. *U.O.I*[169], the Honourable SC of India held that the enjoyment of life and its attainment, including right to life and human dignity encompasses within its ambit, availability of articles of food, without insecticides or pesticides residue, veterinary drugs residue, antibiotic residues and other solvent residues. But the fact remains that many of the food articles like rice, vegetables, meat, fish, milk, fruits available in the market contain insecticides or pesticides residues beyond the tolerable limits, capable of causing serious health hazards and in many cases even death. The two principal soft drinks, Coke and Pepsi have been found to have high volumes of pesticides and insecticides, the effect of these pesticides can result in physiological immaturity among the principal consumers with heavy risk of cancer & other life claiming health hazards. The SC ruled that the Food and Safety Standards Authority of India should gear up their resources with their counter parts in all the States and Union Territories to hold and conduct periodical inspections in corporations dealing with the manufacturing of food and beverages. If any corporation is found to abuse the provisions of the Prevention of the Food Adulteration Act of 1954 resulting in death of likely consumers then the same will be held accountable for homicide.[170]

Lastly, we shall discuss the case of *Dr. Balram Prasad* v. *Dr. Kunal Saha*[171]. In this case the SC of India observed that in this age of corporate-hospitals with world class medical facilities, the burden of negligence should be pulled hard

168 See: Rebecca Samervel, *Record Rs.6 crore payout for lift accident in Delhi,* The Times of India, 28 January 2014, http://timesofindia.indiatimes.com/city/mumbai/Record-Rs-6cr-payout-for-lift-accident-in-Delhi/articleshow/29460794.cms, Visited on: 18-06-2014; Also see: *NCDRC Judgement 2014: Enhanced Compensation using Anuradha,* http://pbtindia.com/wp-content/uploads/2014/02/NCDRC-Judg-2014-Enhanced-compensation-using-Anuradha-SC-judg.pdf, Visited on: 17-06-2014

169 WP(C) No. 681 of 2004; Decided on 22-10-2013 (SC); K.S. Radhakrishnan and Dipak Misra, JJ.

170 See: Rita Aryan, *Latest Supreme Court Judgements- Soft Drinks: Preserves of Pesticides,* The Lawyers Update: Magazine for Legal Professionals & Students, Universal Book Traders, Volume XIX, Part 12, December 2013, p.51

171 C.A. No. 2867 of 2012; Decided on 24-10-2013 (SC); Chandramauli Kr. Prasad and V. Gopala Gowda, JJ.

onto the hospital authorities as well as doctors working therein, if found guilty of negligence & lacking reasonable care and pragmatic caution. The SC observed that the number of medical negligence cases against Doctors, Hospitals and Nursing Homes are increasing day by day. With the commercialisation of medical facilities in the eye of huge multi-facility corporate hospitals coming up, the doctors, hospitals, nursing homes and other connected establishments are to be dealt with strictly if they are found to be negligent with the patients who come to them pawning all their money with the hope to live a better life with dignity. This decision acts as a deterrent and a reminder to those doctors, hospitals, nursing homes and other connected establishments who do not take their responsibility seriously. In this case, the doctors and the Hospital (Advanced Medicare & Research Institute Ltd.) were held negligent in treating the wife of the claimant. The deceased, a resident of the U.S. had contracted a rare skin disease while on vacation in India and she died due to poor diagnosis and prescription of overdose of steroids. The National Commission held three doctors and the hospital criminally negligent for the homicide. A compensation of Rs. 13,466,000/- was awarded. The SC enhanced the amount to Rs. 60,800,550/- with 6% interest per annum from the date of the filing of the complaint.[172]

3.5. Chapter Conclusion:

The problem in India, of late, we people are facing is a lack of legislation that holds corporations accountable for gross negligence manslaughter. The ways and means to combat the gross negligence corporate atrocities is very much there in India but it is spread across various legislations with the Indian Penal Code of 1860 forming the primary base. Hence, when the law is spread across legislations the loopholes can be sought for and can be taken benefit of.

A comprehensive piece of legislation in India which deals with corporate crimes, particularly in the nature of gross-negligence manslaughter and homicide will be a very thoughtful exercise, moreover India apart from taking inspiration from the Corporate Manslaughter and Corporate Homicide Act of 2007 (U.K.) must move a step further, by enacting a legislation by virtue of

---

172 See: *Dr. Balram Prasad v. Dr. Kunal Saha*, http://judis.nic.in/supremecourt/imgs1.aspx?filename=40897, Visited on: 19-06-2014

which crimes committed by corporation in the nature of 'terrorist conspiracy' or 'furthering the goals which the terrorists intend to achieve, must be strictly punished, condemned and if required such corporations must be dissolved compulsorily. Judgment rendered as in the case of *Kalpanath Rai* v. *State*[173] must no more hold the ground. In this case, a company, accused and arraigned under the Terrorist and Disruptive Activities Prevention Act of 1978 was alleged to have harboured terrorists. In a bench trial, the trial court convicted the company of the offence punishable under Section 3(4) of the TADA. On appeal, the Indian SC referred to the definition of the word "harbour" as provided in Section 52A of the IPC and pointed out that there was nothing in TADA, either express or implied, to indicate that the mens rea element had been excluded from the offence under Section 3(4) of TADA. Court referred its earlier decisions in *State of Maharashtra* v. *Mayer Hans George*[174] and *Nathulal* v. *State of M.P.*[175] observed, that there was a plethora of decisions by Indian courts which had settled the legal proposition that unless the statute clearly excludes mens rea in the commission of an offence, the same must be treated as an essential ingredient of the act in order for the act to be punishable with imprisonment and/or fine. Taking this reasoning a step further, the Indian SC held that an accused corporation could not possess the requisite mens rea, even if any terrorist had been allowed to occupy the rooms in its hotel.[176]

---

173 AIR 1998 SC 201

174 AIR 1965 SC 72

175 AIR 1966 SC 43

176 See: Dr. Girjesh Shukla, *Criminology: Crime Causation, Sentencing and Rehabilitation of Victims,* Lexis Nexis Publication, 2013, Chapter 8: Sentencing and Penal Policy, p.189; Also see: *Kalpanath Rai* v. *State* [(1997) 8 SCC 732]

Chapter 4

Corporate Manslaughter and Corporate Homicide: Comparative analysis of standards prevailing in the major jurisdictions

4.1. Introduction:

In this chapter, the Researcher shall be exploring the corporate manslaughter laws as such prevailing in the jurisdictions of U.K., New Zealand, U.S., Canada and Australia. The reasoning behind the selection of these jurisdictions is two-fold. Firstly, all these nations are commonwealth nations and India too being a commonwealth nation shares a common colonial heritage with them, with laws having a more than similar resemblance and structural outlines. Secondly, it was only in these countries of U.K., New Zealand, U.S., Canada and Australia that the consciousness in regards to punishing the corporations for the crimes of manslaughter first arose. These countries have been the forerunners so far as the enactment of laws for punishing corporations for the crime of corporate manslaughter is concerned.

A corporate crime may be defined as an illegal act or omission, punishable by State under administrative, civil or criminal law. These acts and omissions are a result of deliberate decision-making or culpable negligence within the kaleidoscope and the institutional framework of a legitimate formal organisation. These acts and omissions are rooted in the eye-wash of a 'business organisation' pursuing its legitimate, formal, normative goals as per the standard operating procedures and practices seen in close nexus with the cultural norms of the organisation which are intended to benefit the corporation and all others associated with it or as may be affected by its operations.[177]

---

177 See: Eugene Mc Laughlin & John Muncie, *The Sage Dictionary of Criminology*, Sage Publications, Second Edition, p.74-76

Of all the corporate crimes committed, the most serious of them is the crime of corporate manslaughter and homicide. When persons are injured or are killed by corporate activities, it may be possible for the State to initiate a criminal prosecution against the company but, a criminal prosecution for corporate manslaughter will only succeed if it can be proved that the action undertaken by the organisation was deliberately fashioned to cause such a result, and additionally that a senior executive within a company could be pin-pointed as having been responsible for a particular incident. In most of the cases the pity is that the breach of health and safety regulations is most often labelled as an unfortunate accident and is therefore subject to a lesser charge.[178]

Corporate manslaughter is a form of corporate violence, where by decisions rendered or strategies put forth by executives of respective business corporations kill and maim individuals, owing to gross negligence exercised on behalf of such executives and other policy initiators and implementers. The tools of violence include, autos fitted with defective parts resulting in their explosion, defective medical devices, inadequately tested drugs and other hazardous products manufactured and marketed despite knowledge of the corporate officials that such products can injure and kill consumers. Lately, there has been rise in consciousness world-over in regards to corporate crimes in the nature of corporate killings owing to the reports of toxic chemicals dumps that have poisoned drinking supplies, caused leukemia in children, and destroyed entire communities; of cover-ups of asbestos- induced cancer, and the gradual suffocation of workers from inhaling cotton dust; of radioactive water leaking from improperly maintained nuclear reactors; of mangled bodies and lives snuffed out in unsafe coal mines and steel mills and other dangers to individual health and safety.[179] This has in-turn resulted in consolidation of efforts by respective government in power in various nations to enact a legislation that punishes corporations for the crimes of manslaughter and homicide. The most recent and aspiring example is that of the U.K.

---

178 See: Peter Joyce, *Criminal Justice: An introduction to crime and the criminal justice system*, William Publication Co., 2006 Edition, Chapter 2: Crime and crime prevention, p.78

179 See: Frank E. Hagan, *Introduction to Criminology: Theories, Methods, and Criminal Behaviour*, Sage Publications Inc., Seventh Edition, Chapter 10: White Collar Crime, p.327-328

4.2. U.K.:

In U.K., over a period of time it was realised that the rule of "determining mind and will of the company" as laid down by Lord Reid in the case of *Tesco Supermarkets Ltd.* v. *Nattrass*[180], suffers from a defect that finding a personal representative to whom the acts of the corporation can be attributed can be done successfully in regards to very small companies only and not in regards to the large ones. The unfair consequence of this rule was that, small companies were held criminally liable much easily than the large corporations. Sometimes the problem was overcome by using Lord Hoffmann's "attribution rules" that assisted in finding individuals whose mental element could be attributed to account for the mental element of the company.[181] Thereafter it was realised that it is not possible to make a company vicariously liable for crimes with mental element as this in effect will result in making the company criminally liable for all the criminal intents of anyone associated with the company.[182] Therefore, need was felt for a comprehensive piece of legislation that deals exclusively with the crimes in the nature of corporate killings.

Under the rule of the Conservative government in 1996, the Law Commission in the U.K. produced a report namely, *Legislating the Criminal Code: Involuntary Manslaughter,* this report highlighted the in-effectiveness of law as such prevailing and the lack of jurisprudential development in the area of

180 (1972) AC 153 (House of Lords)

181 See: The Meridian Global Case [(1995) 2 AC 500 (Privy Council)]. In this case, funds of Meridian Global Funds Management Asia Ltd. were used by two senior investment managers to provide finance for an attempted takeover of a New Zealand company. The funds were used to purchase shares. The New Zealand legislation required immediate notification of acquisition of more than 5 percent of the shares of a public company. Meridian was held liable for non-disclosure despite the fact that the investment managers had been acting without the authority of the directors. The court held that the knowledge of the investment managers was to be attributed to the company. The test of 'directing mind and will' was not appropriate in all cases and here would defeat the purpose of the Act, which was to encourage immediate notification of acquisition of substantial share-holdings and restricting the company's knowledge to the knowledge of those directing the company could encourage the board to pay as little attention as possible to what its investment managers were doing.

182 See: Len Sealy & Sarah Worthington, *Cases and Materials in Company Law,* Oxford University Press, 9th Edition, Chapter 3: Corporate Activity and Legal Liability, p.145

corporate gross negligence manslaughter in the U.K. and there-after, the draft bill that recommended the creation of an offence in the nature of 'corporate killings' was published.

In 1997, the Labour Party manifesto promised that the Labour Party shall legislate, an enactment on corporate manslaughter if it came to power. After the victory of the Labour Party in the elections of 1997, the then Home Secretary, Jack Straw, said that 'the new government believed that those whose criminal negligence caused the death of innocent people should not escape punishment'.[183]

The Confederation of British Industry, however, vigorously opposed the plans for the new legislation, arguing that it would be unworkable. The Crown Prosecution Service was reluctant to bring the proposed corporate manslaughter legislation because it was felt that the corporate manslaughter cases were notoriously difficult to prove and win. The experience showed that there had been only five successful prosecutions and that too all against small companies.

The Labour Party failed to keep the commitments made by it in its manifesto that is, to legislate the corporate manslaughter legislation. But in the year 2000, it commenced a wide consultation exercise in regards to the proposed new offence of corporate manslaughter. Not all the figure-heads in the business world opposed the action. Ruth Lea of the Institute of Directors said (in the year 2002) that, 'for corporations to realise that getting away with murder is an extraordinary situation, it is necessary to make it explicit that it is common justice that if someone is killed due to the gross negligence of the other, then that other should be held responsible and must be put to trial'.

In May of 2003, the then Home Secretary, David Blunkett, announced the intention to publish a draft bill on reform of the law in regards to corporate killings, but critics believed that it will concentrate virtually on punishing the companies, rather than their managers or directors.

---

[183] See: Martin Bright, *Fury over delay to 'corporate killing' law*, The Guardian, 21 July 2002, http://www.theguardian.com/politics/2002/jul/21/immigrationpolicy.observerpolitics, Visited on: 21-06-2014

Efforts were been made since 1965 in the U.K. to pass a corporate manslaughter legislation, more after the bridge on which Glanville Evans was working on collapsed and he fell into the River Wye and the prosecution in this case failed. Since 1965, more than 31,000 people have been killed at work or through commercially related disasters such as train crashes in the U.K. Safety reports have shown that management failures are responsible in most cases.[184] In U.K. in the 1980s and 1990s, there was a spate of disasters leading to major loss of life and serious injuries, in which criminal neglect of safety standards and regulations by public authorities and private companies was commonly alleged and occasionally proved.

These included: the King's Cross Tube Station Fire in 1987 (in this disaster about 31 people died); the sinking of the Herald of Free Enterprise, a passenger ferry, at Zeebrugge in 1987 (in this tragedy about 192 people died); the Piper Alpha North Sea oil rig fire in 1988 (in this environment catastrophe about 168 people died); capsize of Marchioness, the pleasure boat, in the Thames in 1989 (in this tragedy about 51 people died); in the Hillsborough football disaster of 1990 about 96 people lost their lives; the Southall and Paddington railway crashes of 1997 and 1999 claimed about 7 and 30 lives respectively.

A lot of statistical analysis was undertaken before finally the Corporate Manslaughter and Corporate Homicide Act of 2007 was pulled through. The rising consciousness among the masses and in the media opined that deaths and injuries at the workplaces is a matter of serious concern and must be dealt with an iron fist. By virtue of the research undertaken by the commissions appointed and the government authorities in the U.K., it was found that in the last 10 years preceding the year 2000, nearly 3,759 people were killed in sudden deaths and over 205,000 suffered major injuries at the workplace. It was estimated that each year 20,000 people died from industrial diseases, including 3,000 to 12,000 from occupational cancer. Each year over 1,100 people were killed and 1,390,000 were injured as the result of using home-based consumer products such as furniture, cooking appliances or toys. It had been estimated that almost 400 people were killed and other 36,000 suffered injuries from

184 See: Neil Hodge, *British Government accedes to demands for new corporate killing offence*, 25 February 2002, http://www.wsws.org/en/articles/2002/02/man-f25.html, Visited on: 16-06-2014

the use of medicines. Further between 1992 and 1997, 144 crew members working on merchant ships or fishing vessels were killed; also between 1993 and 1997, 2,424 crew members and 486 members of the public were injured on merchant ships. No figures relating to the number of people killed or injured as a result of the public being exposed to toxic chemicals emitted through corporate activities was made available but it was likely to be in thousands. It was realised that very few incidents resulting from corporate harm were made subject of any criminal investigations.[185]

Professor Gary Slapper welcomed the new Act, the Corporate Manslaughter and Corporate Homicide Act, 2007, noting that globally more people are killed each year at work than are killed in wars and that this legislation makes prosecution and conviction an easier prospect than was previously. This is not to say that the "threshold of guilt" has been lowered, as the Act criminalises only an organisation whose gross negligence has resulted in death. The new law applies not just to the 2.3 million companies in the U.K. but also to partnerships, other employers like trade unions, and to some non-commercial organisations.[186] After much debate in the Parliament, the new law now is also applicable if the death of someone takes place in the custody, as a result of gross negligence of the prison service or of those controlling police cells.[187]

Analysis of the Corporate Manslaughter and Corporate Homicide Act, 2007: As discussed already, the issue of corporate manslaughter attracted wider attention when the Law Commission of England and Wales published their Report, *Legislating the Criminal Code: Involuntary Manslaughter*. This Report included proposals for a new offence of corporate killing that would act as a stand-alone provision for prosecuting companies to complement offences primarily aimed at individuals. This provided the basis for the Government's

---

185 See: David Bergman, *The Case for Corporate Responsibility: Corporate Violence and the Criminal Justice System*, London: Disaster Action (May 5, 2000)

186 See: Gary Slapper, *Corporate manslaughter Law is a vast improvement*, The Times, 18 July 2007, http://www.thetimes.co.uk/tto/law/article2209921.ece, Visited on: 03-05-2014; See also: Section 1(2) of the Corporate Manslaughter and Corporate Homicide Act of 2007

187 See: Eamonn Carrabine, Pam Cox, Maggy Lee, Ken Plummer & Nigel South, *Criminology: A Sociological Introduction*, Routledge Publications, Second Edition, Chapter 13: Organisational and Professional Forms of Crime, p.254-255

subsequent consultation paper in the year 2000; *Reforming the Law on Involuntary Manslaughter: The Government's Proposals.* It was not until 2005 that the Draft Bill was published. This Draft Bill was eventually enacted in 2007 as the Corporate Manslaughter[188] and Corporate Homicide[189] Act of 2007.[190] The Act received the Royal Assent on 26th July, 2007 but it was a year later that the Act completely came into force.[191]

The organisations to which the Act applies include corporations[192], certain departments or other bodies[193], a police force[194] and a partnership[195], trade union or employers association that is an employer[196]. With the enactment of this legislation in the U.K., an organisation will be guilty of an offence if the way in which its activities are managed or organised causes a person's death and amounts to a gross breach of a relevant duty of care owed by the organisation to the deceased.[197] A case of corporate manslaughter can be made out, as per the provisions of the Act, only if the way in which the organisation's activities are managed or organised by its senior management is a "substantial element" in the breach. The crucial elements for the attribution of the liability

---

188 See: Section 1(5) (a) of the Corporate Manslaughter and the Corporate Homicide Act of 2007.

189 See: Section 1(5) (b) of the Corporate Manslaughter and Corporate Homicide Act of 2007.

190 See: Celia Wells, *Corporate Manslaughter: Why Does Reform Matter?;* (2006) 122 South African L.J. 648; David Ormerod & Richard Taylor, *The Corporate Manslaughter and Corporate Homicide Act,* (2008) 8 Criminal L.R. 589; Stephen Griffin, *Corporate Killing- the Corporate Manslaughter and Corporate Homicide Act of 2007,* [2009] L.M.C.L.Q. 73

191 Most of the Act came into force from 6th April, 2008. See: The Corporate Manslaughter and Corporate Homicide Act of 2007, (Commencement No. 1) Order 2008 (SI 2008/401).

192 See: Section 1(2) (a) of the Corporate Manslaughter and Corporate Homicide Act of 2007

193 See: Section 1(2) (b) of the Corporate Manslaughter and Corporate Homicide Act of 2007 read with Schedule 1 of the Act.

194 See: Section 1(2) (c) read with Section 13 of the Corporate Manslaughter and Corporate Homicide Act of 2007

195 See: Section 14 of the Corporate Manslaughter and Corporate Homicide Act of 2007

196 See: Section 1(2) (d) of the Corporate Manslaughter and Corporate Homicide Act of 2007

197 See: Section 1(1) of the Corporate Manslaughter and Corporate Homicide Act of 2007

are that of causing death and that to owing to the gross breach of the relevant duty of care. A gross breach is conduct alleged to amount to a breach of duty which falls below what can reasonably be expected of an organisation in the circumstances.[198] The 'relevant duty of care' as elaborated in the Act, owing to the 'law of negligence' brings to light the following main points[199]:

1. A duty is owed to the employees and to other persons working for the organisation or performing services for it;
2. An organisation owes a duty as the occupier of the premises;
3. A duty is owed in connection with the supply, by the organisation, of goods or services (whether for consideration or not); the carrying on by the organisation of any construction or maintenance operations; the carrying on by the organisation of any other activity on a commercial basis; or the use or keeping by the organisation of any plant, vehicle or other thing.[200]

Whether a duty of care is owed to a particular individual is a question of law but the judge may make any findings of fact necessary to decide that question.[201] Once it is established that an organisation, such as a company, owed a relevant duty of care, it falls to the jury to decide whether there was a "gross breach" of that duty[202] and in doing so, the jury must consider whether the evidence shows that the organisation failed to comply with any health and

---

198 See: Section 1(4) (b) of the Corporate Manslaughter and Corporate Homicide Act of 2007

199 These points have been discussed after taking into consideration the following legislations- the Occupiers' Liability Act of 1957, the Defective Premises Act of 1972 and the Occupiers' Liability Act of 1984. These legislations need to be read with Section 2(4) and Section 2(6) of the Corporate Manslaughter and Corporate Homicide Act of 2007, for better analysis of the points stated above.

200 See: Section 2(1) of the Corporate Manslaughter and Corporate Homicide Act of 2007

201 See: *R* v. *Evans (Gemma)* [(2009) EWCA Crim. 650; (2009) 1 W.L.R. 1999]; See also: Section 2(5) of the Corporate Manslaughter and Corporate Homicide Act of 2007

202 See: Section 8(1) of the Corporate Manslaughter and Corporate Homicide Act of 2007

safety legislation that relates to the alleged breach and, if so, how serious that failure was and how much of a risk of death it posed[203].[204]

Before the enactment of the Corporate Manslaughter and Corporate Homicide Act of 2007 in the U.K., the offence was governed by the ordinary principles of the common law and required the prosecution to prove beyond reasonable doubt not only that an unlawful killing had taken place but also that, a responsible person the so-called "controlling mind" within the company controlled the activities resulting in the death of the individual; and that a person was grossly negligent so as to be responsible for the death and hence could be - and generally is - prosecuted, as an individual, for the offence of manslaughter.[205] The question that always arises from death caused by corporate activity is whether the company can be held liable for crimes related to killing, namely murder and manslaughter. As the mandatory sentence for murder is life imprisonment, a company cannot commit murder as clearly it cannot go to jail. However, manslaughter, the involuntary killing of an individual as a result of the gross negligence of the accused[206] can be punished by fine or incarceration and, formally at least, could be committed by a company. This same idea has been advanced by the corporate manslaughter legislation of the U.K., as enacted in the year 2007.

As per the 2007 legislation, corporations will no longer be prosecutable for the common law offence of gross negligence manslaughter. The Act abolishes the common law offence of manslaughter by gross negligence in its application to

---

203 See: Section 8(2) of the Corporate Manslaughter and Corporate Homicide Act of 2007

204 See: Stephen Girvin, Sandra Frisby and Alastair Hudson, *Charlesworth's Company Law,* Thomas Reuters (Legal) Limited 2010, Eighteenth Edition, Chapter 23: Criminal and Civil Liability of Companies, p.577-578

205 See: Peter Thompson, *Implications of Corporate Manslaughter Bill,* The Faculty of Finance and Management, http://www.icaew.com/en/technical/legal-and-regulatory/business-crime-and-misconduct/the-corporate-manslaughter-and-corporate-homicide-act-2007/fm128-legal-implications-of-the-corporate-manslaughter-bill, Visited on: 20-06-2014

206 Evidence of mens rea i.e. the required state of mind, although is relevant but is not necessary to convict a person of manslaughter or involuntary killing; what must be demonstrated is that the gross negligence of the accused resulted in the death. See: *R* v. *Adomako* [(1994) 3 All ER 79]

corporations and also any application it has to other organisations to which the Act applies.[207] Corporations will commit the new statutory offence of "corporate manslaughter and corporate homicide" only if the way in which its activities are managed or organised by its senior management is a substantial element in the death.[208] There has been criticism of the Act on the grounds of it being unnecessarily complex as the Act requires: that the management failure caused the death; there was a gross breach of a relevant duty of care owed by the organisation to the deceased; and, the consent of the DPP (Director of Public Prosecutions).[209]

Although public bodies are included within the ambit of the Act, most deaths in custody are not covered, however deaths while detained in the custody area of police stations stand covered.[210] Under the provisions of the Act, there shall be a "gross breach" only if the failure in question constitutes the conduct falling far below what can reasonably be expected of the organisation in the circumstances prevailing.[211]

The economic, political and social factors which make agencies and governments reluctant to press prosecutions against powerful interests remain in play because the Act presses in a requirement that DPP's consent must be gained before prosecution can proceed, this the scholars say is particularly worrying. The Director of Public Prosecution's reluctance to take risks in sensitive cases contrasts sharply with the Crown Prosecution Service's usual willingness to interpret the evidential test broadly. It is being said that the thinking behind the Act fails to take into account the fact that deaths are the tip of the iceberg in regards to the dangerous practices leading to thousands of serious injuries each year. Legislation targeting these injuries, rather than

---

207 See: Section 20 of the Corporate Manslaughter and Corporate Homicide Act of 2007

208 See: Section 1(3) of the Corporate Manslaughter and Corporate Homicide Act of 2007

209 See: Section 17 of the Corporate Manslaughter and Corporate Homicide Act of 2007

210 See: Section 2(2) of the Corporate Manslaughter and Corporate Homicide Act of 2007

211 See: Section 1(4)(b) of the Corporate Manslaughter and Corporate Homicide Act of 2007

deaths would have been more useful.[212] Many scholars are of the opinion that the Act is more symbolic in nature than instrumental.[213]

In relation to the 'rules of attribution' the Act adopts an approach similar to but clearly less demanding than the 'directing mind and will' or the 'identification' doctrine approach. The identification doctrine requires that the gross negligence causing the death in a particular case be committed by a person who operated at the very top of the corporate hierarchy but the Act refers to senior participants in the company's management and not necessarily only those at the managerial hierarchy. Pursuant to the Act, the senior management includes not only senior managers for the 'whole' of the organisation but also for a 'substantial part of its activities' suggesting that senior managers of important divisions of a company would fall within the definition of senior management.[214] Under the Act it is now possible that the company could be liable for corporate manslaughter when no one individual member of the company's senior management could be held individually liable for manslaughter. By virtue of Section 18 of the Act, it has been stated that, an individual cannot be held guilty of aiding, abetting, counselling or procuring the commission of an offence of corporate manslaughter and, an individual cannot be accounted guilty of aiding, abetting, counselling or procuring, or being art and part in, the commission of an offence of corporate homicide.[215]

It is essential to note that in some situations, the relevant duty of care owed for the offence of corporate manslaughter is excluded. Thus, the duty of care owed by a public authority in respect of a decision in regards to the matters of public policy, including in particular the allocation of public resources or

212 See: Gobert, *The Corporate Manslaughter and Corporate Homicide Act of 2007,* [(2008) 71 MLR 413]

213 See: Andrew Sanders, Richard Young & Mandy Burton, *Criminal Justice,* Oxford University Press, Fourth Edition, Chapter 7: Prosecutions, p. 416-417

214 Section 1(4)(c)(i) and Section 1(4)(c)(ii) make it clear that 'senior management' refers to both the board of directors making decisions about the delegation of authority and appointment of managers as well as the actual senior managers themselves.

215 See: David Kershaw, *Company Law in Context,* Oxford University Press, 2009 Edition, Chapter Four: Corporate Actions, p.158-159

the weighing of competing public interests is not a "relevant duty of care".[216] Other exclusions include certain types of military activities[217], policing and law enforcement activities[218], emergency circumstances[219], and child protection and probation functions[220].

Sentencing, the corporations for 'corporate crimes' committed by them has always been an issue of debate. The problems of finding an appropriate form of punishment was been dealt with by Professor Gary Slapper in *the Corporate Punishment* [(1994) 144 NLJ 29]. The Court of Appeal too gave guidance on sentencing for offences under the Health and Safety at Work Act of 1974, in *R* v. *F. Howe and Son (Engineers) Ltd.*[221], and revisited the question in *R* v. *Balfour Beatty Rail Infrastructure Services Ltd.*[222]. In between those cases, the Criminal Justice Act of 2003, Section 142 created a statutory statement for the purposes of sentencing as for: the punishment of offenders; the reduction of crime (including its reduction by deterrence); the reform and rehabilitation of offenders; the protection of the public; and the making of reparation by offenders to persons affected by their offences.

In the *Balfour Beatty* case the Court of Appeal observed that most of the above stated propositions [from (a) to (e)] can be applied to a company offender, but said that there are obvious difficulties in looking for reform and rehabilitation. This was observed to be dispiriting, as companies convicted of offences typically continue to carry on their businesses even after conviction. In *R* v. *Rollco Screw and Rivet Co. Ltd.*[223], the court observed that imposing a fine on a company necessarily punishes its shareholders. It is common for the shareholders and directors of a small company to be the same individuals. If both company and directors have been convicted of an offence and the directors are fined, the fine imposed on the company should not in effect be a double punishment

---

216 See: Section 3(1) of the Corporate Manslaughter and Corporate Homicide Act of 2007

217 See: Section 4 of the Corporate Manslaughter and Corporate Homicide Act of 2007

218 See: Section 5 of the Corporate Manslaughter and Corporate Homicide Act of 2007

219 See: Section 6 of the Corporate Manslaughter and Corporate Homicide Act of 2007

220 See: Section 7 of the Corporate Manslaughter and Corporate Homicide Act of 2007

221 (1999) IRLR 434

222 (2006) EWCA Crim. 1586; (2007) Bus LR 77

223 (1999) IRLR 439

of the shareholder-directors. A large company can be required to pay a fine immediately; this was observed in the case of *R* v. *B & Q PLC*[224].[225]

The law in regards to corporate killings eventually got streamlined with the enactment of the Corporate Manslaughter and Corporate Homicide Act of 2007. The punishment for the offence of corporate manslaughter is "fine" as per Section 1(6) of the Corporate Manslaughter and Corporate Homicide Act, 2007.[226] Also, by virtue of Section 9 of the Act, the court may order the company to take specified steps, within a specified time, to remedy the breach of duty and other resultant cause of the victim's death. There is also a provision for the court to make a publicity order requiring the company to publicise the conviction, particulars of the offence, the amount of the fine and the terms of any remedial order.[227] The Sentencing Guidelines Council issued a definitive guideline on the 'Corporate Manslaughter & Health and Safety Offences Causing Death' in February of 2010.[228] Hence, the Corporate Manslaughter and Corporate Homicide Act of 2007 has been instrumental in streamlining all laws as contained in different statutes (the Health and Safety at Work Act of 1974 & the Criminal Justice Act of 2003) for the attribution of liability in regards to the offence of corporate killings.

There are a number of precautions that a company or an organisation can take in light of the Corporate Manslaughter and Corporate Homicide Act of 2007. One recommendation would be to increase the health and safety training for senior management and to ensure that there is board scrutiny of health and safety compliance. In addition, the company or organisation should regularly review internal policies and procedures to ensure compliance

---

224 (2005) EWCA Crim. 2297

225 See: Derek French, Stephen Mayson & Christopher Ryan, *Company Law,* Oxford University Press, 27th Edition (2010-2011), Chapter 19: Acting For a Company-Agency & Attribution, p.637-644

226 The amount of fine usually runs between 2.5% to 10% of the company's annual turnover (and not profit). See: Corporate Manslaughter, http://www.kensingtonswan.com/KSPublicWeb/media/Documents/Corporate-Manslaughter.pdf, Visited on: 23-06-2014

227 See: Section 10 of the Corporate Manslaughter and Corporate Homicide Act of 2007

228 See: Corporate Manslaughter & Health and Safety Offences Causing Death, http://sentencingcouncil.judiciary.gov.uk/docs/web_guideline_on_corporate_manslaughter_accessible.pdf, Visited on: 23-06-2014

with existing health and safety laws. Ensuring that the employees and the management of the corporation is properly and is regularly trained in the health and safety compliance procedures, and periodic reviews of these policies and procedures for ensuring the overall compliance with the law, will make a material difference to the company or the organisation if in any eventuality it finds itself in the court of law.

4.3. New Zealand:

In New Zealand, the identification doctrine is the accepted standard for the attribution of criminal liability over the corporations. There is, as of date, no way of holding a corporation liable for manslaughter as per the wordings of the Crimes Act of 1961. The Act defines 'homicide' as an act of killing one human being by another. The Act throws the artificial legal persons out of the ambit of the definitional parameters set for defining 'homicide'.[229] In New Zealand, a corporation can be convicted of a criminal offence under the Crimes Act of 1961. Section 2 of the Act defines a "person" to include, "the Crown & any public body or local authority, and any board, society, or company and any other body of persons, whether incorporated or not."[230]

It is due to the case of *R* v. *Murray Wright Ltd.* that a corporation cannot be prosecuted for manslaughter under the Crimes Act of 1961. In the case of *R* v. *Murray Wright Ltd.*[231], a chemist company incorrectly prepared some medicine. As a result of this incorrect preparation the patient who received

---

229 The New Zealand criminal law (unlike the U.K. common law approach) is codified in the Crimes Act of 1961. The original criminal code of New Zealand in 1893 was based on the Criminal Code (Indictable Offences) Bill of 1879 by Sir James Fitzjames Stephen, which was drafted for the U.K. but never got enacted. The Crimes Act of 1961 is based on the Crimes Act of 1908, which closely followed the Criminal Code of 1893.

230 The definition of "person" needs to be read in consonance with Section 30 of the Interpretation Act of 1999, which defines "person" for the purposes of the Acts passed prior to the Interpretation Act of 1999, as "a corporation sole, and also a body of persons, whether incorporated or unincorporated". Section 30 of the Interpretation Act of 1999 is qualified by Section 4(1) (a) and Section 4(1) (b) of the Interpretation Act of 1999, which states that the definition of "person" does not apply where 'the provision' or 'the context of the provision points to a different meaning'.

231 (1970) NZLR 476

the prescription died after taking the drugs. A manslaughter prosecution was brought against Murray Wright Ltd. under Section 160(2) (b) of the Crimes Act of 1961, convicting the company for killing the patient by virtue of lack of reasonable care employed by it. "Homicide" is defined in Section 158 of the Crimes Act as "the killing of a human being by another, directly or indirectly, by any means whatsoever". Under Section 160 of the Act, homicide can be either culpable or non-culpable. Non-culpable homicide is not an offence.[232] It was held in this case that, "those responsible for the drafting of the Crimes Act of 1961, failed to appreciate that even a corporation can commit the crime of homicide, the Crimes Act of 1961 expressly describes the crime of homicide as the killing of one human being by another, thereby intentionally excluding the artificial legal persons from governing ambit". It is necessary to emphasise that the Court of Appeal in this case left open the possibility of a company to be prosecuted for the crime of manslaughter by virtue of Section 66 of the Crimes Act of 1961.

In some sense of the term, the corporations in New Zealand can be held accountable for corporate-manslaughter by virtue of the Health and Safety in Employment Act of 1992. The Health and Safety in Employment Act of 1992 is the key health and safety regulation that corporations must adhere to in New Zealand.[233] Section 5 of the Act states that, the objective of this legislation is to promote the prevention of harm to all persons at work and other persons in and around the vicinity of the place of work. This is to be achieved (legislatively speaking in line with the language of Section 5 of the Act) by promoting excellence in health and safety management or, by defining hazards and harms in a comprehensive way and by imposing various duties on persons who are responsible for work and those who do the work. This legislation has replaced a number of statues that were merely prescriptive in nature, such as the Coal Mines Act of 1979 and the Agricultural Workers Act of 1977.

The Health and Safety in Employment Act of 1992 places a number of duties on the employers of a business organisation by virtue of Section 6 of the Act. Section 6 of the Act requires that every employer should take all practicable steps to ensure that the safety of the employees is assured and is not

---

232 See: Section 160 (2) and Section 160 (4) of the Crimes Act of 1961

233 The Health and Safety in Employment Act of 1992 came into force on 1st April, 1993.

compromised while they are on the work-front; also that the employers should take all rational steps to provide employees with safe working conditions. As per the provisions of the Act, the employers are to be held legally responsible for providing and maintaining for employees facilities that ensure their safety and good health. Employers are to ensure that the tools and equipments used by the employees on the work-front are so arranged, designed, made & maintained that it is safe for the employees to use them. The Act provides that a business organisation should develop 'comprehensive procedures' for dealing with emergencies that may arise while employees are at work.

In the year 2002, the comprehensive amendment of the Health and Safety in Employment Act, 1992 was complete. After the 2002 amendment, the penalty for breach of Section 49[234] has been increased to a fine of $500,000 or imprisonment for up to 2 years or both. Hence, the amendment has increased the level of the fine by five times and has doubled the length of imprisonment. Also, after the 2002 amendment, the fine for breach of Section 50[235] of the Act has been increased to a maximum of $250,000, which is a five-fold increase in the penalty in comparison to the proposition of law that existed prior to such amendment. These new levels of fines have to be considered in the light of the Sentencing Act of 2002 and Section 51A of the Health and Safety in Employment Act of 1992 which talks about the 'sentencing criteria'. The ability of the court to award fine, partly or wholly, to the victim or victim's family is removed by the Sentencing Act of 2002. This has been replaced by the new sentence of reparation in Section 32 of the Sentencing Act of 2002. By virtue of Section 32(2) of the Sentencing Act of 2002, the court can impose a sentence of reparation in respect of emotional harm or loss or damage consequential on emotional harm, if the person who suffered the emotional harm is a person described as "victim" in Section 4(a) of the Sentencing Act of 2002.

Therefore in a situation where a person has died and the employer is found guilty of an offence under the Health and Safety in Employment Act of 1992, the immediate family of the person can receive reparation for emotional harm

---

[234] See: Section 49: Offences likely to cause serious harm; The Health and Safety in Employment (Amendment) Act of 2002

[235] See: Section 50: Other offences; The Health and Safety in Employment (Amendment) Act of 2002

suffered. The immediate family or any other person can, on bringing upon the information necessary, level prosecution under the Health and Safety in Employment Act of 1992; where an inspector has failed to initiate an enforcement action against any possible defendant, or where an enforcement authority has not taken prosecutorial action under any other relevant statute on the matter in issue.[236]

It is incumbent for us to take note of the following case, *Linework Ltd.* v. *Department of Labour*[237]. In this case, advancing the jurisprudence of Section 6 of the Health and Safety in Employment Act of 1992, the court held that an employer under the Health and Safety in Employment Act of 1992 does not need to be identified as the "directing mind and will" of the company to be held liable under the provisions of the statute.

To be a complete and comprehensive piece of legislation, the Health and Safety in Employment Act of 1992 needs to provide protection not only to employees but also to consumers and members of public in general. The long title of the Act states that the Health and Safety in Employment Act of 1992 is enacted to reform the law in regards to the health and safety of employees, and other people at work, or affected by the work of the employees of the business organisation. Persons affected by the work would include consumers & members of public whose death may have been caused by the company functioning negligently. Section 15 of the Health and Safety in Employment Act of 1992, is the closest provision which covers this situation by stating that an employer has a duty to take all practicable steps to ensure that no action or inaction of any employee should harm any person whilst the employee is working.[238]

An interesting case, exploring the ambit of Section 15 of the Health and Safety in Employment Act of 1992 is that of *Department of Labour* v. *Nelson Dive*

236 See: Section 54-A of the Health and Safety in Employment Act of 1992

237 (2001) 2 NZLR 639

238 See: Aaron Sweet, *Making a Killing: A Separate Corporate Manslaughter Offence for New Zealand?;* Faculty of Law, University of Otago, Dunedin, 2006, http://www.otago.ac.nz/law/research/journals/otago036249.pdf, Visited on: 25-06-2014

Centre Ltd.[239]. In this case Nelson Dive Centre Ltd., carrying the business of training potential divers, was charged under Section 15 of the Act. The charge was that the defendant failed to take all practicable steps to ensure that no action of the employee (the dive trainer), Mr. Andrew David Stuart, while at work harmed any person namely in respect of training divers at the French Pass.

In this case, six student divers and the instructor, Mr. Stuart entered the water at the French Pass with the intention of completing a 'drift dive'. The dive went tragically wrong and the divers were pulled by a strong current into the deep waters. Two of the divers died, one was never found and three others survived but were severely injured. The court observed that the area in which Mr. Stuart took his student divers should never have been used for drift diving instruction. Mr. Stuart carrying out the drift dive lessons in the French Pass should have known the dangers. The court held that the defendant did not take all practicable steps to ensure that no action of an employee while at work harmed any other person. This case substantially confirms that the Health and Safety in Employment Act of 1992 takes account of a situation where a member of the public dies as a result of the action of an employee.

An important aspect of the Health and Safety in Employment Act of 1992 is the ability of the Crown to bring a manslaughter prosecution against a director of a company where a death as so happening breaches the Health and Safety in Employment Act of 1992. This issue was decided affirmatively after the death of a worker from a trench collapse at Wellington Airport. In 1999, manslaughter charges were laid against the sole director of a small drainage company, David Spencer Ltd. The company was convicted and a fine of $25,000 under the Health and Safety in Employment Act of 1992 was imposed over the company. The death of the employee in this case as a result of a trench-collapse resulted in Mr. Spencer, the sole-director of the company been convicted, but the decision was later overturned by the Court of Appeal on procedural grounds. This case also asserts that the Health and Safety in Employment Act of 1992 does not suffice to deal with problem of corporate killings.

---

239 DCR (2001) 1079, 1082

In nutshell, in New Zealand, a company cannot be charged with homicide, only a person can be. However a company, and its directors, can be charged over a fatality under the Health and Safety in Employment Act of 1992. The fines are capped with a maximum of up to $250,000 where the breach was unintentional, or up to $500,000 for a "knowing" offence.[240] There have been many cases resulting in the death of people, owing to the lack of reasonable care & caution exercised by the accused companies but the legal, regulatory and judicial practice has been to convict the accused companies with fines and necessary hours of community service. This can be seen in several cases as for example in the year 1990, a bungy-jumpmaster at Rainbow's End was convicted of manslaughter for failing to attach the bungy-cord after he and the victim had been smoking cannabis. He was sentenced to 200 hours community service. Also in 2003, a tandem hang glider pilot was convicted and was sentenced to 350 hours of community service plus a $10,000 reparation payment after he failed to attach his passenger's harness to the glider, resulting in her felling and dying. More recently, a case was levelled against an adventure sports company after a bridge swing operator, owing to his negligence, failed to secure the harness on the jumper and thus resulting in her falling 20 metres onto the rocks and dying. The accused received 400 hours of community service and the company was ordered to pay $10,000 as reparations.[241]

After the Pike River Mine Disaster[242], the Royal Commission on the Pike River Coal Mine Tragedy submitted its report to the Governor-General on 30th October of 2012, expressing the need for a legislation dealing exclusively with the crime of corporate manslaughter and corporate homicide taking inspiration

240 See: Angela Gregory, *Corporate manslaughter law the answer?*, 10th April 2012, http://insider.thomsonreuters.co.nz/2012/04/corporatemanslaughter/comment-page-1/, Visited on: 25-06-2014

241 See: Jackie Brown-Hayson, *Does New Zealand need a new crime of corporate manslaughter?;* Safeguard- Thomas Reuters, http://www.safeguard.co.nz/backissues/136-story1.asp, Visited on: 25-06-2014

242 In the Pike River Mine Disaster, an explosion took place inside the Pike River Mine on 19th November, 2010. This explosion resulted in the death of 29 miners. In the April of 2013, Pike River Coal Limited was convicted of nine charges of breaching the Health and Safety in Employment Act of 1992. It was ordered to pay $110,000 to the family of each victim and survivor. It was also fined to the tune of $760,000.

from the U.K. legislation that is the Corporate Manslaughter and Corporate Homicide Act of 2007.[243]

4.4. U.S.:

One of the first American statutes that created a mechanism for indicting corporations by imputing criminal liability over them was passed in New Jersey in the year 1837. The statute provided that summons could be issued against a corporation for indicting it (in its corporate name) for crimes committed by it. But the statute eventually failed to comprehensively enumerate the offences for which a corporation could be indicted or could be held liable.[244] In consonance with this statute of 1837, the Supreme Court of New Jersey in the case of *State* v. *The Morris and Essex R.R.*[245] held that, a corporation could be indicted for criminal nuisance. The Court, however, observed that a corporation cannot commit certain crimes, such as perjury, for such crimes can be committed only by individuals in their respective "human capacity", and that corporations cannot be held guilty of crimes in the nature of a murder because they cannot form the so-called 'criminal intent' or *mens rea,* which is an essential ingredient of crime along with the *actus reus.*

In the same year, that is 1852, the New Hampshire Court decided the case of *State* v. *Gilmore*[246]; it was the first American case in which it was held that, a corporation could be held criminally liable for wrongful deaths in the nature of gross negligence manslaughter. In this case, a person was fatally injured by a train. The Court relied on the 1850 statute that provided that if a person died because of the railroad's negligence, the 'proprietors' of the railroad shall

243 See: The Report of the Royal Commission on the Pike River Coal Mine Tragedy, Volume 1, http://pikeriver.royalcommission.govt.nz/vwluResources/Final-Report-Volume-One/$file/ReportVol1-whole.pdf, Visited on: 25-06-2014; Also see: The Report of the Royal Commission on the Pike River Coal Mine Tragedy, Volume 2, http://pikeriver.royalcommission.govt.nz/vwluResources/Final-Report-Vol2-Part1-only/$file/Report-Vol2-Part1-only.pdf, Visited on: 25-06-2014

244 See: David J. Reilly, *Murder, Inc.: The Criminal Liability of Corporations for Homicide,* 18 SETON HALL L. REV. 378, 381 (1988) [Citing the Act of February 10, 1837, 1837 N.J. ACTS 125]

245 1852 WL 3499 (Sup. Ct. 1852)

246 1852 WL 2109 (Sup. Ct. 1852)

be liable to a 'fine'. The issue in this case was, whether the legislature intended to impose this fine on the railroad itself or on the stockholders of the railroad? The Court held that the indictment must be against the corporation and not against the individual stockholders. The primary goal of the legislation was not to punish the corporation but to compensate the victim's family for the loss suffered.

Moving a step further, in the year 1900, a Pennsylvania Court in *Commonwealth* v. *Punxsutawney St. Passenger Ry.*; quashed the indictment for homicide against the corporation and held that no precedent existed for imposing liability on a corporate entity for a crime for which criminal intent or *mens rea* was necessary. The court also held that the criminal act of manslaughter by an agent of a corporation was *ultra vires* as it contravenes all the accepted principles in the criminal law that are used for making the same, the act of the principal. Few years after this decision, the New York court in the case of *United States* v. *Van Schaick*[247] set a contrary precedent by holding that a corporation could be indicted for manslaughter. This case arose out of the 1904 tragedy when about nine-hundred-people travelling by the steamboat "General Slocum" drowned in an attempt to escape the flames when a fire erupted onto the ship. The issue before the court was whether the Knickerbocker Steamboat Company, the owner of the General Slocum, was liable for the manslaughter. The court answered this question in a "yes" and held that, the corporation allowed the steamboat to navigate without life-preservers, and hence for the deaths caused due to the tragedy, it was the corporation that was to be held responsible. The Court also stated that under the statute it was "not necessary to show that there was an intention to kill'.

In 1909, in a landmark case of *New York Central & Hudson River R.R. Co.* v. *United States*[248], the United States Supreme Court held that a corporation can be indicted for the acts done by its agents provided, "the agent is acting within the scope of his employment and within the scope of authority conferred onto him by the principal, and the virtues of justice, equity and good conscience

247 134 F. 592 (S. Dist. N.Y. Cir. Ct. 1904)
248 212 U.S. 481 (1909)

requires that the latter should be held responsible for damages to the individual who has suffered by such a conduct."[249]

In 1909 itself, despite the ruling of the Supreme Court, the New York Court of Appeals held in the case of *People* v. *Rochester Ry. and Light Co.*[250], that New York's Criminal Code Act defining the term "homicide" could not apply to corporations because "homicide" as lexically defined meant "the killing of one human being by another human being".

In 1961, the Supreme Court of Oregon, similarly, declined to hold a corporation criminally liable for manslaughter on statutory grounds stating that corporations exist only in the contemplation of law and hence a juridical person devoid of flesh and blood is incapable of committing a crime of manslaughter or homicide. In this case *State* v. *Pacific Powder Co.*[251], the employee of the corporation had parked a truck with explosives near a wooden building. The building caught fire and this eventually caused the explosives to explode, killing a bystander.

In the 1980s, the jurisprudence in regards to corporate culpability advanced and the tide turned. The American courts began to hold that a corporation could, indeed, be prosecuted for manslaughter. In the year 1980, the Kentucky Court held that a corporation could be held criminally liable for manslaughter or homicide, in the case of *Commonwealth* v. *Fortner LP Gas Co.*[252]. In this case, a driver employed by the corporation was unable to stop his truck because of the defective brakes and there by fatally injured a child.

In 1987, the Court of Criminal Appeals of Texas decided in the case of *Vaughn & Sons, Inc.* v. *State*[253], where two persons died in a motor vehicle collision caused owing to the gross negligence of the agent of the corporation, that the defendant (corporation) could be prosecuted for gross negligence homicide

---

249 In this case the judgement was rendered principally by citing the case of *Lothrop* v. *Adams* [133 Mass. 471 (1882)]

250 195 N.Y. 102 (N.Y. 1909)

251 226 Or. 502 (Or. 1961)

252 610 S.W. 2d 941 (Ky. Ct. App. 1980)

253 737 S.W. 2d 805 (Tex. Crim. App. 1987) (en banc)

under the Texas Penal Code. The Vaughn Court acknowledged assertively that the area of corporate criminal liability was undergoing reform and stated that the emerging view is that a corporation can be held liable for specific crimes requiring *mens rea* and for offences of gross negligence manslaughter."

The 1990s witnessed a shift in the legal thought which favoured the holding of corporations liable for the crimes of intent, in particular gross negligence manslaughter.[254] The courts in the U.S. began to accept the idea that corporations can be guilty of various crimes requiring intent (*mens rea*), including comprehensive crimes in the nature of manslaughter and homicide. The courts, however, still strained themselves to progressively interpret the criminal statutes to convict the accused corporations for crimes of manslaughter and homicide. The efforts of the courts were directed to include corporations within the ambit of the penal statutes by literally interpreting the penal statutes with a progressive attitude. Despite efforts made by courts to interpret the penal statutes with a progressive attitude, the plain lexicological interpretation of the terms 'homicide' and 'manslaughter' appeared to exclusively apply to human beings. The contention as stated can comprehensively be explained through the case of *State* v. *Richard Knutson Inc.*[255]. In this case, the Wisconsin Court of Appeals held that a corporation could be prosecuted under the homicide statute of the State for crimes of manslaughter and homicide. In this case, one of the construction employees of the Richard Knutson, Inc. was fatally electrocuted while attempting to attach a chain to a backhoe's bucket. Knutson was charged with negligent vehicular homicide, and the jury found the corporation guilty of the crime of manslaughter. The Wisconsin Supreme Court initially accepted this case upon the certification from the appellate court to decide whether or not, can a corporate entity could be prosecuted under the penal statute of the State that provided, "whoever causes the death of another human being by the negligent operation or handling of a vehicle is guilty of a Class E felony." The Supreme Court of Wisconsin returned the case to the appellate court opining that it could not render a substantive opinion on the matter because

---

254 See: Richard M. Dunn, *Criminalization of Negligent Acts by Employees of U.S. and Foreign Corporations,* 69 DEF. COUNS. J. 17, 18 (January 2002) [Citing: Sean Bajkowski & Kimberly R. Thompson (Note), *Corporate Counsel Liability,* 34 AM. CRIM. L. REV. 445 (1997)]

255 537 N.W. 2d 420 (Wis. Ct. App. 1995)

it was equally divided on, whether to affirm or reverse the judgement of Knutson's conviction. On appeal, Knutson argued that the word "whoever" and the correlative phrase "another human being" in the statute necessarily referred to a human being and that the homicide statute could not apply to a corporate entity. After extensive review of the penal statute, the appellate court concluded that a corporation could be liable for vehicular homicide and affirmed Knutson's conviction. Explaining its holding, the Court noted:

"Our conclusion conforms to the modern trend of the law. A leading treatise on corporations acknowledges that a corporation may be held to answer for its criminal acts, including homicide and manslaughter. It is almost universally conceded that a corporation may be criminally liable for actions or omissions of its agents in its behalf."[256]

In December, 2005, the Indiana state lawmaker announced that he shall seek the passage of the legislation in the 2006 session of the Indiana General Assembly. The legislation will penalise corporations for safety violations in the workplace that lead to bodily injuries and fatalities.[257] The working title of the proposed Bill was, "the Corporate Manslaughter Act". This Bill is still to see the light of the day but some commentators indicated, as when the Bill was lined for passage, that Indiana was only a starting point.[258] The primary goal of this Bill was to make the prosecution and the conviction of the corporations easier in the cases of manslaughter and homicide.[259] Indiana seems to be the first state in the U.S. among all other 50 states to have risen up

---

256 See: Laurel J. Harbour & Natalya Y. Johnson, *Can-a-corporation-commit-manslaughter? Recent developments in the United Kingdom and the United States,* Shook Hardy & Bacon LLP, Defence Counsel Journal- July 2006, http://www.shb.com/practiceareas/International/Pubs/Can%20a%20Corporation%20Commit%20Manslaughter.pdf, p.230-234

257 See: House Bill 1144, 114th Gen. Assembly, 2d Sess. (Ind. 2006), http://www.in.gov/apps/lsa/session/billwatch/billinfo?year=2006&session=1&request=getBill&docno=1144, Visited on: 20-06-2014

258 See: The Corporate Manslaughter Act, New Bill in Indiana, 18 January 2006, http://www.unbossed.com/index.php?itemid=590, Visited on: 20-06-2014

259 The penalties provided in this Bill range **from** a "Class A misdemeanor", punishable with imprisonment up to one year and a maximum fine of $5,000 in regards to corporate negligence leading to bodily injury, **to** a "Class C felony" punishable with imprisonment up to 8 years and a maximum fine of $10,000 in regards to an

to the consciousness that crimes in the nature of corporate manslaughter and corporate homicide must be punished and that a specific legislation seeking conviction of flouting corporations must be in place. However, the U.S. is fast drawing inspiration from its neighbour in the north that is, Canada to bring on paper a federal corporate manslaughter law, holding companies liable for crimes in the nature of corporate manslaughter and corporate homicide.

It is of vital importance to share the Canadian experience as the U.S. seeks to take inspiration from the progressive legislative steps taken by the Canadian Government post the Westray coal mine tragedy of 1992.

Despite several efforts made by the Canadian Government, it was not ascertained as to what happened on the 9th of May, 1992 which triggered the explosion in the Westray coal mine in the Canadian province of Nova Scotia. Studies undertaken post the incident, indicate that a spark ignited a cloud of methane gas, which eventually on blasting, tore through the Westray coal mine, leaving at least 26 men dead. The subsequent enquiry conducted by the government revealed of a workplace culture where by the health and the safety standards had been pushed aside in a desperate attempt to meet the new mine's production targets. Ventilation through the shafts had been poor; methane detectors had been tampered; safety inspections had been woefully inadequate; and unsafe work practices were allowed to become the norm.

This event in particular, coupled with the significant media attention the tragedy of 1992 got, provoked the public to demand the government to enact corporate manslaughter legislation in Canada. The Canadian government responded to the same by enacting an amendment to the country's Criminal Code Act, there by introducing Bill C-45, popularly known as the Westray Act of 1992. Under this progressive piece of legislation, the corporations could be convicted for criminal negligence causing the death or injury of an individual, if the individual is harmed in circumstances where one or more of the corporation's representative displays wanton or reckless disregard for the lives and safety of the fellow workers, and where there has been

---

employee dying as a result of a knowing or intentional violation of administrative rules.

a significant failure by senior officers of the corporation to prevent this occurring.

If convicted, the companies are to face unlimited fines coupled with publicity orders. But an individual can be fined only up to $100,000 coupled with imprisonment for a term up to 10 years in cases involving injury, or for life, in the event of a fatality.

When the amendments took effect in 2004, public indignation about the mine tragedy was somewhat assuaged. Scholars opine that it is Canada's legislative experiment that has been repeated in other jurisdictions, in the wake of their own high profile workplace tragedies, particularly in the United Kingdom and the Australian Capital Territory.

Under the U.S. federal law, corporate criminal liability is ordinarily confined to offences: Committed by the officers, employees, or agents of the corporation; within the scope of their employment and authority explicitly conferred onto them; and at least in part, if not in totality for the benefit of the corporation.

The test for whether an activity falls within the scope of authority of an individual is that whether the individual engages himself in activities on behalf of the corporation in performance of his general line of work. These acts so performed must be motivated, at least in part- if not in whole, by the intent to benefit the corporation. If this standard is met, the corporation will be liable notwithstanding the fact that the corporation expressly directed its agents, employees, or officers not to commit the offence at issue.

In U.S. (at present) there is no specific statute operational at the central level, where by corporations can be brought to conviction for their misdemeanour or gross negligence resulting in corporate killings. A corporation can, however, be prosecuted under the Occupational Safety and Health Act of 1970, if the operations of a corporation result in injury or death of an employee, during the course of his employment.[260]

---

[260] See: The Occupational Health and Safety Act of 1970, [29 U.S.C. §651 et. seq. (1970)]

In U.S., the Congress had passed the Occupational Safety and Health Act in the year 1970 to ensure "worker" and "workplace" safety. The goal of this legislation was to make sure that the employers provide their workers with a place of employment that is free from recognized hazards in the nature of exposure to toxic chemicals, excessive noise levels, mechanical dangers in regards to tools and equipments used, heat or cold stress and unsanitary conditions. In order to establish standards for workplace health and safety, the Act created the National Institute for Occupational Safety and Health (NIOSH), a research institution for the Occupational Safety and Health Administration (OSHA).[261] OSHA became a division of the U.S. Department of Labour that looked into the administration of the Act and enforced standards prescribed by the Act, in all the 50 states.

In case of death of an individual in the capacity of a consumer of food, drugs or cosmetics, liability can be attributed on to a corporation through the Federal Food, Drug & Cosmetic Act[262]. The introduction of this act was influenced by the death of more than 100 patients due to a sulfanilamide medication where diethylene glycol was used to dissolve the drug and make a liquid form.[263] This Act prohibits the commerce of adulterated and misbranded food, drugs, devices and cosmetics.

There have been cases of corporate gross negligence manslaughter in the nature of environment crimes committed by corporations. To deal with corporate killings in this niche and to impute criminal liability over corporations, charges are framed under various legislations owing to the nature of crime committed. These legislations are: the Clean Air Act[264], the Clean Water Act[265], the Safe

---

261 See: Occupational Safety & Health Administration, United States Department of Labour, https://www.osha.gov/law-regs.html, Visited on: 20-06-2014

262 21 U.S.C. Ch. 9 § 301 et. seq.

263 See: Sulfanilamide Disaster, http://www.fda.gov/aboutfda/whatwedo/history/productregulation/sulfanilamidedisaster/default.htm, visited on: 23-06-2014. See also: Product Regulation: Sulfanilamide Disaster http://www.fda.gov/aboutfda/whatwedo/history/productregulation/sulfanilamidedisaster/default.htm, visited on: 26-06-2014

264 See: [42 U.S.C. 7401 et. seq.]

265 See: [33 U.S.C. §§ 1251-1387]

Drinking Water Act[266] and the Federal Insecticide, Fungicide & Rodenticide Act[267]. These legislations are framed and are subsequently amended to provide necessary punishment for both environmental tort as well as crime, in regards to individuals as well as corporations. The United States Environmental Protection Agency, came into existence in 1970, it acts as a regulatory body to prevent and to convict, individuals and corporations alike for environmental misfeasance.

In cases of corporate-gross-negligence-manslaughter in U.S., a "corporate officer" acting alone on behalf of the corporation, may not be convicted of conspiring with the corporation. This was held in the cases of *U.S.* v. *Stevens*[268] and *U.S.* v. *Peters*[269]. This assures that the principle of "Respondeat Superior" is followed in U.S. with great efficacy. Hence, what can be made out is that, the 'determining mind and will of a company' cannot be held legally accountable because they are acting in capacity of mere agents of the corporation and, a corporation can be punished within set legal parameters because it has no body to kick but only a soul to damn, doctrine of separate legal entity comes into operation. In cases where it is demanded that the corporate veil needs to be lifted to find the individual perpetrators, often the result is that, not a single individual but a group of individuals are to be blamed and attribution of criminal liability in such cases requires a lot of intellectual debate, more because the standard for attribution in criminal cases is that of "blameworthiness to be pitted beyond reasonable doubt" for conviction to take place.

Hence, the U.S. faces the same problem that is conviction of corporations is a complex issue, more because corporations cannot be incarcerated. Nor can they be put to death. If corporations were bodies of flesh and blood, then like individuals, they too would have been made to face the same consequences following the convictions. Corporations can be fined.[270] They can be placed

---

266 See: [42 U.S.C. § 300 f]

267 See: [7 U.S.C. Ch. 6 § 136 et. seq.]

268 909 F. 2d 431, 432-34 (11th Cir. 1990)

269 732 F. 2d 1004, 1008 n.6 (1st Cir. 1984)

270 See: Title 18 Crimes and Criminal Procedure, 18 U.S.C. 3571 [Designating maximum fines for organisations convicted of felonies and various misdemeanours], http://www.gpo.gov/fdsys/pkg/USCODE-2010-title18/pdf/USCODE-2010-title18-partII-chap227-subchapC-sec3571.pdf, Visited on: 23-06-2014

on probation.[271] They can be ordered to pay restitution.[272] Their property can be confiscated.[273] They can be barred from engaging in various types of commercial activity.[274] But for crimes of corporate killing, all these measure seem to be non-deterrent because in today's United State's multi-national-corporate culture, corporations take the penalties in the nature of fines or confiscation of property as the cost of carrying out business or the operational cost of business.

In nutshell it can be said that U.S. has recognised the crime of corporate killings through case-laws but not by way of statutory enactments. The rising awareness in regards to crimes of corporate manslaughter and inspiration drawn from the Westray Act of Canada and the Corporate Manslaughter and Corporate Homicide Act of the U.K., is creating a level playing field in the U.S. to pass a legislation in this regard; the recent example of the Corporate Manslaughter Bill as formulated in the state of Indiana in U.S. talks in volume in this regard.

4.5. Australia:

The Esso Longford explosion which occurred in Victoria in 1998 is just one example among many that shows that corporate manslaughter incidents akin to those that have occurred in the U.K. can also occur in Australia.[275] The crime

---

271 See: 18 U.S.C. 3561 (a) (1); U.S.S.G. § 8D1.1

272 See: U.S.S.G. § 8 B 1.1; The statutes that authorize restitution orders refer to simply to "victims" or "defendants" rather than to "individuals," "organizations," or "corporations", 18 U.S.C. 3663, 3663A, 2248, 2259, 2264, 2327.

273 See: U.S.S.G. §§ 8 E1.2, 5E1.4

274 See: Congressional Research Service, Corporate Criminal Liability: An Overview of Federal Law, http://fas.org/sgp/crs/misc/R43293.pdf, Visited on: 23-06-2014

275 The 1998 Esso Longford Gas Explosion was a catastrophic industrial accident which occurred at the Esso natural gas plant at Longford in the Australian state of Victoria's Gippsland region. On 25th September 1998, an explosion took place which eventually killed two workers and injured eight others. A Royal Commission was called into the explosion at Longford. The Commission sat for 53 days, commencing with a preliminary hearing on 12th November 1998. The Commission reported that the cause of the accident was a failure to provide and maintain safe and risk free work environment. The Commission charged the company (Esso Longford) for the breach of Section 21 of the Occupational Health and Safety Act of 1985.

of corporate manslaughter is recognised in the Australian State and Territory jurisdictions but it is extremely difficult to successfully prosecute corporations due to the frequently insurmountable difficulties associated with identifying a senior individual in the corporation who is or was both the "directing mind and will" of the corporation and also someone personally guilty of the crime of gross negligence manslaughter.[276]

Attribution of liability, whether civil or criminal depend on "substantial reasons" considering which courts allow piercing of the corporate veil. The courts in Australia pierce the corporate veil only if the corporate form has been used for fraud, to shield the parent company from an existing legal obligation or for corporate groups where the level of control 'is so complete that the parent company is deemed to be directly liable for activities' of the subsidiary.[277] In U.S., the courts are more willing to pierce the corporate veil than in Australia.[278] Australia does not have any extensive or growing 'laundry list' of factors justifying veil piercing. Courts have considered at the broadest, factors such as fraud and misrepresentation for veil piercing.[279] Corporate-veil-

---

Esso was taken to the Supreme Court of Victoria by the Victorian Work Cover Authority. The jury found the company guilty of eleven breaches of the Occupational Health and Safety Act of 1985, and Justice Philip Cummins imposed a record fine of $2 million in July of 2001. In addition to this, a class action was taken on behalf of businesses, industries and domestic users who were financially affected by gas crises, post the disaster. The class action went to trial in the Supreme Court on 4th September 2002, and was eventually settled in December 2004 when Esso was ordered to pay $32.5 million to businesses which suffered property damage as a result of the incident.

276 See: The Criminal Code (Queensland), Section 303 and, the Crimes Act of 1900 (New South Wales), Section 18(1) (b). See also: *Nydam* v. *The Queen* [(1977) VR 430]

There is no federal offence of corporate manslaughter. The High Court of Australia confirmed in *Hamilton* v. *Whitehead* [(1988) 166 CLR 121] that the identification theory applies in Australia.

277 See: John Kluver, *Entity* v. *Enterprise Liability: Issues for Australia*, (2005) 37 Connecticut Law Review, p. 765, 766

278 See: Ian M. Ramsay & David B. Noakes, *Piercing the Corporate Veil in Australia*, [(2001) 19 Company and Securities Law Journal], p. 250, 261; Also see: Robert B. Thompson, *Piercing the Corporate Veil: An Empirical Study*, 76 Cornell Law Review 1048 (1991)

279 See: Stephen M. Bainbridge, *Abolishing Veil Piercing*, (2001) 26 Journal of Corporation Law 510; Also see: *Associated Vendors Inc.* v. *Oakland Meat Co. Inc.* [26 Cal Rptr 806, 813-815 (Molinari, J) (Cal Dist Ct App, 1962)]; Also see: D.S. Chopra & Nishant

piercing for attribution of criminal liability in cases of corporate killings is a tedious task in Australia, less because of lack of substantive and procedural laws in this regard but more because the judicial attitude has been conservative.

Attribution of criminal liability over corporations in Australia takes place based on the identification doctrine.[280] A company as a separate person is not considered a 'human person' and therefore it cannot itself do things which require human thought or action. A legal penalty or detriment for an act- particularly a criminal liability- is usually thought of as deserved only by a person who consciously chose to act in the way that attracts the penalty. It has been found to be expedient to make companies liable to penalties for wrongful acts by attributing to a company the wrongful acts and thoughts of humans identified with the company.[281] In Australia, it has been held that it is not possible to aggregate the knowledge of various individuals identified with a company and infer from the aggregate knowledge that the company was dishonest.[282] This is consistent with the rejection of aggregation in order to create a criminal state of mind for a company but may be contrasted with aggregation in order to create vicarious liability for tort.

Over a period of time shift has been witnessed from the identification principle (commonly known as the organic theory in Australia) to the doctrine of "corporate culture". The doctrine of "corporate culture" says that criminal liability can be imputed over a corporation if it can be proved beyond reasonable doubt that a "corporate culture" existed within the body corporate which directed, encouraged, tolerated or led to non-compliance with the rational and reasonable standards which the corporation ought to have adhered to, for having acted with reasonableness and pragmatism, there by not risking the safety and also the lives of the workers, consumers and members of public in general. A body corporate which fails to create and maintain a "corporate

---

Arora, *Company Law: Piercing the Corporate Veil*, Eastern Law House, 2013 Edition, Chapter 7: A Comparative Study, p.221

280 Australia being a common-wealth nation has from the very inception, reposed its faith in the identification doctrine. See: *Hamilton* v. *Whitehead* [(1988) 166 CLR 121]

281 See: Derek French, Stephen Mayson & Christopher Ryan, *Company Law*, Oxford University Press, 27th Edition (2010-2011), Chapter 19: Acting For a Company-Agency & Attribution, p.631

282 See: *Macquarie Bank Ltd.* v. *Sixty-Fourth Throne Pty Ltd.* [(1998) 3 VR 133]

culture" which respects- human life, health and safety along with the principles of sustainable development, must necessarily be punished with fines and publicity orders, when found guilty. This "corporate culture" approach is based on Section 12.3(2) (d) of the Commonwealth Criminal Code Act of 1995.[283]

Only to a limited extent can the corporations be convicted in Australia through the Commonwealth Criminal Code Act of 1995.[284] In Australia, the concept of corporate criminal responsibility has been codified in Commonwealth legislation, but this codified method of attributing criminal responsibility only applies to the crimes of federal level. In 2004 there was a failed attempt, using the Private Member's Bill, to create a new offence of "industrial manslaughter" in the Commonwealth legislation. The position within individual States and territories in Australia varies so far as crimes in the nature of corporate manslaughter and corporate homicide are concerned. So, for instance, in the Australian Capital Territory the enactment of Part 2.5 of the Criminal Code Act of 2002 (ACT) brought the Commonwealth Criminal Code Act of 1995 into power, but because its provisions did not apply to 'pre 2003' offences, it was necessary to re-enact new provisions pertaining to manslaughter and homicide.[285] Other Australian States have approached this issue in various ways and with different degrees of success.[286] No prosecution has yet been reported

---

283 Section 12.3 of the Commonwealth Criminal Code Act of 1995, speaks of "Fault elements other than negligence"; Section 12.3(2) (d) of the Commonwealth Criminal Code Act of 1995 states: "proving that the body corporate failed to create and maintain a corporate culture that required compliance with the relevant provision".

284 See: Australian Law Reform Commission in the Criminal Code Act of 1995; Also see: Jennifer Hill, *Corporate Criminal Liability In Australia: An Evolving Corporate Governance Technique*, J.B.L. 2003, JAN, 14; Alice Belcher, *Corporate Killing as a Corporate Governance Issue*, Corporate Governance 2002, 10(1) 47-54.

285 However, the same State has also enacted the Crimes (Industrial Manslaughter) Amendment Act of 2003. The 'employer offence' included in this Act applies only to the death of an employee, and can be committed by corporate and non-corporate employer organisations. So, there is some confusion as to which provisions will be used in a prosecution.

286 See: Parliament of Australia, *Workplace Death and Serious Injury: A Snapshot of Legislative Developments in Australia and Overseas*, Research Brief no. 7, 2004-2005, http://www.aph.gov.au/library/Pubs/rb/2004-05/05rb07.htm; Also see: Karen Wheelwright, *Corporate Liability for Workplace Deaths and Injuries- Reflecting on Victoria's Laws in the light of the Esso Longford Explosion*, (2002) 7 Deakin Law Review 323.

(in Australia) that employs the "corporate culture test" to attribute corporate criminal liability over the corporations accused of the crime of corporate manslaughter.

Corporate manslaughter prosecutions in Australia, like in other common-law jurisdictions, can be brought when any individual is killed in any activity carried out by a corporation owing to the gross negligence employed by the corporation. But, these cases have rarely been successful in Australia.[287] The most notable case regarding corporate manslaughter prosecution in Australia is the case of *R* v. *Denbo Pty Ltd.*[288] In this case Denbo Pty Ltd. was prosecuted for the crime of manslaughter when one of its drivers was killed, when the brakes of the truck failed. Upon examination, the prosecutors found that the company's vehicle service record was appalling. The company (through its directors) pleaded guilty and was fined $80,000. At the time of its conviction, Denbo Pty Ltd. was in liquidation. The company was dissolved about six months before the sentencing and thus never paid the fine. Later, it was reborn as another company, and recommenced its operations. The successor company did not pay the fine either.

The success rate, measured by a "guilty verdict" in manslaughter prosecutions against corporations and individual officers in Australia, is very poor indeed. Scholars in the likes of Jim Gobert and Maurice Punch assert that, the criminal law in Australia was not developed with the intention of attributing crimes or criminal conduct onto the corporations. Concepts such as *mens rea* and *actus reus*, which make perfectly rational sense when applied to individuals, do not translate easily to an inanimate fictional entity, such as a corporation which exists only in the contemplation of the law.

Over the years, thousands of deaths have taken place, as a result of activities carried out by the producers of asbestos and asbestos related products in Australia. CSR Ltd., mined asbestos from Wittenoom for more than two decades and Jim Hardie Industries Ltd., manufactured asbestos products in Australia for over a century. It has been proved in various civil action suits

---

287 See: Celia Wells, *Corporate Criminal Liability: Developments in Europe and Beyond*, 2001, 39 (7) Law Society Journal 62

288 Supreme Court of Victoria, Unreported, 14 June 1994

that the directors of the companies knew that asbestos causes lung diseases such as lung-cancer, even at very low levels of exposure but the directors of the companies conspired to keep this knowledge away from the public as well as their employees. In recognition of the fact that, the directors of the companies knew about the ills of asbestos, the companies were forced to pay only a "just compensation" which in rational and reasonable terms seemed un-just. Both the companies (CSR Ltd. and JHI Ltd.) continued to earn billions of dollars for their shareholders. Both the companies were able to successfully hide behind the corporate veil of fiction and are now registered even overseas. It is somewhat shocking to know that the directors in Australia do not owe a general duty to act in the interests of the employees.[289] However, the company and its directors are subject to specific legal obligations in respect of employees arising, for example, under various laws concerning employee welfare and labour entitlements, and prohibited conduct such as unlawful discrimination.[290] Nonetheless, there are precedents in Australian law for making companies liable because of their corporate culture and for making individuals liable along with the company by reason of their being part of the company's senior level management.

The matter of current debate in Australia is the relative efficacy of the new 'industrial manslaughter' law that is to apply to the Australian Capital Territory. 'Industrial manslaughter' is a new offence that came into being in 2004 to deal with deaths that took place at the workplace, owing to the gross negligence of the corporations that were not being imputed with criminal liability by the then existing corporate manslaughter provisions of the general criminal law, nor by existing occupational health and safety laws. However, it is immediately necessary to acknowledge that there are few problems with the legislation, namely, the effectiveness of the industrial manslaughter legislation of the Australian Capital Territory has been largely negated by subsequent Commonwealth legislation which has prevented the Australian Commonwealth Territory legislation from having any application to matters in the federal area. The Commonwealth Government did this by amending the Occupational Health and Safety (Commonwealth Employment) Act of 1991.

---

289 See: *Parke* v. *Daily News Ltd.* [(1962) 2 All ER 929]

290 See: Edward Smerdon (Consulting Editor), *Directors' Liability and Indemnification,* A Global Guide, Global Business Publishing Ltd., 2007 Edition, Chapter on Australia by Richard Midgley, Jodie Potts & Anthony Scott, p.24

Also, as a matter of fact, the industrial and commercial sectors of the Australian Capital Territory are extremely small and that, to date, there do not appear to have been any prosecutions for industrial manslaughter under the corporate manslaughter legislation in the Australian Capital Territory.

The matter worth highlighting is that, under the industrial manslaughter laws, the potential for corporate executives to be sent to prison for the death of a worker, notwithstanding their lack of direct culpability, is now much greater in the Australian Capital Territory than in other jurisdictions.[291] The Crimes (Industrial Manslaughter) Act of 2003, enacted by the Australian Capital Territory Legislative Assembly includes a specific statute for 'industrial manslaughter', which would allow manslaughter to be attributed to a corporation through the provisions of the Commonwealth Criminal Code Act of 1995. Hence, with all positivity, the tides of legislative-progressive-institutional changes, advancing the realms of corporate criminal jurisprudence in the area of corporate killings have touched the Australian shores; now what is to be seen is how effectively the legislative implementation of these changes take place in the Australian Capital Territory and how positively does these changes influence the laws in other Australian jurisdictions.

4.6. Chapter Conclusion:

With the comparative analysis of the corporate manslaughter laws in the jurisdictions of U.K., New Zealand, U.S., Canada and Australia, we reach the following conclusions:

4.6.1. The law in regards to corporate killings is of very recent origin. None of the countries had framed their respective criminal law statutes with the foresight to attributing criminal liability over the corporations. Initially, it was the efforts made to interpret the existing criminal law statutes by judges of progressive stature that helped in convicting companies to some extent. Over a period of time need has been felt for a progressive piece of legislation

---

291 See: Rick Sarre, *Sentencing those convicted of industrial manslaughter,* National Judicial College of Australia, The Australian National University, http://njca.anu.edu.au/Professional%20Development/programs%20by%20year/2010/Sentencing%202010/Papers/SARRE.pdf, Visited on: 29-06-2014

that specifically targets corporations, making them liable for their criminal conduct.

4.6.2. It was a series of industrial catastrophes that took place in each of these countries that brought about the awareness that no longer can we go by the notion that, 'a company has no body to kick but a soul to damn'. So far as penalising the corporations for their criminal conduct is concerned, the popular methods have been- unlimited fines and publicity orders.

4.6.3. It is popularly believed that it is the U.K. that first came up with the idea of convicting the corporations for manslaughters and homicides. But the truth is that, the awareness came about quite early, as for example see the case of the Indiana State of U.S. or the Australian Capital Territory, the only lacking was that these states were not able to push the legislation through before the awareness came about in U.K. and was thereafter given the legislative form. Also, the Westray Law in Canada, as so enacted in 2005, precedes the Corporate Manslaughter and Corporate Homicide Act of 2007.

Chapter 5

Corporate Manslaughter and Corporate Homicide in India: The-Rising-Jurisprudence

5.1. Introduction:

With the emergence and development of the concept of "Corporate Governance" globally, India too was responsive enough to adapt to the new situation and likewise made rapid strides in this area. The important Committees on Corporate Governance at the national level in India have been the following: Confederation of Indian Industry (CII)- Desirable Corporate Governance- A Code, 1988; SEBI- Kumar Mangalam Birla Committee of 1999; The Companies (Amendment) Act of 2000; Advisory Group on Corporate Governance- Reserve Bank of India; SEBI- Narayanamurthy Committee on Corporate Governance (Clause 49 of the Listing Agreement dealing with compliance of conditions of Corporate Governance for listed entities); Naresh Chandra Committee on Corporate Audit and Governance; and Dr. J.J. Irani Committee on Simplification of Company Law.[292] With the concept of corporate governance hitting Indian shores, soon there was rise in awareness in India in regards to the concept of "corporate civil liability" and "corporate criminal liability", because corporate governance in particular speaks of responsive corporate culture, where corporations aim towards growth, not by means of profit maximisation but through the means of promoting ideals in the form of 'sustainable economic growth and development', 'employee welfare', 'consumer welfare' and 'welfare of all stakeholders without giving any special priority to shareholders in particular'. "Corporate civil liability" and "corporate criminal liability", lexically speaking, draw their existence from the conceptual framework of "negligence". Differentiation can be created between

---

[292] See: Dr. Justice A.R. Lakshmanan, *The Judge Speaks*, Universal Law Publishing Co., 2009 Edition, Corporate Governance, p.377

both these terms based on the degree of negligence. Gross negligence on behalf of a corporation can result in corporation being held criminally liable and this eventually may end in imputation of criminal liability upon the corporation.

Corporations can be held criminally liable and are capable of forming *mens rea;* this was recognised lately in India with the decisions rendered by the Hon'ble Supreme Court of India in the following two cases: *Standard Chartered Bank* v. *Directorate of Enforcement*[293] and *Iridium India Telecom Ltd.* v. *Motorola Inc.*[294] From the conceptual framework of "corporate criminal liability" arises another dimension of law that advances the idea in regards to corporate culpability a way further. This dimension of law is that of "corporate manslaughter and corporate homicide". Awareness in regards to the need of a law that punishes corporations for gross-negligence-manslaughter has always prevailed in India since the Bhopal Gas Tragedy and the Oleum Gas Leakage case, but legislative enactment that punishes companies for corporate killings is yet to materialise. India seeks to take inspiration from the Westray Law (2005) in Canada, the Corporate Manslaughter and Corporate Homicide Act of 2007 in U.K. and the corporate manslaughter law as has been lately enacted in the Australian Capital Territory. Judgements post the Bhopal Gas Tragedy, in the nature of Oleum Gas Leakage case, Standard Chartered Bank case, Iridium Motorola case and the Uphaar Cinema case, signify that judicial activism in India is trying to do what the legislature in India must had done post the Bhopal Gas Tragedy, taking into account that the 'Deep-pocket theory' and the Public Liability Insurance Act of 1991 failed to deliver what was required of them.

5.2. Corporate Crimes in India:

Corporate crimes in India are well recognised in the niches of money laundering, fraud and misrepresentation but crimes resulting in death of individuals, may them be workers, customers or members of public in general, are not legally provided for sufficiently and legal remedies to the same are spread across various legislation providing for labour, consumer, public and environment welfarism. Black's Law Dictionary defines "corporate crime" as- a crime committed by a corporation's representative acting on its behalf. More succinctly, a corporate

293 AIR 2005 SC 2622

294 (2011) 1 SCC 74

crime can be defined as the conduct of a corporation or of employees acting on behalf of a corporation, which is proscribed and punishable by law.[295] Thus, crime committed by persons who are in-charge of the affairs of the company, making company vicariously liable for their alleged acts, brings to light the notion of "corporate criminal liability".

The development of the law relating to corporate criminal liability in India is similar to that of the English law and is remarkably influenced by the English law. Corporations have often been viewed as convenient shields for evasion of liability. Under India's present penal regime, for a criminal offence both the corporation as well as its officer can be held liable and accountable. The law in regards to corporate criminal liability in India is not restricted to just the Indian Penal Code of 1860 or the Criminal Procedure Code of 1973, but is scattered over a plethora of statutes with specific provisions for the same. However, over the period of time, need has been felt for a special piece of legislation that focuses solely on the principle of corporate criminal liability in India with special emphasis on the crime of corporate manslaughter and corporate homicide.[296]

In the case of *Charan Lal Sahu* v. *Union of India*[297], the Apex court observed as follows:

"In India, the need for industrial development has led to the establishment of a number of plants and factories by the domestic companies & undertakings as well as by Transnational National Corporations. Many of these industries are engaged in hazardous or inherently dangerous activities which pose potential threat to life, health and safety of persons working in the factory, or residing in the surrounding areas. Though working of such factories and plants is regulated by about six-hundred-and-fourteen laws of our country, there is no special legislation providing for compensation and damages to outsiders who may suffer on account of any industrial accident."

---

295 See: John Braithwaite, *Corporate Crime in the Pharmaceutical Industry,* Routledge and Kegan Paul, First Edition, London, 1984, p.6

296 See: Prachi Manekar, *Insights into the new company law,* Lexis Nexis Publication, 2013 Edition, Chapter XXI: Corporate Criminal Liability, p.339

297 AIR 1990 SC 1480

Broadly speaking, the law relating to Corporations in India is codified in the Companies Act of 1956, as amended in 2013. The definition of "corporation" as given in the 1956 Act under Section 2(7) includes a "company". Under the Indian law, like in the English law, liability both- civil and criminal can be imputed on companies. A company exists only in the contemplation of law and on incorporation it acquires a separate legal entity distinct and independent of its members. When a company is incorporated, all dealings happen in the name of the body corporate. This separate legal personality of the company is a statutory privilege conferred on it; however in cases necessary (usually of fraud and misrepresentation) the court can break through the corporate shell and apply the principles of "lifting of the corporate veil".[298] In *P.C. Agarwala* v. *Payment of Wages Inspector*[299], the Supreme Court observed that the judicial approach of cracking open the corporate shell in India is somewhat cautious and circumspect. Corporate veil is lifted only in cases where legislative provisions justify or, in exceptional cases where courts themselves feel that to meet the ends of justice and to prevent the miscarriage of justice, it is essential to ignore the legal fiction of corporate-separate-legal-entity. The Companies Act of 1956, as amended in 2013, contains many provisions which empower the courts to lift the corporate veil to reach the individual perpetrators who are in fact responsible for the culpable or the wrongful act.[300]

Prior to the decision of the Supreme Court in the case of *Standard Chartered Bank* v. *Directorate of Enforcement*[301], the Indian courts were of the opinion that corporations could not be held criminally liable for offences requiring *mens rea*, as artificial-legal-persons are not individuals possessing flesh and blood, or mind and will, to take decisions on their own.[302] In this case, the Standard Chartered

298 See: Dalal Praveen, *Corporate Entity in Existing Legal System- Its Rights and Liabilities under the Constitution and other Enactments,* (2004) 61 CLA 96 (Mag).

299 (2005) 63 SCL 109 (SC)

300 See: Section 45 of the 1956 Act, Sections 62 & 63 of the 1956 Act [Sections 2(69), 35 & 34 of the 2013 Act], Section 113 of the 1956 Act [Section 56 of the 2013 Act], Section 147 of the 1956 Act [Section 12 of the 2013 Act], Section 212 of the 1956 Act, Section 242 of the 1956 [Section 224 of the 2013 Act], Section 247 of the 1956 Act [Section 216 of the 2013 Act] and Section 542 of the 1956 Act [Section 339 of the 2013 Act]

301 AIR 2005 SC 2622

302 For example in the case of *A.K. Khosla* v. *T.S. Venkatesan* [1992 Cr LJ 1448], two corporations were charged with having committed fraud under the Indian Penal

Bank was being prosecuted for violation of the Foreign Exchange Regulation Act of 1973. The Supreme Court of India held that the corporation could be prosecuted and punished, with fines, regardless of mandatory punishment of imprisonment required under the respective statute.[303] The court further observed that, the Criminal Procedure Code of 1973 contains no provision for the exemption of corporations from prosecution when it is difficult to sentence them according to a statute. The court held that the FERA statute was clear, that the corporations are vulnerable to criminal prosecution, and allowing corporations to escape liability based on the difficulty in sentencing would do violence to the statute. However, the court did not develop its reasoning far enough so as to specifically hold that a corporation is capable of forming mens rea and acting pursuant to it. The court further observed that corporations are liable for criminal offences and can be prosecuted and punished, at least with fines, if not with imprisonment. Plethora of offences punishable by fines, do have mens rea as necessary element of the offence. By implication, it can be said that post *Standard Chartered* decision, corporations are capable of possessing the requisite mens rea. Also, in prosecution of economic crimes, intention

---

Code of 1860. The Magistrate issued process against the corporations. In the Calcutta High Court, the counsel for the defendants argued, inter alia, that the corporations as juristic persons could not be prosecuted for offences under the Indian Penal Code for which mens rea is an essential ingredient. The court agreed. The court pointed out that there were two pre-requisites for the prosecution of corporate bodies, the first being that of mens rea and the other being the ability to impose the mandatory sentence of imprisonment. Each of these pre-requisites rendered the prosecution of the defendant corporations futile. Court held that a corporate body could not be said to have the necessary mens rea, nor can it be sentenced to imprisonment as it has no physical body.

303 The Supreme Court of India referred to the United States Supreme Court decision, *United States* v. *Union Supply* [215 U.S. 50 (1909)]. In this case, a corporation was indicted for wilfully violating a statute that required the wholesale dealers in oleomargarine to keep certain books and make certain returns. Any person who wilfully violated this provision was liable to be punished with a fine of not less than $50 and not exceeding $500 and imprisonment for not less than 30 days and not more than six months.

Justice Holmes held that if the breach is by a "corporation" in regards to the statute in question, then it is necessary for us to free our minds of all legal orthodoxy and go by the natural inference. When a statute prescribes two independent penalties, then we are to inflict the penalties so far as we can; if one of them is impossible, it does not mean, on that account, to let the defendant escape scot free.

could very well be imputed to a corporation and may be gathered from the acts and/or omissions of a corporation.[304]

Attribution of criminal liability on corporations based on the common law principle of "vicarious liability" was very much present in the Indian-corporate-law-jurisprudence since the 1970s.[305] As in the case of *State of Madras* v. *C.V. Parekh*[306], when the question arose as to whether officers of the company can be prosecuted and punished without being ranged with the company in the said prosecution? The court clarified that such prosecution is possible only when the company is found in violation of certain provisions of the respective statute in question. It was made clear that, "vicarious liability" holds that company shall be liable for all acts of its officers, performed for the benefit of the company, during the course of their respective employment and for officers acting within the authority conferred onto them. Hence, if the company itself cannot be blamed, there can be no fastening of guilt on officers of the company. However, no principle of vicarious liability or respondeat superior is to apply in cases where the officers of the company acted outside the scope of authority expressly conferred to them.

Another case of similar nomenclature is that of *Anil Hada* v. *Indian Acrylic Limited*[307], the question that arose for consideration in this case was, if a company eludes prosecution for an offence committed under Section 138 of the Negotiable Instruments Act, can the Director of such a company be prosecuted for the offence committed? The Court held that under Section 141 of the Negotiable Instruments Act, the company shall be the principal offender

---

304 See: Dr. Girjesh Shukla, *Criminology: Crime Causation, Sentencing and Rehabilitation of Victims,* Lexis Nexis Publication, 2013 Edition, Chapter 8: Sentencing and Penal Policy, p.191-192

305 It is important to note that, the doctrine of vicarious liability in India, is more frequently invoked under special enactments such as the Consumer Protection Act of 1986, the Prevention of Food Adulteration Act of 1954 and the Drugs Act of 1940. A master is held criminally liable for the violation of rules contained under the aforesaid statutes, provided that his agent or servant, during the course of his employment, committed such act. If the statute imposes strict liability, a master is held responsible for criminal acts of his servants or agents even where he had no knowledge of the act performed and for which he had given no authority.

306 AIR 1971 SC 447

307 AIR 2000 SC 145

and the directors shall merely be the deemed offenders. Therefore, a finding that a company is guilty of an offence is a condition essential for the operation of the deeming provision to apply to the prejudice of the Director.

In regards to India it can be said with assertiveness that at one time it was thought that a penal liability could not be fastened on a corporation for the acts of its servants or agents. It was contended that a corporation, being devoid of mind and body, cannot have the necessary guilty mind to commit a crime and that the corporation cannot be sentenced to imprisonment. A corporation acts through its resolutions at a meeting and the resolutions must not be ultra vires its constitution. Any resolution for doing a criminal act is bound to be ultra vires and hence the corporation was not subject to criminal liability.[308] However, over a period of time it was realised that a corporation is a legal entity that is incorporated by law for preserving certain rights in perpetual succession and in light of Section 11 of the Indian Penal Code of 1860,[309] a corporation is a group of human beings, authorised by law to act as a legal unit, endowed with legal personality and having a seal of its own.[310] However, a corporation, owing to its peculiarity, is not put on the same footing for its deeds with respect to criminal liability as a human being. A corporation's penal liability depends on the nature of the offence, the relative position of the individual vis-à-vis the corporate body and other relevant facts which could show that the corporate body, as such, meant or intended to commit that act. In other words, the jurisprudence developed in India so far indicates that, a corporation is only

308 See: Professor K.D. Gaur; *Criminal Law- Cases and Materials,* Lexis Nexis Publication, 7th Edition, Chapter 4: Vicarious Liability, p.186

309 According to Section 11 of the Indian Penal Code (IPC) the word "person" includes any company or association or body of persons whether incorporated or not. Similarly Section 3(42) of the General Clauses Act of 1897 provides that "person" shall include any company or association or body of individuals, whether incorporated or not. While the context of most of the provisions of the IPC referring to a person being punishable for doing or failing to do a specific thing, would normally exclude their application to a body of individuals, there is no doubt that a company or association can be prosecuted for certain offences under the IPC and other laws which are punishable with fine. Certain special laws specifically provide for the application of the penal provisions contained in them to companies and associations.

310 See: Section 11 of the Indian Penal Code of 1860; See also: Livington Hall, *Cases on Criminal Law and Its Enforcement,* 1958, p. 43, 439; Law Commission (Published) Working Paper (U.K., No. 14) for Corporate Liability.

liable for those acts of officers, directors or employees, which could reasonably be conceived of as having been undertaken in the corporate interest and in addition, for which they had the power to represent the corporation in that particular field of authority in which the criminal act was done.[311] Fair trial requires that the accused person should be tried in his own physical presence; evidence as to the trial should be taken in the presence of the accused; and the accused person should be made to know the accusations levelled against him. Questions arise as to how these requirements can be satisfied when the accused person is a company or any association. Section 63 of the Criminal Procedure Code of 1973, provides specifically how service of summons on corporate bodies and societies, can be effected. But other questions to arise, as to how the corporation is to appear in court through a representative, how the person who may come forward as a representative of the corporation is to be recognised as such by the court, what will happen if after due service no one appears in court as the authorised representative of the corporation. These issues are very ticklish, but with some amount of certainty are resolved through Section 305 of the Criminal Procedure Code of 1973, which expressly talks about, 'procedure when corporation or registered society is an accused'.[312]

5.3. Corporate Criminal Jurisprudence Developed in the West and the Standards Prevailing in India:

The corporate criminal jurisprudence which has developed in the West is of the opinion that there are broadly speaking, four ways of punishing a corporation for crimes committed by it. These are unlimited fines; publicity orders; blacklisting the corporations from government tenders; and restricting the scope and the area of operations of the corporations. The jurisprudence in India has not developed much. Initially there were cases where by the criminal liability imputed over corporations, called for a mandatory sentence of fines as well as imprisonment. The courts in India, going by literal interpretation

---

311 See: S.S. Huda, *Principles of Criminal Law in British India,* TLL, 1902, p.20-33; See also: Canfield, *Corporate Responsibility for Crimes,* Columbia Law Review, No.14, 1914, p. 469-480; Francis, *Criminal Responsibility of the Corporation,* (1924) 18 LR 305; See also: *Kenny's Outlines of Criminal Law*, 19th Edition, 1966, p.75-78

312 See: Dr. K.N. Chandrasekharan Pillai, *Criminal Procedure*, Eastern Book Company, Fifth Edition, Chapter 14: Trial Procedures- Courts and Parties, p.366

said that the corporations existing only in the contemplation of law cannot be incarcerated and the word used in the statute book been "and" that is, "fine and imprisonment", thus punishment of 'fine' is to go necessarily with 'imprisonment' and as the sentence of imprisonment cannot be imposed, hence fines should also not be imposed.[313] Over a period of time jurisprudence as to corporate crimes in India advanced and the foundation for the same was laid down in the case of the *Assistant Commissioner, Assessment II, Bangalore* v. *Velliappa Textiles Ltd.*[314]. In this case B.N. Srikrishna J. was of the opinion that corporate criminal liability cannot be imposed without making the necessary legislative changes in the required statutes. As for example, the imposition of fine in lieu of imprisonment is required to be introduced in many sections of the penal statutes. The Court opined, not in assertive but in a reflective terms, that where a company is prosecuted for an offence which calls for 'fine' and a mandatory sentence of 'imprisonment', then the company should be made liable to pay the necessary fine, and in lieu of imprisonment, the individuals acting as the determining mind and will of the company should be put behind bars. If the determining mind and will of the company cannot be ascertained then the company must be made liable to pay 'extra fines' in lieu of the imprisonment sentence.

---

313 In the case of *Velliappa Textiles* [(2004) 1 Comp. L.J. 21], a private company was prosecuted for violation of certain sections under the Income Tax Act (ITA). Sections 276-C and 277 of the ITA provided for a sentence of imprisonment and a fine in the event of a violation. The Indian Supreme Court held that the respondent company could not be prosecuted for offences under certain sections of the ITA because each of these sections required the imposition of a mandatory term of imprisonment coupled with a fine. The sections in questions left the court unable to impose only a fine. Indulging in a strict and literal analysis, the court held that a corporation did not have a physical body to imprison and therefore could not be sentenced to imprisonment. Further, the Supreme Court of India was of the view that the legislative mandate was to prohibit the courts from deviating from the minimum mandatory punishment prescribed by the Act. The court also noted that when interpreting a penal statute, if more than one view is possible, the court is obliged to lean in favour of the construction that exempts an accused from penalty rather than the one that imposes the penalty.

The cases of similar nomenclature are: *State of Maharashtra* v. *Syndicate Transport* [(1963) Bom. L.R. 197]; *Oswal Vanaspati & Allied Industries* v. *State of Uttar Pradesh* [(1993) 1 Comp. L.J. 172]

314 (2004) 1 Comp. L.J. 21

In the *Standard Chartered Bank* case, the line of argument adopted by the Hon'ble Supreme Court of India was not only rational and reasonable but was also realist. The Supreme Court held that, when a corporation is convicted of a sentence that calls for fine as well as mandatory imprisonment then least of all the corporations must be punished with fines if not with imprisonment. The court observed, if mandatory sentence of imprisonment cannot be imposed, this does not mean that no fines can be imposed on the corporations, as the legislative intent of the penal statutes under which they are convicted no-where indicate that the corporations can go scot free. This same line of argument was appreciated in the *Iridium Motorola* case. In case of: *Iridium India Telecom Ltd.* v. *Motorola Inc.*[315] it was observed that in all jurisdictions across the world governed by the rule of law, companies and corporate houses can no longer claim immunity from criminal prosecution on the ground that they are not capable of possessing the necessary *mens rea* for commission of criminal offences. It has been observed that the legal position in England and United States has now been crystallised to leave no manner of doubt that the corporation would be liable for crimes of intent. For the crimes committed by corporations, which call for mandatory sentence of fine and imprisonment, the court held that it was obliged to read the phrase 'imprisonment and fine' as 'imprisonment or fine'. Hence, there is no immunity to the companies from prosecution merely because the prosecution is in respect of offences for which the punishment is mandatory imprisonment and fine. Finally the court observed- the company can have criminal liability and further, if a group of persons that guide the business of the companies have criminal intent that could be imputed to the body corporate.

From the notion of "corporate criminal liability" arises the lexicological term "corporate manslaughter". Holding the corporations liable for corporate killings is what corporate manslaughter and corporate homicide is all about. Corporate manslaughter is also known as corporate-gross-negligence-manslaughter. So far as India is concerned instances of corporate manslaughter are not few but are many in number, however the primary instances are that of the Bhopal Gas Tragedy, the Oleum Gas Leakage case and the Uphaar Cinema Tragedy.

---

315 (2011) 1 SCC 74

5.4. Rise in awareness in regards to crimes of "corporate killings" in India:

Rise in awareness in regards to the corporate killings in India took place post the Bhopal Gas Tragedy. There is no consensus on how to label the Bhopal Gas Leakage.[316] Many different terms have been used to describe what happened in Bhopal on the night of 2nd of December 1984- incident, accident, disaster, tragedy, catastrophe, crises, industrial genocide, sabotage, and massacre.[317] What Bhopal Gas Tragedy today represents is- the impunity of MNCs for human rights violations, the timid response of a government to such impunity, and the continuing misery of the victims.[318] According to the official government figure, about 3,000 people died immediately after the tragedy. This figure was revised to 15,248 in the 2003 report of the Bhopal Gas Tragedy Relief and Rehabilitation Department, State of Madhya Pradesh. However, according to Amnesty International's estimate 'between 7,000 and 10,000 people died within three days of the gas leak' and over

---

316 On the night of 2nd of December 1984, there was a massive leakage of toxic gases from the MIC storage tank of the Bhopal chemical plant. The immediate cause of the reaction and the consequent leakage of gases was the penetration of water into the MIC storage tank. There is no consensus on how water entered the tank. UCC tried to explain this using a sabotage theory, while the Indian government suggested that water might have entered the tank during the routine washing of pipes on that night. Although there are gaps and anomalies in the two conflicting explanations of how water might have entered the tank, it seems more plausible that UCC invoked the sabotage theory as a line of defence, or at best as a 'convenient conclusion'. A number of factors jointly contributed to the gas leakage but gross negligence on the part of UCC cannot be ruled out. After the gas leak, in a plant that was presented as a symbol of 'state of the art technology', UCC started shifting all the blame for Bhopal to its subsidiary UCIL. See: Jamie Cassels, *The Uncertain Promise of Law: Lessons from Bhopal,* University of Toronto, Toronto, 1993, p.4, 8-11, 12-25, 315; See also: Amnesty International, *Clouds of Injustice: Bhopal Disaster 20 years on,* Amnesty International, London, 2004, p.40; See also: Dan Kurzman, *A Killing Wind: Inside Union Carbide and the Bhopal Catastrophe,* McGraw-Hill, New York, 1987, p.181, 185-189

317 See: William Bogard, *The Bhopal Tragedy: Language, Logic, and Politics in the Production of a Hazard,* Boulder, Colorado: Westview Press, 1989, p. viii; See also: Paul Shrivastava, *Bhopal: Anatomy of a Crises,* Massachusetts, Ballinger Publishing Co., 1987, p.85

318 See: Dr. Surya Deva, *From 3/12 to 9/11: Future of Human Rights?;* Economic and Political Weekly, 2004, Volume 39, 5198, at 5200

20,000 to date.[319] Perhaps more tragic is the plight of survivors of Bhopal and their post- Bhopal children. It is estimated that about two-thirds of the total population of Bhopal was affected by the gas leakage. Many survivors still suffer from a range of medical conditions- from respiratory illness to eye disease, immunity impairment, neurological damage, neuromuscular damage, cancers, gynaecological disorders, miscarriages and compromised mental health.[320] Bhopal also led to environment pollution in the vicinity of the plant, including contamination of the ground water.

The peculiar problem regarding the claim of compensation was involved because of a large number of victims, most of those belonging to the lower economic strata. On behalf of the victims, a large number of cases were filed in Bhopal, and also in U.S.A. against the UCC. There was an effort for an out of court settlement between the Government of India (GOI) and the UCC but that failed. The GOI then proclaimed an Ordinance, and thereafter passed "the Bhopal Gas Leak Disaster (Processing of Claims) Act of 1985".[321] Section 3 of the Act conferred an exclusive right on the Central Government to represent, and act in place of every person who has made a claim, or is entitled to make a claim arising out of, or connected with, the Bhopal gas leak disaster. Empowered by Section 9 of the Act, the GOI also framed "the Bhopal Gas Leak Disaster (Registration and Processing of Claims) Scheme, 1985". In pursuance of the power conferred on it under Section 3, the Union of India filed a suit on behalf of all the claimants, against the UCC in the United States District Court of New York.[322] The UCC pleaded for the dismissal of the suit on the grounds of *forum non conveniens,* that is the suit could be more conveniently be tried in India, as India was the place of the catastrophe, and the plant personnel, victims, witnesses, documentary and all related evidence were located here in India. The Union of India, however, maintained that the Indian judiciary is yet to reach an intelligible level of maturity to be capable

---

319 See: Amnesty International, *Clouds of Injustice: Bhopal Disaster 20 years on,* Amnesty International, London, 2004, p.10, 12

320 See: Dinham and Sarangi, *The Bhopal Gas Tragedy of 1984 to? The Evasion of Corporate Responsibility,* Environment and Urbanization, 2002, Volume 14, 89, at p.92-96

321 Published in the Gazette Of India on 29th March, 1985

322 All the suits earlier filed in U.S.A. by some American lawyers were superseded and consolidated in this action.

enough to handle issues of such sort. Judge Keenon accepted the plea of *forum non conveniens* put forth by the UCC and thereby he rejected the plea of the Union of India and dismissed the action.

After the dismissal of the suit in U.S.A., the Union of India filed a suit in the District Court of Bhopal. The District and Sessions Judge, Mr. M.W. Deo, ordered the UCC to pay an interim relief of Rs. 350 crores to the victims. On a Civil Revision Petition filed by the UCC in the Madhya Pradesh High Court against the order of the Bhopal District Court, Justice S.K. Seth reduced the quantum of "interim compensation" payable from Rs. 350 crores to Rs. 250 crores. UCC decided to go in appeal against the decision requiring it to pay interim compensation and simultaneously it devised a strategy for manoeuvring the Indian Government by a direct settlement with the gas tragedy victims through their lawyers in India and U.S.A. Against this move of direct settlement by UCC, on a prayer made by the Union of India, the District and Session Judge of Bhopal, Mr. M.W. Deo passed an interim order directing the UCC not to make any settlement or compromise with any individual until further orders.

During the course of litigation in the Bhopal Gas Tragedy case, India came across another gas tragedy in the form of Oleum Gas Leakage case.[323] The Supreme Court of India in *M.C. Mehta* v. *Union of India*[324] observed as follows:

---

323 In *M.C. Mehta* v. *Union of India* [AIR 1987 SC 1086], the Supreme Court of India was dealing with claims arising from the leakage of oleum gas on 4th and 6th of December, 1985 from one of the units of Shriram Foods and Fertilizer Industries, in the city of Delhi, belonging to Delhi Cloth Mills Ltd. As a consequence of this leakage, it was alleged that one advocate practising in Tis Hazari Court had died and several others were affected by the same. An action was brought through a writ petition under Article 32 of the Constitution by way of public interest litigation. The court had in mind that within a period of one year, this was a second case of large scale leakage of deadly gas in India, as a year earlier due to the leakage of MIC gas from the Union Carbide plant in Bhopal more than 3,000 people died and several others were seriously injured. The court held that it was not obliged to depend on the Western Jurisprudence of "strict liability" and it can coin an indigenous remedy in the form of "absolute liability" as the circumstance demand that judiciary in India should play an activist role.

324 AIR 1987 SC 1086

"We would also like to point out that the measure of compensation in cases in which an enterprise was carrying on hazardous activity must be correlated to the magnitude and capacity of the enterprise because such compensation must have a deterrent effect. The larger and more prosperous the enterprise, greater must be the amount of compensation payable by it for the harm caused on account of an accident in the carrying of the hazardous or inherently dangerous activity by the enterprise."

With the decision in the case of Oleum Gas Leakage, India equipped itself with the "deep-pocket theory" and the "absolute liability principle". In view of the decision rendered in this case, the Supreme Court of India hoped that the victims of the Bhopal Gas Tragedy will be able to get relief, without further delay. After a long drawn litigation for over 4 years, there was a settlement between the Union of India and Union Carbide Corporation and in terms thereof, the Supreme Court in *Union Carbide Corporation* v. *Union of India*[325], passed an order on February 14 and 15, 1989 directing the payment of a sum of U.S. $470 million or its equivalent Rs. 750 crores. The court observed that the payment of Rs. 750 crores by the Union Carbide as compensation cannot be said to be void under the provisions of the Civil Procedure Code of 1908, on the ground that the recording of the settlement was not preceded by a notice to the persons interested in the suit. It was also observed that the quashing of criminal proceedings along with the settlement did not amount to compounding of an offence, and there was no stifling of the prosecution and thus the settlement was not void by virtue of Section 23 and/or Section 24 of the Indian Contract Act of 1872.[326]

Resort to the Alien Tort Claim Act (ATCA) and the continuing quest for criminal liability: The ATCA provides that 'the district courts shall have original jurisdiction of any civil action by an alien for a tort only, committed in violation of the law of nations or a treaty of the United States'.[327] There is an unusual degree of uncertainty about the origin, exact scope, and the

325 AIR 1990 SC 273

326 See: Dr. R.K. Bangia, *Law of Torts,* Allahabad Law Agency, Nineteenth Edition, 2006, Chapter 16: Rules of Strict and Absolute Liability, p.395-398

327 The Alien Tort Claims Act [28 U.S.C. 1350 (2004)]

legislative intent behind the enactment of the ATCA.[328] Yet it is relatively non-contentious that in its current form the jurisdiction of district courts to entertain civil actions is limited by three factors: only an alien can invoke this provision; there should be an allegation of the commission of a tort; and the alleged tort should have been committed either in violation of the *law of nations* or a *treaty* of the U.S.

Companies have been sued under the ATCA for a wide range of issues such as environmental pollution;[329] beating, arbitrary arrest and detention, torture, and execution;[330] drug experimentation without informed consent;[331] breach of the rights of life, health and sustainable development;[332] extra-judicial killing, forcible displacement and aiding/abetting genocide;[333] Holocaust war crimes;[334] participation in, or abetting, the regime of apartheid;[335] personal injury and property damage due to chemical pollution;[336] forced dislocation, torture, forced labour, murder and rape;[337] knowingly and wilfully aiding and abetting the commission of torture for exercising the right to freedom of speech and expression;[338] detention-cum-interrogation at the Abu Ghraib prison as well

---

328 In the case of *Hanoch Tel-Oren* v. *Libyan Arab Republic* [726 F. 2d 774, at 812 (1984)], Justice Bork observed:

"I have discovered no direct evidence of what congress had in mind when enacting the provision. The debates over the Judiciary Act in the House- the Senate debates were not recorded- nowhere mention the provision, not even, so far as we aware, indirectly… Historical research has not yet disclosed what section 1350 was intended to accomplish."

329 See: *Aguinda* v. *Texaco, Inc.* [945 F. Supp. 625 (SDNY 1996)]

330 See: *Wiwa* v. *Royal Dutch Petroleum Co.* [1998 U.S. Dist. LEXIS 23064]

331 See: *Abdullahi* v. *Pfizer* [2002 U.S. Dist. LEXIS 17436 (SDNY, 2002)]

332 See: *Flores* v. *Southern Peru Copper* [253 F. Supp. 2d 510 (SDNY, 2002)]

333 See: *The Presbyterian Church of Sudan* v. *Talisman Energy* [244 F. Supp. 2d 289 (SDNY, 2003)]

334 See: *Abrams* v. *Societe Nationale Des Chemins de fer Francais* [175 F. Supp. 2d 423 (EDNY, 2001)]; *Bodner* v. *Banque Paribas* [114 F. Supp. 2d 117 (2000)]; *In re Holocaust Victim Assets Litigation* [105 F. Supp. 2d 139 (EDNY, 2000)]

335 See: *In re South African Apartheid Litigation* [2004 U.S. Dist. LEXIS 23944]; *Khulumani* v. *Barclay National Bank Ltd.* [504 F. 3d 254 (2007)]

336 See: *Sajida Bano* v. *UCC* [2000 U.S. Dist. LEXIS 12326]; *Janki Bai Sahu* v. *UCC* [418 F. Supp. 2d 407 (2005)]

337 See: *Deo* v. *Unocal* [963 F. Supp. 880 (CD Cal., 1997)]

338 See: *Wang Xiaoning* v. *Yahoo!* [2007 U.S. Dist. LEXIS 97566 (ND Cal.)]

as unlawful killing and beating;[339] extra-judicial killings and war crimes;[340] and cultural genocide.[341] Although the recourse to the ATCA for redressing corporate human rights abuses did raise high hopes initially, the final results to date do not seem to be too encouraging.[342]

The Bhopal Gas Tragedy also led to environmental pollution in the vicinity of the plant, including contamination of ground water.[343] The plant site has not been cleaned yet, hence the toxins continue to seep through and contaminate community water sources. Being disappointed by the lack of will shown by the Government of India to respond effectively to the miseries of the Bhopal Gas victims generally and to the contamination of the plant site specifically, victim-groups once again approached the U.S. Courts in November 1999 under the ATCA and the Common Law. This time, specific claims were also made for environmental contamination including that of land and water wells, before as well as after the gas leak. A review of numerous judgements and orders passed by the U.S. Courts- dealing with diverse pleas like veil piercing, discovery of documents and assignment of the case to another judge- reveals that this time too litigation initiated, failed to deliver any significant outcome to the victims.[344]

---

339 See: *Haider Muhsin Saleh* v. *Titan Corp.* [436 F. Supp. 2d 55 (DDC, 2006)]

340 See: *Estate of Himoud Saed Atban et al.* v. *Blackwater* [611 F. Supp. 2d 1 (DDC, 2009)]; *In re Xe Services Alien Tort Litigation* [665 F. Supp. 2d 569 (2009)]

341 See: *Tom Beanal* v. *Freeport- McMoran, Inc.* [197 F 3d 161 (5th Cir., 1999)]

342 See: Dr. Surya Deva, *Regulating Corporate Human Rights Violations: Humanizing Business,* Routledge Research In Human Rights Law, Routledge Publications, 2012 Edition, Chapter 4:Existing regulatory initiatives- An evaluation of (in)adequacy, p. 66-67

343 Greenpeace Reports of 1999 and 2002 amply document the level of contamination of soil and water on and around the plant site. See: Labunska *et al.*, *The Bhopal Legacy: Toxic Contaminants at the Former Union Carbide Factory Site, Bhopal, India- 15 Years after the Bhopal Accident,* Greenpeace, November, 1999;

See also: Stringer *et al.*, *Chemical Stockpiles at Union Carbide India Limited in Bhopal: An Investigation,* Greenpeace, November, 2002

344 See: *Sajida Bano* v. *UCC* [2000 U.S. Dist. 12326]; *Sajida Bano* v. *UCC* [273 F. 3d 120 (2d Cir. N.Y., 2001)]; *Sajida Bano* v. *UCC* [2003 U.S. Dist. LEXIS 4097]; *Sajida Bano* v. *UCC* [361 F. 3d 696 (2d Cir. N.Y., 2004)]; *Sajida Bano* v. *UCC* [2005 U.S. Dist. LEXIS 32595]; *Sajida Bano* v. *UCC* [2005 U.S. Dist. LEXIS 22871]; *Janki Bai Sahu* v. *UCC* [418 F. Supp. 2d 407 (2005)]; *Janki Bai Sahu* v. *UCC* [2006 U.S. Dist. LEXIS 714]; *Janki Bai Sahu* v. *UCC* [2006 U.S. Dist. LEXIS 944]; *Sajida Bano*

The outcome of efforts to fix criminal liability on UCC-UCIL has not been much different from the struggle faced for the imputation of civil responsibility. Although the Indian Central Bureau of Investigation (CBI) did file a charge sheet against UCC-UCIL and their personnel in December 1987, nothing much happened and the Supreme Court's settlement order then quashed all pending criminal proceedings in February 1989.[345] The quest for criminal liability gained some momentum again after the court reinstated the criminal proceedings in October 1991.[346] But even after this, the criminal proceedings moved at a snail's speed and faced many encumbrances. To begin with, Warren Anderson, the chief executive officer of UCC- who was arrested soon after landing in India and then released on bail on the same day- did not appear before the court and was declared a proclaimed offender.[347] Later, the Indian Attorney General advised the Government of India that the proceedings in the U.S. for extradition of Anderson, is not likely to succeed and, therefore, the same should not be pursued. The Supreme Court of India, by reversing the judgement of the High Court, diluted the charges levelled at UCIL and its Indian officers (but not against Anderson) from "culpable homicide not amounting to murder" under Section 304 Part II of the Indian Penal Code (IPC) to causing death by a "rash or negligent act" under Section 304-A.[348]

More than 25 years after the gas leak, on 7th of June, 2010, a criminal court convicted eight persons (UCIL and seven of its officials) for causing death by negligence under Section 304-A, the IPC of 1860.[349] Whereas the Court directed

v. *UCC* [2006 U.S. App. LEXIS 21022]; *Janki Bai Sahu* v. *UCC* [2006 U.S. Dist. LEXIS 84475]; *Janki Bai Sahu* v. *UCC* [548 F. 3d 59 (2d Cir. 2008)]; *Janki Bai Sahu* v. *UCC* [262 F.R.D. 308 (SDNY, 2009)]; *Janki Bai Sahu* v. *UCC* [746 F. Supp. 2d 609 (2010)]; *Janki Bai Sahu* v. *UCC* [2010 WL 532307 (SDNY)]

345 See: *Union Carbide Corporation* v. *Union of India* [AIR 1990 SC 273]

346 See: *Union Carbide Corporation* v. *Union of India* [AIR 1992 SC 248]

347 See: S. Murlidhar, *Unsettling Truths, Untold Tales: The Bhopal Gas Tragedy Victims,* "Twenty Years" of Courtroom Struggles for Justice, IELRC Working Paper 2004/5, p. 36-39. The courts can declare a person who faces criminal charges but neither appears before it nor responds to its summons as a 'proclaimed offender'.

348 See: *Keshub Mahindra* v. *State of Madhya Pradesh* [(1996) 6 SCC 129]

349 See: Suchandana Gupta, *Bhopal Gas Case Verdict: Justice Delayed, Denied,* The Times of India, 8th of June, 2010, http://timesofindia.indiatimes.com/india/Bhopal-gas-case-verdict-Justice-delayed-denied/articleshow/6021821.cms, Visited on: 06-07-2014

UCIL to pay Rs. 500,000 (approximately U.S. $11,000) in fines, others were sentenced to two years in prison and a fine of about Rs. 100,000 (approximately U.S. $2,200) each. In response to the public outrage that the verdict attracted, the Central Government proposed several steps to pacify public sentiment. The government filed a special leave petition (SLP) in the Supreme Court seeking review of the 1996 judgement that had diluted the criminal charge from "culpable-homicide-not-amounting-to-murder" to "death-by-negligence".[350] Although the Court rejected this SLP, it allowed- in an unprecedented move- a curative petition to revisit the 1996 judgement.[351] But this ray of hope did not last long, as the court subsequently rejected this curative petition on account of a long delay of 14 years in filing the petition.[352] Arguably, the Indian government failed to live up to the expectations of victims on this front too. It did not vigorously pursue the extradition of Anderson and in fact supported the dilution of the criminal charge against the Bhopal defendants. It was only in July 2010 that the government initiated the process of decontaminating and remedying the Bhopal plant site.[353] This overall inability and unwillingness of the Indian government to bring UCC and others to justice seem to indicate that the Indian government has considered the creation of an MNC- friendly environment to be more important than safeguarding the rights of its own populace.

The quest for justice of the victims of Bhopal Gas Tragedy can be summarised in five phases[354]:

---

350 See: *Supreme Court Sore Over Delay in Bhopal Gas Tragedy Case,* The Hindu, 8th of August, 2010, www.hindu.com/2010/08/08/stories/2010080859750400.htm, Visited on: 06-07-2014

351 See: Dhananjay Mahapatra, *SC Reopens Bhopal Case, Notices to Accused on Homicide Charge,* The Times of India, 1st of September, 2010, http://articles.timesofindia.indiatimes.com/2010-09-01/india/28217038_1_s-b-majmudar-curative-petition-devadatt-kamat, Visited on: 07-07-2014

352 See: *SC Dismisses CBI petition, Rejects Harsher Punishment for Bhopal Gas Tragedy Accused,* The Times of India, 11th of May, 2011, http://archive.today/76k4, Visited on: 07-07-2014

353 See: Ministry of Environment and Forests, *Press Release: Bhopal Environmental Remediation Oversight Committee Constituted,* 7th of July, 2010, http://envfor.nic.in/sites/default/files/PM_Bhopal-1.pdf, Visited on: 07-07-2014

354 See: Dr. Surya Deva, *Regulating Corporate Human Rights Violations: Humanizing Business,* Routledge Research In Human Rights Law, Routledge Publications, 2012 Edition, Chapter 2: Understanding Bhopal afresh, p.37-45

	Place of Struggle	Objective and Time Span
Phase I	India	How and where to litigate? (December 1984 to March 1985)
Phase II	U.S. Courts	Going after the 'parent' in the U.S. (April 1985 to January 1987)
Phase III	Indian Courts	Struggle to fix responsibility in India. (September 1986 to December 1989)
Phase IV	Both U.S. and Indian Courts Indian Courts	Trying to overturn the settlement. (1990-1993) Seeking compensation and medical care. (1993-2004)
Phase V	U.S. Court Indian Courts	Resort to the Alien Tort Claims Act and Common Law (2000-) Quest for criminal liability (1992-)

Activities carried out by UCC in the state of Bhopal presents a gloomy picture of administration of justice in India, particularly in reference to the MNC culture which the Government of India is persistently supporting in the shield of lending support to a culture that promotes economic growth and development. Bhopal Gas Disaster portrayed the following picture of India on the international forefront:

"India is a country where: there is lack of specific human rights obligations for corporations; the regulatory frameworks are inadequate and fragile; there is general unwillingness or incapacity of states to vigorously pursue MNCs; economic leverage that MNCs enjoy can influence regulatory initiatives; there is non-liability of a parent corporation for human rights abuses by its subsidiaries; the corporate misuse the doctrine of *forum non conveniens*; the MNCs use litigation delay as defence; large number of victims, many of whom could be poor and/or illiterate are left to suffer as claiming interim relief in cases of industrial disasters is not very easy; there is absence of, and difficulties in imposing, effective sanctions against MNCs and there are inherent hurdles in criminal prosecution of MNCs and their executives."[355]

Bhopal Gas Tragedy led to the enactment of three statutes in India- the Environment Protection Act of 1986[356], the Public Liability Insurance Act of 1991[357] and the Protection of Human Rights Act of 1993[358].

The objective of **the Environment Protection Act of 1986** is to protect and improve the environment in the country. It is a comprehensive legislation that lends support to the provisions of the Air Act of 1981 (as amended in 1987) and the Water Act of 1974 (as amended in 1988). Series of environmental disasters (in the likes of the Bhopal Gas Tragedy) prodded the Indian Government to pass this comprehensive piece of legislation, complemented with rules relating to storing, handling and use of hazardous waste.

The Environment Protection Act of 1986 empowered the Indian Government to make necessary rules and regulations to fulfil its objectives. It is under this Act and its rules that government takes all necessary steps such as the formulation of national environmental standards, to prescribe procedures for managing hazardous substances, to regulate industrial locations, to establish safeguards for preventing accidents and to collect and disseminate information regarding environmental pollution. It also empowered the government to set up parallel regulatory agencies to seek environment protection. As for example under the provisions of the Act, the government is empowered to set up agencies for the protection of coastal resources.[359]

---

355 See: Dr. Surya Deva, *Regulating Corporate Human Rights Violations: Humanizing Business,* Routledge Research In Human Rights Law, Routledge Publications, 2012 Edition, Chapter 2: Understanding Bhopal afresh, p. 25

356 See: The Environment Protection Act of 1986, http://www.moef.nic.in/sites/default/files/eprotect_act_1986.pdf, Visited on: 08-07-2014

357 See: The Public Liability Insurance Act of 1991, http://labour.nic.in/upload/uploadfiles/files/ActsandRules/Others/ThePublicLiabilityInsuranceAct1991.pdf, Visited on: 07-07-2014

358 See: The Protection of Human Rights Act of 1993, http://www.refworld.org/pdfid/474e89cf2.pdf, Visited on: 08-07-2014

359 See: P.M. Prasad [Edited by: Pushpam Kumar & B. Sudhakara Reddy], *Ecology and Human Well- Being,* Sage Publications, 2007 Edition, Chapter 18: Environmental Protection- The Role of Regulatory System in India, p. 306

Under Section 3 of the Act, the Central Government has the power to take all such measures as it deems necessary for the purpose of protecting & improving the quality of environment and preventing, controlling & abating environmental pollution. In the case of: *F.B. Taraporawala* v. *Bayer India Ltd.*[360], the Supreme Court ordered the relocation of chemical industries located in the densely populated area of Thane in Mumbai. Since, the Supreme Court generally does not possess any information to decide upon the question of relocation of industries, it directed the Central Government to constitute an authority under Section 3(3) of the Environment Protection Act within one month of the hearing of the suit. The Authority was required to submit its report to the Central Government within 3 months after examining and deciding upon all the relevant issues on the matter in question, but after affording reasonable opportunity of been heard to the parties concerned.

The Act by virtue of Section 15 provides for civil and criminal penalties for the violation of its provisions. It imposes the penalty with fine up to Rs. 100,000 or with imprisonment up to five years or with both. In the case of continuous violation (after the first conviction), it imposes an additional fine up to Rs. 5,000 every day. Section 37 of the Act imposes fine and imprisonment up to 7 years if the violation continues for over one year.

The Environmental Protection Rules of 1986 empowers the formulation of standards for emission of environmental pollutants. In general, these rules were formulated by the government for regulating the working and the conduct of business under the Environment Protection Act of 1986. The formulated rules are- the Hazardous Waste (Management and Handling) Rules of 1989 and the Biomedical Waste (Management and Handling) Rules of 1998.

The objective of the Hazardous Waste (Management and Handling) Rules of 1989 is to regulate and control the generation, collection, treatment, import, storage and handling of hazardous waste. The Biomedical Waste (Management and Handling) Rules of 1998 make it binding on the health-care-institutions to streamline the process of proper handling of hospital waste, such as segregation, disposal, collection and treatment of the same.

---

360 (1996) 6 SCC 58

The Public Liability Insurance Act of 1991 was enacted to provide immediate relief to the victims of an accident involving a hazardous substance.[361] To achieve this object the Act imposes 'no-fault' liability upon the owner of the hazardous substance and requires the owner to compensate the victims irrespective of any neglect or default on his part.[362] "Hazardous substance" means any substance or preparation which, by reason of its chemical or physicochemical properties or handling, is liable to cause harm to human beings, other living creatures, plants, micro-organisms, property or the environment.[363] The Act stipulates the maximum compensation for injury or death at Rs. 25,000 and limits compensation in respect of damage to private property to Rs. 6,000.[364] The right of a victim to claim additional relief under any other law is expressly reserved.

---

361 In the background of the absolute liability principle of the Oleum Gas Leak Case [AIR 1987 SC 982], this Act was passed to consolidate the law relating to product liability particularly in relation to hazardous activity. This Act also seeks to provide relief to the members of the general public who become the victims of industrial catastrophes. In effect, the Act is also an answer to the reflections of the Supreme Court in the case of *Charan Lal Sahu* v. *Union of India* [1990 SCC 613, Para 129], where necessity of such an Act was expressed.

362 See: The Preamble of the Public Liability Insurance Act of 1991, http://labour.nic.in/upload/uploadfiles/files/ActsandRules/Others/ThePublicLiabilityInsuranceAct1991.pdf, Visited on: 07-07-2014

363 See: Section 2(d) of the Public Liability Insurance Act of 1991 & Section 2(e) of the Environment Protection Act of 1986. It is interesting to note that the Madhya Pradesh High Court in *Madhya Pradesh State Electricity Board, Jabalpur* v. *Collector, Mandla* [AIR 2003 MP 156] held that electricity is a hazardous substance for the purpose of application of the Public Liability Insurance Act of 1991. The petitioner, electricity board, challenged the award of compensation for a death by electrocution on the ground that electricity is not a hazardous substance as defined under PLIA. It was contended that electricity is hazardous when it is not used with proper care and caution, but it is not a substance. The court repelled the plea and held that electricity consists of electron, which is a substance and hence, electricity itself is a substance. The court said that once when something is hazardous, irrespective of quantity, it is not necessary for the Central Government to issue a notification under Section 2(d) of PLIA fixing its quantum that makes it hazardous. The court observed: "Whatever irrespective of proportion is hazardous has to be treated as hazardous one. Some article may not be hazardous in small quantity but electricity is not one such article."

364 See: The Schedule annexed to Section 3(1) of the Public Liability Insurance Act of 1991; Section 3 of the Act states, "Liability to give relief in certain cases on the principle of no-fault".

The Act obligates every owner to take out an insurance policy covering potential liability from an accident. An 'accident' is defined to cover a sudden unintended occurrence while 'handling' any hazardous substance resulting in continuous, intermittent or repeated exposure leading to death or injury to any person, or damage to property or the environment. Accidents by reason of war or radioactivity are excluded from the scope of the Act. The expression 'handling' is defined widely include manufacture, trade, and transport of hazardous substances.[365]

Along with the insurance premium, every owner must make a contribution to an Environment Relief Fund established by the Central Government.[366] The fund is designed to provide relief to the victims of an accident.[367] The principal administrative authority under the Public Liability Insurance Act of 1991 is the Collector, who is required to verify the occurrence of the industrial accident, give publicity to the event and invite applications for compensation and award relief.[368]

The Act was amended in 1992 to introduce provisions relating to the relief fund. Rules framed in 1991 lay down the procedure for inviting and processing compensation applications; and also cap the potential liability of an insurer at Rs. 45 crores.[369]

Effective legal remedies for addressing the consequences of mass disasters are the need of the hour. The Public Liability Insurance Act of 1991 aims at providing an immediate temporary relief only. Moreover, the shortcomings of the Act can be summed up as follows:

Firstly, the Act is limited to accidents arising out of handling of hazardous substances. Accidents arising out of equally perilous factors such as radioactivity

---

365 See: Section 2(c) of the Public Liability Insurance Act of 1991

366 See: Section 4(2C) of the Public Liability Insurance Act of 1991

367 See: Section 7A (1) read with Section 7A (2) and Section 7A (3) of the Public Liability Insurance Act of 1991. Section 7A (1) provides that the Central Government may, by notification, establish a Fund, known as the Environmental Relief Fund.

368 See: Section 5 read with Section 6(1) of the Public Liability Insurance Act of 1991

369 See: Shyam Divan & Armin Rosencranz, *Environmental Law and Policy in India*, Oxford University Press, Second Edition, Chapter 3: Constitutional and Legislative Provisions, p.62

and other non-hazardous substances are not covered under the Act. Also, under the provisions of the Act, only over-dose of exposure to hazardous substances, exceeding such quantity as may be prescribed by notification by the Central Government is prohibited. The "routine" exposure to hazardous substances and its deleterious effect on the health and property of people in general has been ignored.

Secondly, the limitation period of five years to make a claim under the provisions of the Act may not be sufficient, because many times the deleterious effects of hazardous substances take a longer time to appear.

Thirdly, the exemption of government owned & controlled corporations from "no fault liability" principle has been criticised as it may lead to dilution of the concept of mandatory insurance under the Act. Further, the discretionary powers conferred onto the Central Government under the Act in all eventualities can lead to arbitrariness.

Fourthly, no scope has been provided for social action litigation and public participation in the claiming of compensation under the provisions of the Act. On one hand, the Act intends to protect innocent victims especially the weaker sections of the society and on the other hand, the Act discourages representative suits, class action and social action litigation; this dichotomy existing within the spirit of the Act is not-understandable.

Lastly, the Act requires a victim to claim relief under this Act and then go to other forums for higher compensation. This is more of an impediment, particularly in cases where the poor victims of the accident will be unable to claim the relief under the law of torts.

It is pertinent to note that even after several years of the Bhopal Gas Leak disaster, the continuing damage to groundwater in Bhopal is appalling. The rehabilitation of the survivors is still clouded in disillusion and despair.[370] The clean-up of the site is a dilemma, as it requires dismantling the plant and the

---

370 See: P. Leelakrishnan, *Environmental Law in India,* Lexis Nexis Publication, Third Edition, Chapter 9: Environmental Hazards- Mass Tort Action, p.272

buildings, and decontaminating soil and groundwater.[371] It has been observed that the aftermath of the disasters like Bhopal Gas Leak demonstrates 'the need for an international human rights framework that can be applied to companies directly, that could also act as catalyst for national legal reform, and serve as a benchmark for national law and regulations'.[372]

The Bhopal Gas Tragedy has not just been an environmental disaster but also a case of gross human rights violation. A slew of international human rights laws and standards were trampled before the gas leak even happened, and Union Carbide, Dow Chemical, and the Government of India have continued to violate the human right laws and standards by refusing to clean up the accident site, refusing to provide compensation, denying people clean water, denying them proper medical care, and generally ignoring the plight of thousands of people in Bhopal who continue to suffer from the effects of the 1984 gas leak and the water contamination that persists to this day. The awareness aftermath the Bhopal Gas Tragedy, led to the enactment of the Protection of Human Rights Act of 1993.

Scholars opine that the adequacy of existing regulatory initiatives that seek to impose and enforce human rights obligations on companies should be judged with reference to their efficacy. The efficacy, however, can be tested by inquiring about the extent to which the regulatory initiatives have achieved the desired objectives; this can be done by comparing the 'actual' effect of a given norm with its 'intended effect'.[373] Regulatory initiatives can secure intended effects if they are able to- encourage companies to comply with their human rights responsibilities and bring to justice those companies that are not so encouraged. Hence, a regulatory initiative related to corporate human rights responsibilities should be considered 'effective' if it can prevent or pre-empt human rights violations by companies- at least in some cases- and could offer

---

371 See: Vibha Varshney, *Flawed plans- India has little idea how to clean up Bhopal,* Down to Earth, 15th of December, 2004, p.7

372 See: Amnesty International, *Summary of 'Clouds of Injustice Bhopal Disaster 20 years on,* ASA 20/104/2004 dated 29th November, 2004.

373 See: Fran Oise Tulkens, *Human Rights, Rhetoric or Reality?,* European Review, 2001, Volume 9, 125, p. 129

adequate relief to victims in cases of violations.[374] This awareness seems to be completely lacking in India if we view this proposition through the lens of the Protection of Human Rights Act of 1993, which is more institutional in nature and less focused on remedial measures.

The Protection of Human Rights Act of 1993 provides for the constitution of a National Human Rights Commission at the central level; State Human Rights Commissions in the various States, and Human Rights Courts for better protection of human rights and for matter connected therewith or incidental there-to.[375] Section 2(d) of the Act states that "human rights" mean the rights relating to life, liberty, equality and dignity of the individuals guaranteed by the Constitution of India or embodied in the International Covenants and enforceable by courts in India. Section 12 of the Act specifically speaks about the functions of the National Human Rights Commission and State Human Rights Commissions. The Section 37 of the Act talks about the constitution of special-investigative-teams for the purpose of investigating various instances of human rights violations. Section 12 read with Section 37 of the Act enables the National and the State Human Rights Commissions to take into consideration incidents such as that of clinical trials carried out by the various pharmaceutical companies on the victims of the Bhopal Gas Tragedy. Pharmaceutical companies such as Quintiles Ltd. and Sanofi-Synthelabo Ltd. have been accused of carrying out clinical trials on the victims of the Bhopal Gas Disaster without acquiring adequate permission from the authorities concerned and without adhering to the rules & regulations required to be complied with before carrying out such trials.[376] Clinical trials carried out by pharmaceutical companies on the Bhopal Gas victims, treating them as

---

[374] Meaning of 'efficacy' is quite different from the effectiveness criteria for non-judicial grievance mechanisms proposed by the United Nations Secretary-General's Special Representative on human rights and transnational corporations and other business enterprises. Human Rights Council, *Guiding Principles on Business and Human Rights: Implementing the United Nations "Protect, Respect and Remedy" Framework,* A/HRC/17/31 [21st of March, 2011], Principle 31

[375] See: The Long Title of the Protection of Human Rights Act of 1993 [As amended by the Protection of Human Rights (Amendment) Act of 2006 (No. 43 of 2006)]

[376] See: *Bhopal Gas Victims Used As Guinea Pigs For Drug Trials*, 17th of December, 2013, http://timesofindia.indiatimes.com/india/Bhopal-gas-victims-used-as-guinea-pigs-for-drug-trials/articleshow/27495772.cms, Visited on: 08-07-2014

guinea pigs, is inhuman and shameful, and deaths resulting from such trials are killings in the nature of corporate manslaughter and corporate homicide.

If the position of law in India is to be assessed so far as corporate crimes in the nature of corporate killings are concerned, the position is not dismal but is rather confused. The rise in awareness in regards to crimes in the nature of corporate killings in India began with the Bhopal Gas Tragedy, and with the Oleum Gas Leakage case, the judicial activism in India brought to forefront the absolute liability principle, which is but an improvement over the strict liability principle. If the judgement in the Oleum Gas Leakage case is to be scrutinised then we can draw an analysis that, absolute liability principle is to be made functional or is to be complemented with the principle of deep-pocket theory. Absolute liability principle on one hand talks about no-fault liability and the deep-pocket theory asserts that compensation for damages in disasters in the likes of Bhopal Gas Tragedy are to be computed taking into concern the size of the corporation and its operational efficiency. The judgement delivered in the Oleum Gas Leakage case was not-so-progressive as it is claimed because when the principle of deep-pocket theory was coined, the Supreme Court concerned itself with an MNC which was operating at an international level, having a huge turnover and making more than substantial profits, hence the court (with all due respect) thought that the deep-pocket theory will result in huge amount of compensation been made payable to the victims, forgetting that in future if an incident in the likes of Bhopal happens and the accused is not an MNC working at an international pedestal but a small company with marginal turnover and operating below the break-even-point, then despite the fact that the disaster so occurring resulting in massive loss of human life and property, the compensation that can be claimed on the set parameters of deep-pocket theory will be hardly satisfactory. Hence, "principle of absolute liability", read with the "deep-pocket theory" makes this "no-fault liability principle" a weak principle.

Secondly, it is important to note that the absolute liability principle is applicable when the corporation accused is dealing with "hazardous substances". What is meant by hazardous substances is debatable as the definition for hazardous substances given in the Environment Protection Act of 1986 and the Public Liability Insurance Act of 1991 is not an exhaustive definition. It is often left to the judiciary to decide as what is meant by hazardous substances, one instance of such a kind is the case of *Madhya Pradesh State Electricity Board, Jabalpur* v. *Collector, Mandla* [AIR 2003 MP 156], where the Madhya Pradesh High Court held that "electricity" too is a hazardous substance and shall fall within the ambit of Section 2(d) of the Public Liability Insurance Act of 1991 and Section 2(e) of the Environment Protection Act of 1986.

Lastly, despite incidents of corporate killings happening in India successively, from *Bhopal Gas Tragedy* to the *Oleum Gas Leakage* case to the *Uphaar Cinema Tragedy*, it was only in the year 2005 that the Indian Supreme Court with its verdict in the *Standard Chartered Bank* case adjudged that "corporations" like other criminal perpetrators are capable of forming the requisite mens rea because for asserting an act to be of criminal orientation, the conditions of mens rea and *actus reus* need to be fulfilled. Re-asserting the fact that crimes can be committed by corporations, the Supreme Court of India in the *Iridium-Motorola* case in 2011 held that corporations are capable of forming a guilty mind and can commit crimes such as cheating and forgery. So here what can be seen is that India has although equipped itself statutorily with enactments such as the Environment Protection Act of 1986, the Public Liability Insurance Act of 1991 and the Protection of Human Rights Act of 1993, post the Bhopal massacre but has hardly realised statutorily or by way of judicial-enactments (also known as judicial-legislations) that "corporate-killing" as a crime needs special attention, as has been given in the U.K., the Indian State of the U.S. and the Australian Capital Territory. India has realised fundamentally as late as in 2005 that corporations can form a guilty mind and can be punished for crimes levying upon the corporations "criminal liability".

It is high time to realise that apart from a comprehensive corporate-manslaughter legislation, what India needs is an awareness that, when the risk of harm from an activity is transnational in character, major in degree and of a nature that cannot be eliminated by exercise of reasonable care, then the state must be held strictly liable and originally responsible for consequent injury. The transnational hazardous nature of a given activity may be determined by way of a contextual multiple factor analysis. It centres on ascertaining whether a significant risk of transnational damage exists, not in the sense of a high probability of minor damage but of severe damage associated even with very low probability. The hazardous nature may be further compounded by lack of State compliance with any incumbent duty of prior information and consultation.[377] Post the Bhopal-Gas-UCC-massacre it is necessary for us to realise that transnational industrial accidents should be treated as "ultra hazardous incidents" justifying not just the application of a principle of absolute liability under the national law but, also incidents which call for making the State jointly liable for the accidents that have so occurred. A crucial element in allocating liability for transnational industrial accidents must be prevention. Such liability must be strict and indeed absolute. A strict liability will force industries and the State to weigh the benefits of a polluting activity against the injury caused by pollution. Thus, the main rationale should be to minimize the possibility of injurious consequences and to provide adequate redress where injurious consequences occur.[378]

Two areas greatly contributing towards corporate manslaughter in India are, firstly, dumping of toxic waste by MNCs in India and importation of toxic waste by corporations in India from abroad; and secondly, dumping of nuclear waste by corporations without adequately treating it, hence, resulting in loss of life or personal injury to persons exposed to such nuclear waste.

Toxic Waste: In the case of *Res. Foundation for Science* v. *Union of India*[379], the Apex Court observed that every day two-thousand-tonnes of hazardous waste is generated in India. The court further observed that a prompt action is required to be taken not only by the Central Government but by all State Governments, as well as the Central and State, Pollution Control Boards to remedy the problem of safe disposal of toxic waste. The court issued appropriate directions, which were necessary to ensure performance of necessary duties by the State Governments, Pollution Control Boards and other concerned authorities.

---

377 See: Justice V.R. Krishna Iyer, *The Indian Law: Dynamic Dimensions of the Abstract*, Universal Law Publishing Co., 2009 Edition, Wounded Nature vs. Human Future, p.363-364

378 See: Report of the International Law Commission, 35 U.N. GAOR, Supp. (No.10), U.N. Doc. A/35/10 (1980), p.365

379 2003 (8) SCALE 258

MNCs operating in India discard their toxic waste on the Indian land and that too without relevantly treating it. Toxic waste dumped in the open ground results in contamination of soil as well as the ground water and when people come in contact with the contaminated soil or water or even the fumes of the toxic waste, they develop life claiming ailments such as nervous breakdown or kidney failure. Hardly any checks and balances have been put in place in India to control such dumping and more-so-over, it is often easy for the corporate giants to circumvent the rules and regulations imposed by municipal corporations that disallow such dumping. One of the recent examples is that of "Unilever".

Unilever, an Anglo-Dutch multinational consumer goods company, having head-quarters in London, England, Rotterdam and Netherlands; claims to be concerned with safety of its operations which it perceives to be environment friendly, but this attitude of this multinational company does not stretch to India. Unilever has been time and again accused by Greenpeace of double standards and shameful negligence for allowing its Indian subsidiary, Hindustan Lever, to dump several tonnes of highly toxic mercury waste in the densely populated tourist resort of Kodaikanal and the surrounding protected natural-reserve of Pambar Shola in Tamil Nadu, Southern India. Greenpeace activists and concerned residents of Kodaikanal have started cordoning off contaminated dump sites in Kodaikanal, to protect people from the mercury wastes that have been recklessly discarded in open by Hindustan Lever which manufactures mercury thermometers for export, mainly to the United States, from United States the thermometers are sold to Germany, U.K., Spain, Australia and Canada. The Unilever factory in India at Kodaikanal was set up in 1977 and the machinery used comprised of second-hand equipments imported from the United States, after the U.S. factory was shut down for the reasons unknown. The workers at the Indian factory in Kodaikanal are not offered any protection from the mercury spills and several workers, over a period, have complained of health problems which, they allege, is caused by their exposure to mercury in the workplace. Mercury is highly poisonous and exposure even to the smallest amount through air or water exerts severe effects on the central nervous system and kidneys of human beings which eventually results in fatality.[380]

---

380 See: *Unilever: Corporate Crimes*, Corporate Watch, http://www.corporatewatch.org.uk/content/unilever-corporate-crimes, Visited on: 09-07-2014

It has been reported that shipping municipal waste to India is about four times cheaper than recycling it, for the developed countries. It is estimated that, it may cost to Britain about Rs. 12,000 to recycle a tonne of rubbish after segregation and shipping the rubbish to India may cost it about just Rs. 2,800. It has been reported that cement factories in Tamil Nadu, import toxic garbage on the pretext of using it as fuel. Also, in 2008, 40 containers of "mixed wastepaper" imported by ITC from U.S. were confiscated after they were found to contain municipal waste of eco-toxic nature. In 2009, 9 containers of toxic waste from Malaysia, Barcelona and Jeddah were imported by the Excel Trading Corporation, Sree Jayajothi Cement and Harbour Petro Chemicals, all these containers were seized for flouting the rules and regulations governing such import of garbage. In 2010, 20 containers of trash from French colony Reunion and Greece imported by Sripathi Paper and Board were confiscated for violating the legal norms governing such import.[381]

Nuclear Waste: The nuclear power plants generate radioactive waste. It is often either the heavy water or the spent nuclear fuel. The radioactive waste is highly hazardous to the environment and to all life forms due to its ability to remain in the environment for long time and affect the genes or the genetic material of life forms thereby affecting the future generations. Handling of radioactive waste is itself hazardous since it can affect the person handling it. Radioactivity is especially dangerous since it can be created, but it cannot be eliminated. It attacks living cells which are the basis and the very building blocks of all forms of life. A "safe radiation level" does not exist, and to arbitrarily fix such a level is extremely difficult.

India is known for its uranium mining. In India, 100% of uranium comes from Jharkhand and Meghalaya. Uranium mining releases both external and internal radiation. Internal radiation is of particular concern, as most of the chemical emissions in uranium mining are from Alpha particles. In internal radiation, Alpha particles like canon-balls have less penetrating power, but more impact that is, when they enter the human body they settle in lungs, kidneys, and other delicate parts and continue to bombard the cells.

---

381 See: Radha Venkatesan, *Is India a global trash can?;* The Times of India, 24th of April, 2010, http://timesofindia.indiatimes.com/india/Is-India-a-global-trash-can/articleshow/5851954.cms, Visited on: 09-07-2014

Radioactive particles pose the greatest threat to human health when they are inhaled or ingested. They are so microscopic that they can enter into the skin via the sweat pores and hair follicles or through food, water and air.

Radium (Radium- 226) is one isotope in uranium waste that is especially dangerous. This is because it is harmful to life-forms at low concentrations and it decays further into the even more dangerous radon gas (Radon- 222). Besides this, as a chemical, radium is similar to calcium so when ingested it migrates to the bones, teeth and breast milk and replaces the calcium. It is a bone seeker and is also readily taken up by vegetation.

In India, in Jadugora, in the State of Jharkhand only 0.02% of the ore has uranium, therefore for production of uranium, huge quantities of radioactive waste, solid, liquid and gases are created. The Uranium Corporation of India Limited (UCIL) has three productive uranium mines namely Jadugora, Batin and Narwapahar which are within a 5 km radius. The ore is mined from underground at a depth of 1,600 feet. It is brought to the surface and through a process of leaching, 'yellow cake' or uranium concentrate is manufactured. The radioactive waste that is produced as a result of uranium processing many times is not effectively disposed of and hence ineffective disposal of the same becomes a real time threat to lives of the plants, animals and human beings.

"Radioactive substances" till recently in India, had been dealt with by the Government of India, itself (or by the Government Companies). The private players have now been allowed to enter this area of activity with the amendment of the Atomic Energy Act of 1962 by the enactment of the Civil Liability for Nuclear Damage Act of 2010. In Jadugora the uranium is extracted from uranium mines leaving behind 85% of the other radioactive by-products which are mixed and made into slurry and pumped to a tailing dam. While the rice fields of the surrounding villages were acquired for the dams, their schools, vegetable gardens and water sources continue to be adjacent to these dams. Besides this, to save cost the dams have been constructed with the radioactive tailings. These dams, each about 400 acres of land and around 100 feet deep have been constructed in between villages and the villagers continue to use them as thoroughfares, these being their traditional routes to the market, etc. As a result, they continually pose a threat to all the surrounding areas including the city of Jamshedpur, which is close by.[382] Also, lately, the plans of the Central Government to dump nuclear waste from the Kudankulam Nuclear Power Plant (in Tamil Nadu), in the disused mines at Kolar Gold Fields has created a lot of public furore.[383]

5.5. Chapter Conclusion:

To conclude it can be said that, India is still realising the ways and means by which corporations in the nature of indigenous companies, transnational companies and multi-national organisations, inflict atrocities on the people. Post the *Bhopal Gas Tragedy, Oleum Gas Leakage case* and *Uphaar Cinema Tragedy*; it was only in 2005 that Indian judiciary became complacent with imposing criminal liability on corporations. Crime in the nature of illegal dumping of nuclear waste in densely populated areas of Jharkhand, Meghalaya and Tamil Nadu, without effectively treating the same is raising questions on the efficacy of laws in India enacted for punishing corporations accused of illegal dumping of nuclear waste in the light of the fact that the Civil Liability for Nuclear Damage Act of 2010 imposes a monetary liability on the flouting corporations, at an amount less than the amount adjudged to be paid as compensation in the Bhopal Gas Disaster to the victims and their respective family, by the Honourable Supreme Court of India, after applying the deep-pocket theory read complimentary to the absolute liability principle.[384]

On the one hand, India is still searching ways to clean the site where Bhopal Gas accident took place; on the other hand, companies in India are importing nearly all the toxic waste from the countries in the likes of Jeddah, Barcelona and Malaysia, to dump the same in India either without treating it or just

---

382 See: Mohammad Naseem, *Environment Law in India,* Wolters Kluwer Law & Business, 2011 Edition, Part I: Pollution Control, Chapter 8: Radiation and Vibrations (Nuclear and Non-nuclear), p.161- 165

383 See: M. Suchitra, *Will Kolar become India's nuclear waste dump-yard?;* Down to Earth, 26 November 2012, http://www.downtoearth.org.in/content/will-kolar-become-indias-nuclear-waste-dumpyard, Visited on: 03-08-2014

384 See: Section 6 of the Civil Liability for Nuclear Damage Act of 2010, http://lawmin.nic.in/ld/regionallanguages/THE%20CIVIL%20LIABILITY%20OF%20NUCLEAR%20DAMAGE%20ACT,2010.%20(38%20OF2010).pdf, Visited on: 03-08-2014

partially treating it. The dimensions in regards to the crime of corporate manslaughter in India seem to be in-exhaustive, more because India is still a developing country and is often lured by the idea of transnational and multinational companies operating in India, earning for it the valuable foreign exchange without realising that sometimes this valuable foreign exchange is the bargain price for the priceless human lives that our country is putting to risk. The need of the hour is a comprehensive piece of corporate manslaughter legislation which in not only progressive but is also futuristic in the sense that as science is progressing hence, an open-textured corporate manslaughter legislation will be capable enough to take care of all situations and adversities that may arise in the future.

Chapter 6

Conclusion and Suggestions

6.1. Conclusion:

Corporate manslaughter and corporate homicide are comprehensive crimes committed by corporations which exist only in the contemplation of law. Doctrine of separate legal entity has done more harm than good. To remedy the ills of the doctrine of separate legal entity, the doctrine of lifting up of the corporate veil was introduced to the corporate legal mainstream. But the doctrine of lifting up of the corporate veil extended itself only to the cases related to forgery and misrepresentation. From the doctrine of lifting up of the corporate veil came about the identification principle and the principle of determining mind and will of the company. Attribution of criminal liability over corporations is the result of these two principles of "identification" and "determining mind and will", these principles emphasise that a body corporate although is an artificial legal person, existing only in the contemplation of law, having a common seal and perpetual succession, still behind the corporate veil, there are individuals of flesh and blood, that manage the affairs of the corporation. Every corporation is managed by a group of individuals that form the head and brain of the body corporate and when a corporation commits a crime, the required *mens rea* requirement needs to be fulfilled by attributing the guilty mind with the knowledge and intentions of the individuals that manage the affairs of the body corporate.

It was as late as in 2005 (*Standard Chartered Bank Case*) that the Supreme Court in India gave recognition to the fact that corporations like other individuals are capable of forming *mens rea* and can be held accountable for crimes, which necessarily require fulfilment of the conditions of *mens rea* and *actus reus*. The Supreme Court re-emphasised and re-reflected on this premise in 2011 when it delivered the *Iridium Motorola* judgement. India still hasn't given any legislative recognition to the crimes in the nature of corporate killings. India is a common law country and has over the years drawn inspiration from legislative enactments in the U.K. and the U.S., the pity is that even though India has seen the Bhopal Gas Tragedy, Oleum Gas Leakage Disaster and Uphaar Cinema Tragedy, still it has failed to draw any inspiration from the U.K. legislation of Corporate Manslaughter and Corporate Homicide Act of 2007 or the Corporate Manslaughter Bill of the Indian State of U.S. or the Westray Law (2005) of Canada or the Corporate Manslaughter Law of the Australian Capital Territory. The Companies Act of 2013, India, doesn't even mention anything about the crime of corporate killings, what to speak of defining the terms "corporate manslaughter" and "corporate homicide".

Corporate killings in India take place primarily because of *five* reasons: adulterated goods produced by corporations, resulting in death of consumers; deaths of labourers and workmen taking place because of unhealthy and unsafe work conditions in which they are forced to work in; deaths taking place due environment disasters triggered by corporations owing to their lack of concern towards the idea of sustainable development; illegal clinical trials taking place in India in the backdrop of pharmaceutical companies lacking in human values and ethics, targeting the illiterate and poor sections of society by using them as guinea pigs; lastly, companies in India, importing toxic waste from foreign countries and disposing the same, either without treating it or partially treating it, on the open land or through water bodies.

Post the Bhopal Gas Tragedy, the legislature in India enacted the Environment Protection Act of 1986, the Public Liability Insurance Act of 1991 and the Protection of the Human Rights Act of 1993. Also, the judicial activism in India led to the dilution of the *locus standi* requirement in cases involving "public interest" which necessarily included cases in the nature of industrial catastrophes and disasters. As a result, the traditional concept of bipolar litigation or adversary type of litigation was supplemented by the social action litigation and public interest litigation under new changing scenario of the adjudication system in India.[385]

---

[385] See: Dr. Indranil Bhattacharyya, *Environment Laws,* Kamal Law House, 2009 Edition, Chapter 9: Conclusion and Suggestions, p. 276-277

Under the Environment Protection Act of 1986, the Ministry of Environment and Forests (MoEF) was established with the following main functions: coordination of activities of various States and Central authorities established under law; laying down minimum emission/effluent standards; obtaining information about industrial processes and inspect plant premises; giving directions for closure, prohibition or regulation of industrial processes; and stoppage or regulation of the supply of water and electricity or any other services to industries violating pollution standards.

The Public Liability Insurance Act of 1991 was enacted to make the owner of an industrial undertaking strictly liable for any injury or damage caused because of pollution and provides for immediate relief in respect of death or injury to any person or damage to any property resulting from an accident while handling hazardous substances. The payment made to the victim under the Act is meant only for providing immediate relief and does not require establishing the claim on merits. The final compensation is paid subsequently by the owner arising out of any legal proceeding in due course.[386] Both the legislation, the Environment Protection Act of 1986 and the Public Liability Insurance Act of 1991 define the term "hazardous substances" as substances having chemical or physiochemical properties. Section 2(f) of the National Green Tribunal Act of 2010 defines "hazardous substance" as "any substance or preparation which is defined as hazardous substance in the Environment (Protection) Act of 1986, and exceeding such quantity as specified or may be specified by the Central Government under the Public Liability Insurance Act of 1991". The legislative definition of the term "hazardous substances" in India is very narrow and in times of scientific and technical revolution, as we are witnessing at present, what is needed a more comprehensive definition of the term "hazardous substances".

The noxious substances in India are dealt with by the Manufacture, Storage and Import of Hazardous Chemical Rules of 1989 and the Chemical Accidents

386 See: Mohammad Naseem, *Environmental Law in India,* Wolters Kluwer Law & Business Publication, 2011 Edition, Part I: Pollution Control, Chapter 2: General Law, Section 3: Fiscal Incentives to Encourage Prevention and Control of Pollution, p.88-89

(Emergency Planning, Preparedness and Response) Rules of 1996. There is no specific legislation that may assertively take action against the flouting industrial corporations that deal with noxious substances, despite the fact that India is exposed to high levels of mercury poisoning from companies producing caustic soda and chlorine, which are in-turn are used to produce products such as- plastics, bulbs, batteries and pesticides. Around 60-70 tonnes of mercury is released every year in the environment in India by the industrial corporations which are engaged in the production of electrical equipments, batteries and thermometers. Mercury poisoning, results in nervous system damage which eventually results in death. Despite hundreds of deaths taking place in the past owing to the operations of industrial corporations dealing in with noxious substances such as mercury, reluctance has been shown by them to switch over to membrane technology.

The Protection of Human Rights Act of 1993 institutionalises the establishment of the National Human Rights Commission at the Centre and the respective State Human Rights Commissions at the State level. The functions to be performed by these respective commissions as per the language of the Act in no way reflect upon their power to deal strongly with crimes in the nature of corporate killings or assert claims where by deaths take place due to gross negligence exercised by industrial corporations resulting in catastrophes in the nature of Bhopal Gas Disaster.

In order to honour the decisions taken at the United Nations Conference on the Human Environment held at Stockholm in June 1972, in which India participated and to ensure that tragedies in the likes of the Bhopal Gas do not happen again in India, the National Green Tribunal Act was enacted in the year 2010. This Act repealed the previous two Acts, the National Environment Tribunal Act of 1995 and the National Environment Appellate Authority Act of 1997. The National Green Tribunal established under the Act has been authorised by virtue of Section 15(1) to provide relief and compensation to the victims of environment pollution; restitution of property damaged; and restitution of the environment polluted. Section 17(1) provides that where death of, or injury to any person (other than a workman) or damage to any property or environment has resulted from an accident or the adverse impact of an activity or operation or process, under any enactment specified in Schedule

I of the Act [387], the person responsible shall be liable to pay such relief or compensation for such death, injury or damage, under all or any of the heads specified in Schedule II of the Act[388], as may be determined by the Tribunal. The Tribunal by virtue of Section 17(3) is to apply the principle of "no-fault" in cases of accidents. This legislation although is progressive in nature but is not free of serious failures. One serious failure is that the term "victim" has not being defined under the Act and the other is that, even though, the legislation came into existence after the Parliament of India took necessary inspiration from the models existing abroad but still the sentencing regime has remained orthodox, no measures have been taken to introduce innovative sentencing regimes such as the ones calling for unlimited fines, publicity order or limiting the areas operation and scope of operations of the flouting corporations.

Corporate criminal wrongdoings in India are primarily punished by reading progressively and not literally; the provisions of the Indian Penal Code of 1860, but the punishments provisioned in the code in no eventuality appear to be deterrent in nature. See for example, in case any person unlawfully or negligently does any act which is, and which he knows or has reason to believe to be, likely to spread the infection of any disease dangerous to life, shall be punished with imprisonment for a term which may extend to six months, or with a fine, or with both (Section 269 of the Indian Penal Code) or, in case the same act is done malignantly punishment will be imprisonment for a term which may extend to two years, or with a fine, or with both (Section 270 of the Indian Penal Code). Other examples can be of, adulteration of any article of food or drink, making such article noxious as food or drink, intending to sell such article as food or drink, or knowing it to be likely that the same will be sold as food or drink, is punishable with imprisonment for a term which may extend to six months, or with a fine which may extend to Rs. 1,000 or with both (Section 272 of the Indian Penal Code); Voluntarily corrupting or

387 Enactments specified under Schedule I of the National Green Tribunal Act of 2010: the Water (Prevention and Control of Pollution) Act of 1974; the Water (Prevention and Control of Pollution) Cess Act of 1977; the Forest (Conservation) Act of 1980; the Air (Prevention and Control of Pollution) Act of 1981; the Environment (Protection) Act of 1986; the Public Liability Insurance Act of 1991 and the Biological Diversity Act of 2002.

388 Schedule II of the National Green Tribunal Act of 2010 specifies the respective heads under which compensation or relief for damage may be claimed.

fouling the water, of any public spring or reservoir, so as to render it less fit for the purpose for which it is ordinarily used, is punishable with imprisonment for a term which may extend to three months, or with a fine which may extend to Rs. 500, or with both (Section 277 of the Indian Penal Code); Use any explosive substance so rashly or negligently as to endanger human life, or to be likely to cause harm or injury to any other person, or knowingly or negligently omits to take such precautions with any explosive substance in his possession sufficient to guard against any probable danger to human life from that substance, shall be punished with imprisonment for a term which may extend to six months, or with fine which may extend to Rs. 1,000 or with both (Section 286 of the Indian Penal Code).

In the light of the jurisprudence developed aftermath the *Standard Chartered Bank* case (2005), and the *Iridium Motorola* case (2011) it can be said that, although the lexicological definition of the word "person" does include a body corporate but the punishments imputed on the corporations as per the relevant provisions of the code extend only to fines and not to the extent of incarceration as an artificial legal person cannot be put behind bars. The penalty imposed over the corporations in the nature of fines only, is accounted by the corporations as just the "cost of operating the business".

To promote the cause of environment protection and to ensure corporate participation in the same the Government of India has come up with various schemes in the nature of "fiscal incentives" from time to time. Over a period of time it has been found that the highlighting cause of corporate killings in India has been the non-compliance with environment protection legislations by the flouting corporations. The fiscal incentives that the government has come up with over a period of time are in the nature of: exemption from income tax, depreciation allowance, investment allowance, exemption from tax on capital gains, excise duty exemption, custom duty exemption, easy loans, sales-tax exemptions and reduced water cess.[389]

[389] See: Mohammad Naseem, *Environmental Law in India,* Wolters Kluwer Law & Business Publication, 2011 Edition, Part I: Pollution Control, Chapter 2: General Law, Section 3: Fiscal Incentives to Encourage Prevention and Control of Pollution, p.90-92

Despite the efforts placed by the Government of India in the past, India still needs a comprehensive piece of legislation primarily targeting crimes in the nature of "corporate manslaughter and corporate homicide". In the light of the same, the following points must be taken into consideration:

- India has seen enough in the past, namely, the Bhopal debacle, the Oleum gas leakage disaster & the Uphaar cinema tragedy and the dilatory practices which corporations adopt to circumvent the prosecution. The past may be tragic but the present is even more gloomy in the light of the practices of Vedanta in Orissa, regarding bauxite mining; atrocities inflicted by Coca-Cola Co. by setting up its bottling plant in Plachimada, Kerala; erosion of natural resources by illegal mining carried out by POSCO in Orissa; activities of Monsanto, a multi-national corporate giant, promoting mono-culture by way to genetically engineered seeds, is blamed for more than 200,000 farmer suicides in India; and, the ostrich like attitude shown by Dow Chemicals, the legal successor of Union Carbide Corporation, in its refusal to clean up the Bhopal Gas Tragedy accident site. India is need of a comprehensive piece of legislation that can fight the corporate-terrorism, India is facing. India at present is eyeing for growth and progress by promoting the multi-national corporate culture, forgetting that growth for the sake of growth is the characteristic of a cancerous cell[390]; much doubt can be imputed on the so-called progressive attitude of the legislature in India in the light of the recently enacted,

[390] See for example, the case of the Dabhol Power Project, commonly known as the Enron Project, initiated in the middle of 1992 by the Enron Corporation. This project was the first major litmus test of the Indian government policy to allow foreign investment in power and electricity sector. But the project remained in controversy from the very inception due to various reasons such as corruption, lack of transparency and competitive bidding, and the high cost of electricity. When people protested against the project, the state government machinery muzzled such protests including through arbitrary arrests, beating, and harassment of protest movement leaders. What was however critical was that, the Enron Corporation provided resources to aid and fund these state operations. Enron is, thus, an example of how even a democratic state could take the side of a foreign investor MNC against its own people, whose human rights it is obliged to protect constitutionally. See: Human Rights Watch, *The Enron Corporation: Corporate Complicity in Human Rights Violations(1999)*, http://www.hrw.org/reports/1999/enron/, Visited on: 18-07-2014

the Companies Act of 2013 which hardly talks about crimes in the nature of "corporate killings".

- Post the Bhopal Gas Tragedy; in the Oleum Gas Leakage case the Supreme Court of India through Justice Bhagwati (speaking for majority) coined the principle of no-fault liability which is an improvement over the *Ryland* v. *Fletcher* Rule, also known as the Rule of Strict Liability. This Rule of Absolute Liability says that the owner of "hazardous substances", in case of any industrial accidents shall be held absolutely liable, regardless of existence of no fault on the part of the owner of hazardous substances. The defences available to the defendant in cases of strict liability, in the nature of, plaintiff the wrong-doer; the act of God; the act done with the consent of the plaintiff; the act of the third party; and the act done under the authority of a statute; are not available to the defendant in the cases of absolute liability. The lacking of this principle is that, it needs to be read with the principle of deep-pocket theory, as a principle complimenting the no-fault liability principle.

The principle of deep-pocket theory says, the amount of compensation in cases of industrial disasters involving hazardous substances will depend on or shall be directly proportional to the size of the business organisation and the volume of profits it makes. This may be so because the Supreme Court, with all due respect, while delivering the judgement was focusing on the corporate giants in the nature of multi-national companies such as the Union Carbide Corporation, as the sentencing came post Bhopal debacle. The Supreme Court failed to reflect on the premise, as to what shall happen if debacle of the size of Bhopal happens and the accused is not a multi-national corporate giant but a small indigenous company, earning low volume of profits.

- Post the Bhopal Gas Tragedy, India came up with the following legislation: the Environment Protection Act of 1986; the Public Liability Insurance Act of 1991 and the Protection of Human Rights Act of 1993; particularly to punish the corporations for the loss of human life and property. Liabilities imputed under these legislations on corporations are merely in the nature of "non-substantial" fines, these legislation do not even carry forward the spirit of the absolute liability principle. India is in need of a comprehensive legislation that recognises crimes in the nature of "corporate killings" and classifies them into the broad categories of "corporate manslaughter" and "corporate homicide". Also, this proposed legislation should introduce sentencing regimes in the nature of- "unlimited fines", "publicity orders", "loss of license", and "loss of statutory and non-statutory benefits". This legislation should take note of corporate killings in regards to labourers working for the corporation, dying as a result of tools, equipments and machinery employed being of obsolete and un-standardised nature and as a reason of work conditions being unhealthy and unsafe. The proposed legislation must impute conviction of "corporate manslaughter" on corporations that cause the death of customers from goods supplied being adulterated or the products marketed being of defective orientation or people dying because of services offered by corporations being nefarious. The proposed legislation must be efficacious to impute criminal liability on pharmaceutical companies for carrying out illegal clinical trials, and should punish with criminal sanctions the companies that import toxic waste from foreign countries under the garb of recycling that waste to produce goods of commercial viability, but in fact dispose of this waste either without treating it or partially treating it.

- Computation of "monetary sanctions" under various legislation in India to make corporations obligated and obliged to pay compensation to the workers, consumers and public in general, suffering from wrongs caused to them by the corporations, infringing their right to life and property, is often done through the "multipliers method"[391], although

---

391 Lord Wright in the case of *Davies* v. *Powell Duffryn Associated Collieries Ltd.* [1942 AC 601 at p.617: (1942) 1 All ER 657 (HL)], enunciating and explaining the "multipliers method" stated as follows:

"It is a hard matter of pounds, shillings and pence, subject to the element of reasonable future probabilities. The starting point is the amount of wages which the deceased was earning, the ascertainment of which to some extent may depend upon the regularity of his employment. Then there is an estimate of how much he expended for his own personal and living expense. The balance will give a datum of basic figure which will generally be turned into a lump sum by taking a certain number

the "interest method" for the assessment of damages and computation of claim was initially recognised in India but this method was never considered satisfactory, just or relevant. According to the interest method the dependents should be paid such lump sum amount of money, the interest from which would be equivalent to loss suffered by them. The interest method was found to be based on wrong and un-scientific assumptions and was labelled as an improper method for computation of damages or loss suffered by the claimants. In the case of *Joki Ram* v. *Naresh Kanta*[392] and *Padmadevi* v. *Kabalsingh*[393], the Punjab & Haryana High Court and the Bombay High Court, respectively held that the "interest method" is an unjust method as it does not takes into consideration the decreasing value of money. Later in the following cases: *Gobald Motor Service Ltd.* v. *R.M.K. Veluswami*[394], *M.C.D* v. *Subhagwanti*[395] and *C.K. Subramania Iyer* v. *T. Kunhikuttan*[396], it was held that "multipliers method" is the most logical and rational method to compute damages, assess the loss of dependency and determine the claim as to compensation, for it does not suffer the unjust intricacies other methods in the nature of "interest method" suffer.

In case of injury suffered, compensation is computed under the multipliers method taking in account the following factors: the age of the individual sufferer; the nature of the injury suffered; how grievous the injury is; the cost of treatment; the loss of earnings on account of injury suffered; and the number of family members that are dependent on sufferer. In case of

---

of years' purchase. That sum, however, has to be taxed down by having due regard to uncertainties, for instance, that the widow might have married again and thus ceased to be dependent and other like matters of speculation and doubt".

Over the years in the common-law countries, the "multipliers method" has came out to be recognised as one of the most logical and scientific method for the evaluation of, damages and compensation payable to the victims of motor vehicle accidents and industrial disasters.

392 AIR 1977 P&H 214 at p.219

393 AIR 1985 Bom. 357 at p.361

394 AIR 1962 SC 1

395 AIR 1966 SC 1750

396 (1969) 3 SCC 64: AIR 1970 SC 376

death of an individual, the compensation is computed taking in account the following factors: the age of the deceased; the number of years the deceased ought to have survived had there been no such accident; the sum of money the deceased was earning or could have been able to earn taking in account his education qualifications and experience; the nature of profession and the likely future professional prospects of the deceased; the number of family members dependent of the deceased; the age of the claimants; and the funeral expenses.

The multipliers method takes into consideration only the quantitative factors and pays no stress or pays negligible stress on factors such as pain suffered by the deceased or the victims injured; the emotional turmoil the family of the deceased went through; and the mental distress the victim and his family suffered owing to the injuries sustained or death of the deceased. Multipliers method is a rational and a pragmatic method for the evaluation of compensation payable as to the victims of motor accidents and industrial disasters, but it is not comprehensive method for the computation of damages in regards to pain suffered by the victim or emotional turmoil that the family of the victim went through. There is a need for legislative creation of sanctions that can be imputed onto the corporations in case of industrial disasters so that the monetary loss that the corporations suffers is recurring in nature such as an "on-going community service"; and it should not be an one-time affair for the corporations to consider the same as the "cost of carrying on the business"; the sanctions imposed should be recurring in nature in the sense that they must be in the nature of certain percentage of profits that the corporations must necessarily invest towards community service each quarter or each year. Monetary sanctions when complemented with publicity orders, act as effective means of corporate punishment as relevant inference can be drawn from the B.P. oil spill accident in the Gulf of Mexico, the publicity orders issued by the U.S. Government as against the B.P. led to the sharp fall in the market value of the share price of the B.P."Goodwill" is often defined as the reputation that the business organisation or the corporation has earned over the years.

- "Goodwill" is an intangible asset of a business organisation and it is shown as an asset is the position statement (Balance Sheet) of the body corporate. Several factors determine the "goodwill" of a business organisation, these factors are: nature of the business, risks involved in

> the business, nature and extent of competition the business organisation faces in the dynamic business environment, managerial ability, consumer recognition the 'trade name' of the business organisation enjoys and quality of products manufactured and marketed. There are several methods through which the "goodwill" of a business organisation can be computed, these methods are- "the average profits method", "the super-profits method" and "the capitalisation method".

In the average profits method, the goodwill is computed by multiplying the average profits earned by a business organisation in the past specific years with the number of years of purchase.

In the super profits method, the goodwill is computed by multiplying the super profits earn with the number of years of purchase. Super profits are calculated by subtracting the "normal profits" from the "actual profits". Normal profits are calculated by multiplying the capital invested with the normal rate of return.

The capitalisation method enunciates two ways for calculating goodwill. One is the capitalisation of average profits method and the other is the capitalisation of super profits method. In the first method, the goodwill is computed by subtracting the capital employed from the capitalised value of average profits. The capital employed is calculated by subtracting the liabilities from the assets, and the capitalised value of average profits is calculated by multiplying the average profits with 100 and dividing the total by the normal rate of return. In the second method, the goodwill is computed by multiplying the super profits earned with 100 and dividing the total by the normal rate of return.

Thus, what can be inferred from the above is that, the goodwill calculated by a business organisation bears a direct relationship with the amount of profits earned by the business organisation, and no material emphasis is placed on the qualitative factors such as: *pro bono public*o work undertaken by a corporation for the overall welfare of the society, the schemes of labour welfarism undertaken by a body corporate, the environment protection measures to which the business organisation strictly complies with, or the preventive measures which the business organisation adheres to for avoiding any kind of industrial disaster that may take place owing to the business organisation dealing with production, manufacturing and sale of substances hazardous in nature. The corporate manslaughter legislation proposed must take note of not only of the quantitative factors but should lay equal emphasis on the qualitative factors for the computation of goodwill of a business organisation. There must be provisions that call for erosion of some percentage of the value of goodwill of a business organisation (say, 25% or 50%) in case the activities of the business organisation result in industrial disasters owing to gross negligence. This erosion in the value of goodwill should be complemented with necessary publicity orders. It must be noted that any monetary loss that a corporation faces as a matter of punishment may be regarded by the corporation as just the "cost of operating the business", but the loss of reputation is something that shall affect the corporation for a over a long period time in the long run.

6.2. Suggestions:

Apart from the points above noted, the proposed corporate manslaughter legislation must provide for the following:

6.2.1. Environment Audit: The Environment (Protection) Rules of 1986 require that every person carrying on any industry, operation or process requiring consent under the Water or Air Act or authorisation under the Hazardous Waste Rules has to submit an environmental audit report for each financial year to the Pollution Control Boards.

Environmental auditing is a self-regulating measure. It is used for checking, whether or not, a company is complying with environmental laws and regulations. It can be used as a valuable tool for assessing a company's environmental management systems, policies compliance & equipment, and hence, the incorporation of this measure should not be "secondary" in the form of rules complementing an Act, but it should be "primary" that is incorporation should be in the main body of the Act. The intended corporate manslaughter legislation must create a statutory authority that should be vested with the responsibility of carrying out environmental audits for all corporations notified to be dealing with the manufacturing, purchase or sale of substances which are of hazardous nature. Also, this statutory authority should see, whether or not there is compliance by the corporations of the rules and regulations formulated under the Environment Protection Act of 1986, the Water Act of 1974, the Air Act of 1981 and the Public Liability Insurance Act of 1991. The report prepared by this statutory authority must necessarily be made public and non-compliance with the statutes concerned must be dealt with fines and publicity orders; also within specified timeframe the corporations must be made obligated to comply with the relevant statutory rules and regulations which they have flouted.

Polluter pays principle and precautionary principle; do play a substantial role in imposing liability over corporations for their failure to adhere to the environment protection legislation. But, the liability imposed is in nature of fines and the same is often seen by the flouting corporations as just the cost of operating the business. Thus, it is necessary that publicity orders must be made complimentary to the monetary fines imposed. Environment protection legislations in India, do provide for "environment impact assessment" to judge the overall ecological feasibility of the operations to be carried out by the corporations in India; however, more or less often corporations sway away from such assessments by offering bribes to the officers concerned, hence to see that the "environment audits" as proposed, do not meet the same fate, provisions in the proposed legislation must provide that the statutory authority (that shall carry out the audits) must comprise of individuals of high repute, having worked with exceptional vigour towards the cause of environment-protection. Individuals in the likes of Mr. M.C. Mehta, Baba Amte, Medha Patkar, Gaura Devi, Sunderlal Bahuguna, Chandi Prasad Bhatt and Arundhati Roy, must be consulted and a high circuit power statutory authority must be effectuated so as to carry out environmental audits.

6.2.2. Human Resource Audit: To fight the menace of workplace deaths and occupational health hazards, the proposed corporate manslaughter legislation must provide for human resource audits by specialised agencies. It shall be rational and pragmatic that such audits are undertaken by the already established specialised institutions in the nature of the National Human Rights Commission and the State Human Rights Commissions. The National Human Rights Commission and the State Human Rights Commissions, must be burdened with necessary duties and responsibilities to undertake annual human resource audit of all corporations which deal in production, manufacturing or sale of hazardous substances, and the report prepared by them after due submission with the respective State Governments and the Central Government, must be published in the official gazette. The audit must take into consideration- the quality of tools and equipments, the workers in the corporation work with; the workplace conditions- how clean, hygienic and well-ventilated the place of work is; in case of production, manufacturing or sale of hazardous substances, what special measures does the corporation undertakes to ensure the safety of life and health of the employees; whether or not the employees are equipped with protective equipment such as goggles, helmets and gloves; whether or not, or, to what extent the lives of the employees of the corporation are insured; what precautionary measures has the corporation undertaken to combat casualties in the nature of fire, short circuits, chemical leakages or gas leakages; whether or not the thermostats are in good working order to control heat and air conditioning; whether or not the smoke & fire alarms, fire extinguishers and carbon monoxide detectors are in good working condition; and whether or not the corporation conducts, on regular intervals, the disaster preparedness drills.

The considerations put forth in this point shall require necessary amendments to be brought forth in the Protection of Human Rights Act of 1993, to enlarge the scope of operations and powers of the National Human Rights Commission and the respective State Human Rights Commissions. Provisions of the proposed Corporate Manslaughter legislation must provide that every year corporations dealing with "hazardous substances" must conduct human resource audit, to impute punishments for failure to comply with legislations (and rules complementing the respective legislations) in the nature of: the Insecticides Act of 1968; the Poisons Act of 1919; the Hazardous Wastes (Management, Handling and Trans-boundary Movement) Rules of 2008; the Manufacture, Storage and Import of Hazardous Chemicals, Rules of 1989 as amended in 1994 (Framed under the Environment Protection Act of 1986); the Municipal Solid Waste (Management and Handling) Rules of 2000; the Recycled Plastic Manufacture and Use Rules of 1999; the Bio-medical Waste (Management and Handling) Rules of 1998; and the Chemical Accidents (Emergency Planning, Preparedness and Response) Rules of 1996. Failure to comply with the necessary legislations must be taken note of in the proposed human-resource-audit and penalty in the nature of fines and publicity orders must be imputed as against the flouting corporations.

6.2.3. State Responsibility: The proposed corporate manslaughter legislation must provide for State scrutiny and licensing regime to be followed in regards to granting of permission to the industries for the establishment of plants dealing in the production and manufacturing of hazardous and poisonous substance such as toxic gas or industrial chemicals. The permission to establish plants dealing in with the production and manufacturing of poisonous substances must be given by the State after looking into the following factors: the density of population in the area where the plant is proposed to be established; the hospital facilities available in the area concerned to combat tragedies in case of industrial disasters; and, means and measures the industrial corporation abides by and voluntarily undertake to ensure workmen safety and environment protection.

An insight must be drawn from the Bhopal Gas Tragedy, where by the permission to establish a plant dealing in with the manufacturing of poisonous gas in a densely populated area such as that of the city of Bhopal with only a meagre of four hospitals operational, was taken from the State by bribing and corrupting the bureaucrats and politicians in power. What can be proposed is institution of necessary liability over the State in case such disasters take place. The appropriate punishment is the imputation of fines which must be unlimited in nature, the corporation must be asked to compensate the victims substantially not in lump-sum but on recurring terms. The State on the other hand must be made party to the crime for allowing the industrial corporation to establish its plant without taking due not of the implications concerned. If the industrial corporation is indicted for gross negligence manslaughter, then the State must also be made necessarily liable for the mishap resulting in the criminal conviction and there by the State must be punished with same strictness as with which the industrial corporation is punished. Such kind of convictions and sentencing regimes will serve two purposes- firstly, the State will be conscious enough in regards to its decision for the grant of permission to the industrial corporations for the establishment of plants dealing in with hazardous substances; and secondly, the corrupt bureaucrats and politicians will think twice before indulging in corrupt activities because of the fear of their respective names coming into the limelight, as the criminal conviction will take place not only against the corporation but also against the State with the respective government authorities granting permission to the malicious industrial corporations, as the party to the suit.

6.2.4. Doctrine of "Cumul": Necessary inspiration can be taken from the French Model, where by the "doctrine of cumul" is applicable to impute criminal liability over the corporation in general and over the corporate executives (acting within or outside the authority conferred on to them) in particular, for the crimes committed by the corporation in the capacity of an artificial legal person, having perpetual succession and common seal, with the management of the corporation forming its "determining mind and will". This doctrine is one of its kind, as on one hand, it holds the corporation liable and punishes it for the crimes committed by it in the capacity of a juridical person; and on the other hand, it lifts the corporate veil to determine the individuals forming the mind and will of the body corporate, to punish them for the irrational and unreasonable decisions taken by them, that led to the gross negligence manslaughter.

This doctrine of *cumul* has its origin in one of the un-reported cases of 1911 of the French jurisdiction. In this case, the victim was assaulted by the staff of a post office for having left the premises of the post office through an exit door which was temporarily closed for the use of the public, but the door was closed prematurely, that is before it officially was occasioned to be closed. The victim on exiting the post office premises through the door prematurely closed for 'public use' was thrashed by the post office staff. The staff broke the leg of the victim. When the case was brought before the administrative tribunal, the presiding members of the tribunal holding the post office (in its administrative capacity) liable announced conviction against the post office staff in concurrence. The administrative tribunal held that in cases of the present nomenclature a distinction needs to be drawn between *faute personnel* and *faute de service*. The administrative tribunal held that the door was prematurely closed and this was the fault of the post office (to be convicted in its administrative capacity) and the post-office-staff having assaulted the victim was liable in its personal capacity for acting violently and outside the course of their respective employment and authority conferred onto them.

Further it was held that the fault of the post-office-staff can be correlated with the fault of the post office (in its administrative capacity), as the post office in its administrative capacity was duty-bound to see that its officials worked within the authority conferred onto them, when they were acting during the course of their employment.[397] There by the doctrine of *cumul* was coined which simply meant "to hold concurrently liable".

Later in 1973, in another un-reported case, one of the courts in the state of France, upheld the conviction of a police officer with the State been made party to the crime. In this case the gun that given to the police officer by the State (in pursuance of rendering of his duties as a police officer), went off accidently when he was off the duty, there by killing one of his flatmates. The police officer was accused of the crime of homicide and hence was sentenced to punishment. The court, applying the doctrine of *cumul*, upheld that this case was maintainable in the administrative tribunal established for the specialised purpose of convicting the accused person(s) in the cases pertaining to public service. The court there by held that, "the State can be held liable for having allowed an off-duty officer to carry his gun with him, thereby creating danger for the third parties".[398]

Doctrine of *cumul* does not permit the victim to obtain damages twice. Rather it gives him a right to obtain judgement both in ordinary courts (often the criminal court in cases of personal injury) against the official for his personal fault and in the administrative courts against the administration for its service fault. Whichever of the two judgement debtor pays the damages awarded then has the right of action against the other for a contribution or complete indemnity. In terms of a body-corporate accused of a crime, the victim can hold the corporation liable generally and the individuals forming the mind and will of the corporation liable in particular. Thereafter, once the claim of the victim is settled, the corporation can sue the individuals forming the mind and will of

---

397 See: L. Neville Brown and John S. Bell, *French Administrative Law*, Oxford University Press, 1998 Edition, Chapter 8: The Substantive Law: The Principle of Administrative Liability, p.187

398 Ibid., p.188

the body corporate for having exercised authority beyond the limits in regards to which the authority was conferred to them.[399]

The doctrine of *cumul* has restricted its application to matter pertaining to "public services" in the French jurisdiction. However, the trend is fast a change with claims against non-state corporate entities fast rising and application of this doctrine taking place in manners innovative.

6.3. Remarks:

India at present needs a strong corporate manslaughter legislation which takes into consideration the necessary reasons owing to which corporate killings happen in India. Also, it must provide reasonable solutions to remedy the problems and must suggest preventive steps to avoid the problems that India faces today in the form of corporate gross negligence homicides. The legislation must focus itself in defining the terms "corporate manslaughter", "corporate homicide" and "corporate killings". The legislation must encourage imputation of criminal liability and sanctions in the nature of imprisonment imposed upon the "senior management" of the industrial corporation which is accused of taking and implementing the decisions which result in crimes in the nature of corporate killings. The term "senior management" must also be defined in definite terms to include all individuals that form the "determining mind and will" of the industrial corporation. The corporate manslaughter legislation must impose sanctions in the nature of publicity orders on to the flouting corporations, as the experience shows that when international media spread across the awareness in regards to the malicious activities undertaken by the Union Carbide Corporation, resulting in the Bhopal Gas Disaster, eventually a steep decline was witnessed in the value of the shares of company and as the corporate history has it, the company was taken-over by the Dow Chemicals. Thus, "publicity orders" can be seen as innovative means to sentence corporations for crimes committed by them.

The corporate manslaughter legislation must enlarge the definitional scope of the term "hazardous substances" and must provide that any corporation

---

399 Ibid., p.189-193

dealing with the production, manufacturing and sale of substance which are be perceived to harmful to the environment in general and the workmen in particular must come under the ambit of the Public Liability Insurance Act of 1991 read with the Environment Protection Act of 1986, and in case of industrial disasters occurring due to the gross negligence exercised by the industrial corporations, unlimited fines must be imposed onto them. The sentencing regime in the nature of "unlimited fines" must also extend to cases involving nuclear substances. The legislation enacted in 2010, the Civil Liability for Nuclear Damage Act, has provisions for providing compensation in cases of nuclear damage based on the "no-fault liability principle", but the manner in which the provisions providing for compensation are tabulated in the Act is fact confusing with leaving one question un-answered, that is, if the Act provides for absolute liability principle as the means for granting compensation then by virtue of the Oleum Gas Leakage judgement rendered by the Supreme Court of India, the deep-pocket theory must necessarily be read in complementation with the absolute liability principle and hence, the 'principal' in regards to the nuclear operations conducted being the State, it is the State that shall be held responsible and accountable; and the paying capacity of the State being un-limited then, will the amount of compensation to be paid will be un-limited? And if so, then the same is not reflected in the language of the Act.

The proposed corporate manslaughter legislation must provide for provisions in regards to black-listing the industrial corporations that do not comply with environmental protection legislation from government tenders and fiscal benefits that the government proposes, to be given to them, in the nature of relaxation from imposition of taxes and other reliefs in the nature of raw materials available at low cost; the Central and the State Government must be empowered to restrict the area of operations and the scope of operations of the flouting industrial corporations. Lastly, the intended legislation must provide provisions that encourage "reversal of burden of proof", that is, when a corporation is accused of a corporate crime, it shall be incumbent upon the corporation to prove that it is not at fault and hence should not be punished.

It is high time for India to realise that, like other developing countries, India too is a lucrative destination point for multi-national corporate giants to invade, so that both, the human as well as the natural resources can be plundered. Powerful implementation of existing laws is one end of the stream, innovative legislative measures in the nature enacting the corporate manslaughter law is the other end of the stream. It is better to take notice of the 'other end' before it's too late, as the rule of law must apply equally to natural persons as to the artificial persons and the norms of "justice, equity and good conscience" cannot be mere stars twinkling in the sky but must call culprits to order, with instant ability to catch the offender with punitive culpability to compel obedience. The researcher hopes that India takes necessary insights from its dynamic past and the present, so as to move towards a future that is bright and shining.

LIST OF ABBREVIATIONS

ACT	Australian Capital Territory
ATCA	Alien Tort Claim Act
CAG	Comptroller Auditor General of India
CBI	Central Bureau of Investigation
CII	Confederation of Indian Industry
DMRC	Delhi Metro Rail Corporation
DPP	Director of Public Prosecutions
EU	European Union
FERA	Foreign Exchange Regulation Act
IPC	Indian Penal Code
MES	Military Engineering Services
MNCs	Multi-National Corporations
MoEF	Ministry of Environment and Forests
NCDRC	National Consumer Disputes Redressal Commission
NHRC	National Human Rights Commission
NIOSH	National Institute for Occupational Safety and Health
NHTSA	National Highway Traffic Safety Association
OSHA	Occupational Safety and Health Act
PLIA	Public Liability Insurance Act

POSCO	Pohang Steel Company
RAW	Research Analysis Wing
SEBI	Securities and Exchange Board of India
SHRCs	State Human Rights Commissions
SLP	Special Leave Petition
TADA	Terrorist and Disruptive Activities Prevention Act
UCC	Union Carbide Corporation
UCIL	Uranium Corporation of India Limited
USAID	U.S. Agency for International Development

TABLE OF CASES

S. No.	CASELAWS REFERRED	CITATION
1.	*A.K. Khosla* v. *T.S. Venkatesan*	[1992 Cr LJ 1448]
2.	*Abdullahi* v. *Pfizer*	[2002 U.S. Dist. LEXIS 17436 (SDNY, 2002)]
3.	*Abrams* v. *Societe Nationale Des Chemins de fer Francais*	[175 F. Supp. 2d 423 (EDNY, 2001)]
4.	*Aguinda* v. *Texaco, Inc.*	[945 F. Supp. 625 (SDNY 1996)]
5.	*Anil Hada* v. *Indian Acrylic Limited*	[AIR 2000 SC 145]
6.	*Anz Grindlays Bank Limited* v. *Directorate of Enforcement*	[Appeal (Civil) 1748 of 1999]
7.	*Assistant Commissioner, Assessment II, Bangalore* v. *Velliappa Textiles Ltd.*	[(2004) 1 Comp. L.J. 21]
8.	*Associated Vendors Inc.* v. *Oakland Meat Co. Inc.*	[26 Cal Rptr 806, 813-815 (Cal Dist Ct App. 1962)]
9.	*Bacha F. Guzdar* v. *Commissioner of Income Tax*	[1955] 27 ITR 1 (SC)]
10.	*Badsha* v. *Income Tax officer*	[1987 (1) KLT 112]
11.	*Baker* v. *Bolton*	[(1808) 1 Camp 493: 10 R.R. 734]
12.	*Barnes* v. *Irwell Valley Water Board*	[(1939) 1 K.B. 21]
13.	*Batcheller* v. *Tunbrige Wells Gas Co.*	[(190) 84 L.T. 765]

14.	*Bodner* v. *Banque Paribas*	[114 F. Supp. 2d 117 (2000)]
15.	*Box* v. *Jubb*	[(1879) 4 Ex. D. 76]
16.	*C.K. Subramania Iyer* v. *T. Kunhikuttan*	[(1969) 3 SCC 64: AIR 1970 SC 376]
17.	*Centre for Public Interest Litigation* v. *U.O.I*	[WP(C) No. 681 of 2004]
18.	*Charan Lal Sahu* v. *Union of India*	[AIR 1990 SC 1480]
19.	*Charing Cross Electricity Co.* v. *Hydraulic Power Co.*	[(1914) 3 K.B. 772]
20.	*Collingwood* v. *Home and Colonial Stores Ltd.*	[(1936) All E.R. 200]
21.	*Commonwealth* v. *Fortner LP Gas Co.*	[610 S.W. 2d 941 (Ky. Ct. App. 1980)]
22.	*Crowhurst* v. *Amersham Burial Board*	[(1878) 4 Ex. D. 5]
23.	*DPP* v. *Kent and Sussex Contractors*	[(1944) K.B. 146]
24.	*Dr. Balram Prasad* v. *Dr. Kunal Saha*	[C.A. No. 2867 of 2012]
25.	*Daimler Co. Ltd.* v. *Continental Tyre & Rubber Co. Ltd.*	(1916) 2 AC 307
26.	*Davies* v. *Powell Duffryn Associated Collieries Ltd.*	[1942 AC 601: (1942) 1 All ER 657 (HL)]
27.	*Deo* v. *Unocal*	[963 F. Supp. 880 (CD Cal., 1997)]
28.	*Department of Labour* v. *Nelson Dive Centre Ltd.*	[DCR (2001) 1079, 1082]
29.	*Donoghue* v. *Stevenson*	[(1932) A.C. 562]
30.	*Eastern and South African Telephone Co.* v. *Cape Town Tramways Co.*	[(1936) A.C. 381]
31.	*Escola* v. *Coca-Cola Bottling Co.*	[24 Cal. 2d 453, 150 P. 2d 436]
32.	*Estate of Himoud Saed Atban et. al.*v. *Blackwater*	[611 F. Supp. 2d 1 (DDC, 2009)]
33.	*F.B. Taraporawala* v. *Bayer India Ltd.*	[(1996) 6 SCC 58]
34.	*Firth* v. *Bowling Iron Co.*	[(1878) C.P.D. 254]

35.	*Fletcher* v. *Ryland*	[(1866) L.R. 1 Ex. 265]
36.	*Flores* v. *Southern Peru Copper*	[253 F. Supp. 2d 510 (SDNY, 2002)]
37.	*Foster* v. *Warblington Urban Council*	[(1906) 1 K.B. 648]
38.	*Gilford Motor Co. Ltd.* v. *Horne*	[(1933) Ch. 935]
39.	*Gobald Motor Service Ltd.* v. *R.M.K. Veluswami*	[AIR 1962 SC 1]
40.	*Green* v. *Chelsea Waterworks Co.*	[(1894) 70 L.T. 547]
41.	*H.L. Bolton Engineering* v. *T.J. Graham*	[(1957) 1 Q.B. 159]
42.	*Haider Muhsin Saleh* v. *Titan Corp.*	[436 F. Supp. 2d 55 (DDC, 2006)]
43.	*Hamilton* v. *Whitehead*	[(1988) 166 CLR 121]
44.	*Hanoch Tel-Oren* v. *Libyan Arab Republic*	[726 F. 2d 774 (1984)]
45.	*Haseldine* v. *Daw*	[(1941) 2 K.B. 343]
46.	*Herschtal* v. *Stewart & Ardern*	[(1940) 1 K.B. 155]
47.	*Hoare & Co.* v. *Mc. Alpine*	[(1893) 1 Ch. 167]
48.	*Howard* v. *Furness Houldar Ltd.*	[(1936) 2 All E.R. 296]
49.	*In re Holocaust Victim Assets Litigation*	[105 F. Supp. 2d 139 (EDNY, 2000)]
50.	*In re South African Apartheid Litigation*	[2004 U.S. Dist. LEXIS 23944]
51.	*In re Xe Services Alien Tort Litigation*	[665 F. Supp. 2d 569 (2009)]
52.	*Indian Council for Enviro-Legal Action* v. *U.O.I*	[AIR 1996 SC 1446]
53.	*Iridium India Telecom Ltd.* v. *Motorola Inc.*	[(2011) 1 SCC 74]
54.	*J.K. Industries Ltd.* v. *Chief Inspector of Factories & Boilers*	[(1996) 6 SCC 665]
55.	*Jackson* v. *Watson*	[(1909) 2 K.B. 193]
56.	*Janki Bai Sahu* v. *UCC*	[418 F. Supp. 2d 407 (2005)]

57.	*Joki Ram* v. *Naresh Kanta*	[AIR 1977 P&H 214]
58.	*Jones* v. *Llanrwst U.D.C.*	[(1911) 1 Ch. 393]
59.	*Kalpanath Rai* v. *State*	[(1997) 8 SCC 732]
60.	*Keshub Mahindra* v. *State of Madhya Pradesh*	[(1996) 6 SCC 129]
61.	*Khulumani* v. *Barclay National Bank Ltd.*	[504 F. 3d 254 (2007)]
62.	*Krishna Gopal* v. *State of M.P.*	[(1986) CRLJ 396 (MP)]
63.	*Lee* v. *Lee's Air Farming Ltd.*	[1961] UKPC 33
64.	*Lennard's Carrying Co.* v. *Asiatic Petroleum Co.*	[(1915) A.C. 705]
65.	*Linework Ltd.* v. *Department of Labour*	[(2001) 2 NZLR 639]
66.	*M.C. Mehta* v. *Kamal Nath*	[1996 1 SCC 38]
67.	*M.C. Mehta* v. *U.O.I*	[AIR 1987 SC 1086]
68.	*M.C.D* v. *Subhagwanti*	[AIR 1966 SC 1750]
69.	*M.P. Electricity Board* v. *Shail Kumar*	[AIR 2002 SC 551]
70.	*Macquarie Bank Ltd.* v. *Sixty-Fourth Throne Pty Ltd.*	[(1998) 3 VR 133]
71.	*Madhya Pradesh State Electricity Board, Jabalpur* v. *Collector, Mandla*	[AIR 2003 MP 156]
72.	*Manchester Corporation* v. *Farnworth*	[(1930) A.C. 171]
73.	*Mar Themotheous* v. *Santosh Raj*	[2001 LLR 164 (Ker HC DB)]
74.	*Miller* v. *Addie & Sons Collieries*	[1934 S.C. 150]
75.	*Modi Industries Limited* v. *B.C. Goel*	[144 ITR 496 (1983)]
76.	*Moore* v. *Bresler*	[(1944) 2 All E.R. 515]
77.	*Mousell Bros.* v. *London and North Western Railway*	[(1917) 2 K.B. 836, 845]
78.	*Nathulal* v. *State of M.P.*	[AIR 1966 SC 43]
79.	*National Telephone Co.* v. *Baker*	[(1893) 2 Ch. 186]
80.	*New York Central & Hudson River R.R. Co.* v. *United States*	[212 U.S. 481 (1909)]

81.	*North Western Utilities Ltd.* v. *London Guarantee and Accident Co.*	[(1936) A.C. 108]
82.	*Nydam* v. *The Queen*	[(1977) VR 430]
83.	*Oswal Vanaspati & Allied Industries* v. *State of Uttar Pradesh*	[(1993) 1 Comp. L.J. 172]
84.	*P.C. Agarwala* v. *Payment of Wages Inspector*	[(2005) 63 SCL 109 (SC)]
85.	*Padmadevi* v. *Kabal Singh*	[AIR 1985 Bom. 357]
86.	*Parke* v. *Daily News Ltd.*	[(1962) 2 All ER 929]
87.	*People* v. *Rochester Ry. and Light Co.*	[195 N.Y. 102 (N.Y. 1909)]
88.	*Ponting* v. *Noakes*	[(1894) 2 Q.B. 281]
89.	*R* v. *Adomako*	[(1994) 3 All ER 79]
90.	*R* v. *B & Q PLC*	[(2005) EWCA Crim. 2297]
91.	*R* v. *Balfour Beatty Rail Infrastructure Services Ltd.*	[(2006) EWCA Crim. 1586; (2007) Bus LR 77]
92.	*R* v. *Denbo Pty Ltd.*	[Supreme Court of Victoria, Unreported, 14 June 1994]
93.	*R* v. *Evans (Gemma)*	[(2009) EWCA Crim. 650; (2009) 1 W.L.R. 1999]
94.	*R* v. *F. Howe and Son (Engineers) Ltd.*	[(1999) IRLR 434]
95.	*R* v. *ICR Haulage Ltd.*	[(1944) K.B. 551]
96.	*R* v. *Murray Wright Ltd.*	[(1970) NZLR 476]
97.	*R* v. *Rollco Screw and Rivet Co. Ltd.*	[(1999) IRLR 439]
98.	*R* v. *Sorsky*	[(1944) 2 All E.R. 333]
99.	*Ratnham Chemical Works* v. *Belvedere Fish Gauno Co.*	[(1921) 2 A.C. 465]
100.	*Re, Sir Dinshaw Maneckjee Pettit*	[(1927) 29 BOMLR 447]
101.	*Res. Foundation for Science* v. *Union of India*	[2003 (8) SCALE 258]
102.	*Read* v. *Croydon Corporation*	[(1938) 4 All E.R. 631]

103.	*Read* v. *Lyons & Co.*	[(1947) A.C. 156; (1946) 2 All E.R. 471]
104.	*Richards* v. *Lothian*	[(1913) A.C. 263]
105.	*Ryland* v. *Fletcher*	[(1868) L.R. 3 H.L. 330]
106.	*Salomon* v. *Salomon & Co. Ltd.*	[(1897) AC 22]
107.	*Sajida Bano* v. *UCC*	[2000 U.S. Dist. LEXIS 12326]
108.	*Sharpe* v. *E.T. Sweepings & Son Ltd.*	[(1963) 1 W.L.R. 665]
109.	*Shiffman* v. *Graud Priory*	[(1936) 1 All E.R. 557]
110.	*Standard Chartered Bank* v. *Directorate of Enforcement*	[AIR 2005 SC 2622]
111.	*State* v. *Gilmore*	[1852 WL 2109 (Sup. Ct. 1852)]
112.	*State* v. *Pacific Powder Co.*	[226 Or. 502 (Or. 1961)]
113.	*State* v. *Richard Knutson Inc.*	[537 N.W. 2d 420 (Wis. Ct. App. 1995)]
114.	*State* v. *The Morris and Essex R.R.*	[1852 WL 3499 (Sup. Ct. 1852)]
115.	*State of Madras* v. *C.V. Parekh*	[AIR 1971 SC 447]
116.	*State of Maharashtra* v. *Jugamander Lal*	[AIR 1966 SC 940]
117.	*State of Maharashtra* v. *Mayer Hans George*	[AIR 1965 SC 72]
118.	*State of Maharashtra* v. *Syndicate Transport*	[1963 Bom LR 197]
119.	*Stennett* v. *Hancock*	[(1939) 2 All E.R. 578]
120.	*T.C. Balakrishnan* v. *T.R. Subramanian*	[AIR 1968 Kerala 151]
121.	*Tenant* v. *Goldwin*	[(1704) 1 Salk, 360]
122.	*Tennent* v. *Earl of Glasgow*	[(1864) 2 M (H.L.) 22]
123.	*Tesco Supermarkets Ltd.* v. *Nattrass*	[(1972) A.C. 153]
124.	*The Presbyterian Church of Sudan* v. *Talisman Energy*	[244 F. Supp. 2d 289 (SDNY, 2003)]

125.	*Tom Beanal* v. *Freeport-McMoran, Inc.*	[197 F 3d 161 (5th Cir. 1999)]
126.	*Triplex Glass Safety* v. *Lancegay Safety Glass*	[(1939) 2 K.B. 395]
127.	*U.S.* v. *Peters*	[732 F. 2d 1004, 1008 n.6 (1st Cir. 1984)]
128.	*U.S.* v. *Stevens*	[909 F. 2d 431(11th Cir. 1990)]
129.	*U.O.I.* v. *Nathmal Hansaria*	[(1997) CPJ 20 (NC)]
130.	*U.P. Pollution Control Board* v. *Modi Distillery*	[(1987) 3 SCR 798]
131.	*Union Carbide Corporation* v. *Union of India*	[AIR 1990 SC 273]
132.	*Union Carbide Corporation* v. *Union of India*	[AIR 1992 SC 248]
133.	*United States* v. *Union Supply*	[215 U.S. 50 (1909)]
134.	*United States* v. *Van Schaick*	[134 F. 592 (S. Dist. N.Y. Cir. Ct. 1904)]
135.	*Vaughn & Sons, Inc.* v. *State*	[737 S.W. 2d 805 (Tex. Crim. App. 1987) (en banc)]
136.	*Vellore Citizen Welfare Forum* v. *U.O.I*	[AIR 1996 SC 2715]
137.	*Wang Xiaoning* v. *Yahoo!*	[2007 U.S. Dist. LEXIS 97566 (ND Cal.)]
138.	*West* v. *Bristol Tramways Co.*	[(1908) 2 K.B. 14]
139.	*Wiwa* v. *Royal Dutch Petroleum Co.*	[1998 U.S. Dist. LEXIS 23064]
140.	*Workmen employed in Associated Rubber Industries Ltd.* v. *Associated Rubber Industries Ltd.*	[AIR 1986 SC 1]

Bibliography

Statutory Legislation and Reports

U.K.

- The Corporate Manslaughter and Corporate Homicide Act of 2007
- The Criminal Justice Act of 2003
- The Defective Premises Act of 1972
- The Health and Safety at Work Act of 1974
- The Occupiers' Liability Act of 1957
- The Occupiers' Liability Act of 1984
- The Railway Clauses Consolidation Act of 1845
- The U.K. Law Commission Report of 1996
- U.K. Conservative Government (Report of 1996), *Legislating the Criminal Code*: *Involuntary Manslaughter*

U.S.

- The Clean Air Act of 1963
- The Clean Water Act of 1972
- The Federal Food, Drug & Cosmetic Act of 1938
- The Federal Insecticide, Fungicide & Rodenticide Act of 1910
- The Occupational Safety and Health Act of 1970
- The Safe Drinking Water Act of 1974

New Zealand

- The Agricultural Workers Act of 1977
- The Coal Mines Act of 1979
- The Crimes Act of 1908
- The Crimes Act of 1961

- The Criminal Code of 1893
- The Health and Safety in Employment Act of 1992
- The Interpretation Act of 1999
- The Sentencing Act of 2002

Canada

- The Westray Act of 2005

Australia

- The Commonwealth Criminal Code Act of 1995
- The Crimes (Industrial Manslaughter) Act of 2003 [Australian Capital Territory]
- The Crimes Act of 1900 [New South Wales]
- The Criminal Code Act of 2002 [Australian Capital Territory]

India

- The Air (Prevention and Control of Pollution) Act of 1981
- The Bhopal Gas Leak Disaster (Processing of Claims) Act of 1985
- The Biological Diversity Act of 2002
- The Biomedical Waste (Management and Handling) Rules of 1998
- The Bonded Labour System (Abolition) Act of 1976
- The Chemical Accidents (Emergency Planning, Preparedness and Response) Rules of 1996
- The Child Labour (Prohibition and Regulation) Act of 1986
- The Civil Liability for Nuclear Damage Act of 2010
- The Companies (Amendment) Act of 2000
- The Companies (Amendment) Act of 2013
- The Companies Act of 1956
- The Consumer Protection Act of 1986
- The Contract Labour (Abolition and Regulation) Act of 1970
- The Criminal Procedure Code of 1973
- The Drugs Act of 1940
- The Employees Provident Fund and Miscellaneous Provisions Act of 1952

- The Employees State Insurance Act of 1948
- The Environment Protection Act of 1986
- The Equal Remuneration Act of 1972
- The Factories Act of 1948
- The Foreign Exchange Regulation Act of 1973
- The Forest (Conservation) Act of 1980
- The Forest (Conservation) Act of 1980
- The General Clauses Act of 1897
- The Hazardous Waste (Management and Handling) Rules of 1989
- The Hazardous Wastes (Management, Handling and Trans-boundary Movement) Rules of 2008
- The Income Tax Act of 1961
- The Indian Contract Act of 1872
- The Indian Penal Code of 1860
- The Industrial Disputes Act of 1947
- The Insecticides Act of 1968
- The Manufacture, Storage and Import of Hazardous Chemical Rules of 1989
- The Maternity Benefits Act of 1961
- The Mines Act of 1952
- The Motor Vehicles Act of 1988
- The Municipal Solid Waste (Management and Handling) Rules of 2000
- The National Environment Appellate Authority Act of 1997
- The National Environment Tribunal Act of 1995
- The National Green Tribunal Act of 2010
- The Negotiable Instruments Act of 1881
- The Payment of Gratuity Act of 1972
- The Payment of Wages Act of 1936
- The Poisons Act of 1919
- The Prevention of Food Adulteration Act of 1954
- The Protection of Human Rights Act of 1993
- The Public Liability Insurance Act of 1991
- The Recycled Plastic Manufacture and Use Rules of 1999
- The Terrorist and Disruptive Activities Prevention Act of 1978
- The Trade Unions Act of 1926

- The Unorganised Workers' Social Security Act of 2008
- The Water (Prevention and Control of Pollution) Act of 1974
- The Water (Prevention and Control of Pollution) Cess Act of 1977
- The Wild Life (Protection) Act of 1972
- The Workmen's Compensation Act of 1923

Books

- Andrew Sanders, Richard Young & Mandy Burton, *Criminal Justice,* Oxford University Press, Fourth Edition, Chapter 7: Prosecutions.
- D.S. Chopra & Nishant Arora, *Company Law: Piercing the Corporate Veil,* Eastern Law House, 2013 Edition, Chapter 7: A Comparative Study.
- David Kershaw, *Company Law in Context,* Oxford University Press, 2009 Edition, Chapter Four: Corporate Actions.
- Derek French, Stephen Mayson & Christopher Ryan, *Company Law,* Oxford University Press, 27th Edition (2010-2011), Chapter 19: Acting For a Company- Agency & Attribution
- Dr. Girjesh Shukla, *Criminology: Crime Causation, Sentencing and Rehabilitation of Victims,* Lexis Nexis Publication, 2013, Chapter 8: Sentencing and Penal Policy.
- Dr. Indranil Bhattacharyya, *Environment Laws,* Kamal Law House, 2009 Edition, Chapter 9: Conclusion and Suggestions
- Dr. Justice A.R. Lakshmanan, *The Judge Speaks,* Universal Law Publishing Co., 2009 Edition, Corporate Governance
- Dr. K.N. Chandrasekharan Pillai, *Criminal Procedure,* Eastern Book Company, Fifth Edition, Chapter 14: Trial Procedures- Courts and Parties
- Dr. Surya Deva, *Regulating Corporate Human Rights Violations: Humanizing Business,* Routledge Research In Human Rights Law, Routledge Publications, 2012 Edition, Chapter 4:Existing regulatory initiatives- An evaluation of (in)adequacy
- Eamonn Carrabine, Pam Cox, Maggy Lee, Ken Plummer & Nigel South, *Criminology: A Sociological Introduction*, Routledge Publications, Second Edition, Chapter 13: Organisational and Professional Forms of Crime.

- Eugene Mc Laughlin & John Muncie, *The Sage Dictionary of Criminology,* Sage Publications, Second Edition
- Frank E. Hagan, *Introduction to Criminology: Theories, Methods, and Criminal Behaviour,* Sage Publications Inc., Seventh Edition, Chapter 10: White Collar Crimes.
- Frank Schmalleger, *Criminology: A Brief Introduction,* Pearson Education Inc. 2011, Chapter 10: White- Collar and Organised Crime.
- John M. Martin and Anne T. Romano, *Multinational Crime- Terrorism, Espionage, Drug & Arms Trafficking,* Sage Publications- 1992 Edition, Chapter 5: Approaching the Study of Multinational Systemic Crime.
- John Braithwaite, *Corporate Crime in the Pharmaceutical Industry,* Routledge and Kegan Paul, First Edition, London, 1984
- Justice V.R. Krishna Iyer, *The Indian Law: Dynamic Dimensions of the Abstract,* Universal Law Publishing Co., 2009 Edition, Wounded Nature vs. Human Future.
- L. Neville Brown and John S. Bell, *French Administrative Law,* Oxford University Press, 1998 Edition, Chapter 8: The Substantive Law: The Principle of Administrative Liability.
- Kamala Sankaran, Mahavir Singh, Anju Vali Tikoo, Alok Sharma & Vageshwari Deswal, *Jurisprudence II: Concepts,* Case Material, Faculty of Law, University of Delhi, January 2013.
- Katherine S. Williams, *Textbook on Criminology,* Oxford University Press, Fifth Edition, Chapter 3: Public conceptions and misconceptions of crime.
- Larry Siegel, *Criminology,* Wadsworth Publishers, Seventh Edition, Chapter 13: White Collar and Organised Crime.
- Len Sealy & Sarah Worthington, *Cases and Materials in Company Law,* Oxford University Press, 9th Edition, Chapter 3: Corporate Activity and Legal Liability.
- Mohammad Naseem, *Environment Law in India,* Wolters Kluwer Law & Business, 2011 Edition, Part I: Pollution Control, Chapter 8: Radiation and Vibrations (Nuclear and Non-nuclear)
- P. Leelakrishnan, *Environmental Law in India,* Lexis Nexis Publication, Third Edition, Chapter 9: Environmental Hazards- Mass Tort Action
- P.M. Prasad [Edited by: Pushpam Kumar & B. Sudhakara Reddy], *Ecology and Human Well- Being,* Sage Publications, 2007 Edition,

Chapter 18: Environmental Protection- The Role of Regulatory System in India

- Paul Shrivastava, *Bhopal: Anatomy of a Crises,* Massachusetts, Ballinger Publishing Co., 1987
- Peter Joyce, *Criminal Justice: An Introduction to Crime and the Criminal Justice System,* William Publishing, Chapter 2: Crime and Crime Prevention.
- Prachi Manekar, *Insights into the new company law,* Lexis Nexis Publication, 2013 Edition, Chapter XXI: Corporate Criminal Liability
- Professor K.D. Gaur; *Criminal Law- Cases and Materials,* Lexis Nexis Publication, 7th Edition, Chapter 4: Vicarious Liability
- R.K. Bangia, *Law of Torts,* Allahabad Law Agency, Nineteenth Edition, 2006, Chapter 16: Rules of Strict and Absolute Liability.
- R.W.M. Dias, *Jurisprudence,* Fifth Edition, 1994
- Ronald J. Berger, Marvin D. Free Jr. & Patricia Searles, *Crime, Justice and Society: An Introduction to Criminology,* Second Edition, Viva Books Private Limited, Chapter 6: Corporate and Organized Crime.
- Shyam Divan & Armin Rosencranz, *Environmental Law and Policy in India,* Oxford University Press, Second Edition, Chapter 3: Constitutional and Legislative Provisions
- Stephen Girvin, Sandra Frisby and Alastair Hudson, *Charlesworth's Company Law,* Thomas Reuters (Legal) Limited 2010, Eighteenth Edition, Chapter 23: Criminal and Civil Liability of Companies.
- Zia Mody, *10 Judgements That Changed India*, The Penguin Books Ltd. 2013, Chapter 5- Justice Delayed: The Loss Through Law.

<u>Articles from the Journals</u>

- *Access to Justice: Human Rights Abuses Involving Corporations,* A Project of the International Commission of Jurists, India, International Commission of Jurists, Chapter 1: Legal Liability for Corporations Under Indian Law
- Amnesty International, *Clouds of Injustice: Bhopal Disaster 20 years on,* Amnesty International, London, 2004
- Amnesty International, *Don't Mine Us Out Of Existence: Bauxite Mine and Refinery Devastate Lives in India,* ASA 20/001/2010, February 2010

- Amnesty International, *Summary of 'Clouds of Injustice Bhopal Disaster 20 years on,* ASA 20/104/2004 dated 29th November, 2004
- Ananthi Bharadwaj, NALSAR University, Hyderabad, *Corporate Manslaughter and Corporate Homicide Act, 2007,* National Law School of India Review, Volume 21(1), 2009
- Canfield, *Corporate Responsibility for Crimes,* Columbia Law Review, No.14, 1914
- Celia Wells, *Corporate Criminal Liability: Developments in Europe and Beyond,* 2001, 39 (7) Law Society Journal 62
- Celia Wells, *Corporate Manslaughter: Why Does Reform Matter?;* (2006) 122 South African L.J. 648
- Dalal Praveen, *Corporate Entity in Existing Legal System- Its Rights and Liabilities under the Constitution and other Enactments,* (2004) 61 CLA 96 (Mag)
- David J. Reilly, *Murder, Inc.: The Criminal Liability of Corporations for Homicide,* 18 SETON HALL L. REV. 378, 381 (1988)
- David Ormerod & Richard Taylor, *The Corporate Manslaughter and Corporate Homicide Act,* (2008) 8 Criminal L.R. 589
- Dinham and Sarangi, *The Bhopal Gas Tragedy of 1984 to? The Evasion of Corporate Responsibility,* Environment and Urbanization, Volume 14, 2002
- Dr. Surya Deva, *From 3/12 to 9/11: Future of Human Rights?;* Economic and Political Weekly, Volume 39, 2004
- Fran Oise Tulkens, *Human Rights, Rhetoric or Reality?,* European Review, Volume 9, 2001
- Francis, *Criminal Responsibility of the Corporation,* (1924) 18 LR 305
- Gobert, *The Corporate Manslaughter and Corporate Homicide Act of 2007,* [(2008) 71 MLR 413]
- Human Rights Council, *Guiding Principles on Business and Human Rights: Implementing the United Nations "Protect, Respect and Remedy" Framework,* A/HRC/17/31, 21st of March, 2011
- Ian M. Ramsay & David B. Noakes, *Piercing the Corporate Veil in Australia,* (2001) 19 Company and Securities Law Journal
- Ilona Bray, Richard Stim and Nolo, *Defective Products that Changed the Law,* The Lawyers Update: Magazine for Legal Professionals &

Students, Universal Book Traders, Volume XIX, Part 10, October 2013

- John Kluver, *Entity* v. *Enterprise Liability: Issues for Australia*, (2005) 37 Connecticut Law Review
- Karen Wheelwright, *Corporate Liability for Workplace Deaths and Injuries- Reflecting on Victoria's Laws in the light of the Esso Longford Explosion,* (2002) 7 Deakin Law Review 323
- Report of the International Law Commission, 35 U.N. GAOR, Supp. (No.10), U.N. Doc A/35/10 (1980)
- Richard M. Dunn, *Criminalization of Negligent Acts by Employees of U.S. and Foreign Corporations,* 69 DEF. COUNS. J. 17, 18 (January 2002)
- Rita Aryan, *Latest Supreme Court Judgements- Soft Drinks: Preserves of Pesticides,* The Lawyers Update: Magazine for Legal Professionals & Students, Universal Book Traders, Volume XIX, Part 12, December 2013
- Robert B. Thompson, *Piercing the Corporate Veil: An Empirical Study,* 76 Cornell Law Review 1048 (1991)
- S. Murlidhar, *Unsettling Truths, Untold Tales: The Bhopal Gas Tragedy Victims,* "Twenty Years" of Courtroom Struggles for Justice, IELRC Working Paper 2004-2005
- Sean Bajkowski & Kimberly R. Thompson (Note), *Corporate Counsel Liability,* 34 AM. CRIM. L. REV. 445 (1997)
- Stephen Griffin, *Corporate Killing- the Corporate Manslaughter and Corporate Homicide Act of 2007,* [2009] L.M.C.L.Q. 73
- Stephen M. Bainbridge, *Abolishing Veil Piercing,* (2001) 26 Journal of Corporation Law 510

Miscellaneous

Aaron Sweet, *Making a Killing: A Separate Corporate Manslaughter Offence for New Zealand?;* Faculty of Law, University of Otago, Dunedin, 2006, http://www.otago.ac.nz/law/research/journals/otago036249.pdf

Ajkia Timfoldgyar Disaster, *The New York Times*, http://www.nytimes.com/2010/10/12/world/europe/12hungary.html?_r=2&pagewanted=all&, Visited on: 03-06-2014

Andrew Malone, *The GM Genocide: Thousands of Indian farmers are committing suicide after using genetically modified crops,* 3 November 2008, http://www.dailymail.co.uk/news/article-1082559/The-GM-genocide-Thousands-Indian-farmers-committing-suicide-using-genetically-modified-crops.html, Visited on: 16-06-2014

Angela Gregory, *Corporate manslaughter law the answer?,* 10th April 2012, http://insider.thomsonreuters.co.nz/2012/04/corporatemanslaughter/comment-page-1/, Visited on: 25-06-2014

Beas River Tragedy: 7 Key Points, *The Times of India,* 10 June 2014, http://timesofindia.indiatimes.com/india/Beas-river-tragedy-7-key-points/articleshow/36357851.cms, Visited on: 14-06-2014

Beas Tragedy: Case Against Dam Project Authorities, Search On, *The Times of India*, 11 June 2014, http://timesofindia.indiatimes.com/india/Beas-tragedy-Case-against-dam-project-authorities-search-on/articleshow/36387471.cms, Visited on: 14-06-2014

Bhopal Case: A Corporate Manslaughter, http://www.ndtv.com/article/india/bhopal-case-a-corporate-manslaughter-sushma-swaraj-43679, Visited on: 09-06-2014

Bhopal Gas Victims Used As Guinea Pigs For Drug Trials, 17th of December, 2013, http://timesofindia.indiatimes.com/india/Bhopal-gas-victims-used-as-guinea-pigs-for-drug-trials/articleshow/27495772.cms, Visited on: 08-07-2014

Case against Coca-Cola Kerala State: India, http://www.righttowater.info/rights-in-practice/legal-approaches/legal-approach-case-studies/case-against-coca-cola-kerala-state-india/, Visited on: 16-06-2014

Celia Wells, *The Millennium Bug and Corporate Criminal Liability,* 2 J.I.L.T. (1999), http://www2.warwick.ac.uk/fac/soc/law/elj/jilt/1999_2/wells/, Visited on: 23-06-2014

Congressional Research Service, Corporate Criminal Liability: An Overview of Federal Law, http://fas.org/sgp/crs/misc/R43293.pdf, Visited on: 23-06-2014

Corporate Manslaughter & Health and Safety Offences Causing Death, http://sentencingcouncil.judiciary.gov.uk/docs/web_guideline_on_corporate_manslaughter_accessible.pdf, Visited on: 23-06-2014

Corporate Manslaughter, http://www.kensingtonswan.com/KSPublicWeb/media/Documents/Corporate-Manslaughter.pdf, Visited on: 23-06-2014

Dhananjay Mahapatra, *SC Reopens Bhopal Case, Notices to Accused on Homicide Charge,* The Times of India, 1st of September, 2010, http://articles.timesofindia.indiatimes.com/2010-09-01/india/28217038_1_s-b-majmudar-curative-petition-devadatt-kamat, Visited on: 07-07-2014

Dr. Vandana Shiva, *The Seeds of Suicide: How Monsanto Destroys Farming,* Global Research, 13 March 2014, http://www.globalresearch.ca/the-seeds-of-suicide-how-monsanto-destroys-farming/5329947, Visited on: 16-06-2014

Ethan A. Huff, *Monsanto connected to at least 200,000 suicides in India throughout past decade,* 4 January 2011, http://www.naturalnews.com/030913_Monsanto_suicides.html, Visited on: 16-06-2014

Gary Slapper, *Corporate manslaughter Law is a vast improvement,* The Times, 18 July 2007, http://www.thetimes.co.uk/tto/law/article2209921.ece, Visited on: 03-05-2014

Gary Slapper, *Corporate Manslaughter,* (1993) 2 Social and Legal Studies 423, http://oro.open.ac.uk/20975/2/1535A240.pdf, Visited on: 25-05-2014

House Bill 1144, 114th Gen. Assembly, 2d Sess. (Ind. 2006), http://www.in.gov/apps/lsa/session/billwatch/billinfo?year=2006&session=1&request=getBill&docno=1144, Visited on: 20-06-2014

Human Rights Watch, *The Enron Corporation: Corporate Complicity in Human Rights Violations(1999),* http://www.hrw.org/reports/1999/enron/, Visited on: 18-07-2014

Impact of POSCO-India's Project on the lives of local people in Jagatsinghpur, Odisha, India, http://www.escr-net.org/sites/default/files/briefing-note-posco-india-private-ltd.pdf, Visited on: 17-06-2014

Indian Committee of the Netherlands; *Monsanto, Unilever use child labour in India,* 14 May 2003, http://www.indianet.nl/a030514.html, Visited on: 16-06-2014

Jackie Brown-Hayson, *Does New Zealand need a new crime of corporate manslaughter?;* Safeguard- Thomas Reuters, http://www.safeguard.co.nz/backissues/136-story1.asp, Visited on: 25-06-2014

Jim Yardley, Report on Deadly Factory Collapse in Bangladesh Finds Widespread Blame, *The New York Times*, 22 May 2013, http://www.nytimes.com/2013/05/23/world/asia/report-on-bangladesh-building-collapse-finds-widespread-blame.html?_r=0, Visited on: 15-06-2014

John Vidal, *Indian Coal Power Plants kill 120,000 people a year, says Greenpeace,* The Guardian, 10 March 2013, http://www.theguardian.com/world/2013/mar/10/india-coal-plants-emissions-greenpeace, Visited on: 15-06-2014

Jonathan Hills, *Coca-Cola in India: A Case Study*, CSR Asia Weekly, http://csr-asia.com/csr-asia-weekly-news-detail.php?id=4146, Visited on: 16-06-2014

Julian Borger, *Rumsfeld 'offered help to Saddam',* The Guardian, 31 December 2002, http://www.theguardian.com/world/2002/dec/31/iraq.politics, Visited on: 16-06-2014

Keith N. Hylton, *The Law and Economics of Products Liability,* Boston University School of Law, http://www.bu.edu/law/faculty/scholarship/workingpapers/documents/HyltonK072512_000.pdf, Visited on: 17-06-2014

Landmark Corporate Manslaughter Cases, http://www.cqms-ltd.co.uk/news/landmark_corporate_manslaughter_case.html, Visited on: 14-06-2014

Laurel J. Harbour and Natalya Y. Johnson, *Can-a-corporation-commit-manslaughter? Recent developments in the United Kingdom and the United States,* Shook Hardy & Bacon LLP, Defence Counsel Journal- July 2006, http://www.shb.com/practiceareas/International/Pubs/Can%20a%20Corporation%20Commit%20Manslaughter.pdf

London Sports Club Sentenced For Corporate Manslaughter Over Banana Boat Ride, *The Crown Prosecution Service,* 22 November 2013, http://www.cps.gov.uk/news/latest_news/london_sports_club_sentenced_for_corporate_manslaughter/, Visited on: 14-06-2014

M. Suchitra, *Will Kolar become India's nuclear waste dump-yard?;* Down to Earth, 26 November 2012, http://www.downtoearth.org.in/content/will-kolar-become-indias-nuclear-waste-dumpyard, Visited on: 03-08-2014

Martin Bright, *Fury over delay to 'corporate killing' law,* The Guardian, 21 July 2002, http://www.theguardian.com/politics/2002/jul/21/immigrationpolicy.observerpolitics, Visited on: 21-06-2014

Metro Crash, *The Frontline,* Volume 26, Issue 16, August 01-14, 2009, http://www.frontline.in/static/html/fl2616/stories/20090814261604200.htm, Visited on: 05-05-2014

Ministry of Environment and Forests, *Press Release: Bhopal Environmental Remediation Oversight Committee Constituted,* 7th of July, 2010, http://envfor.nic.in/sites/default/files/PM_Bhopal-1.pdf, Visited on: 07-07-2014

NCDRC Judgement 2014: Enhanced Compensation using Anuradha, http://pbtindia.com/wp-content/uploads/2014/02/NCDRC-Judg-2014-

Enhanced-compensation-using-Anuradha-SC-judg.pdf, Visited on: 17-06-2014

Neil Hodge, *British Government accedes to demands for new corporate killing offence,* 25 February 2002, http://www.wsws.org/en/articles/2002/02/man-f25.html, Visited on: 16-06-2014

Parliament of Australia, *Workplace Death and Serious Injury: A Snapshot of Legislative Developments in Australia and Overseas,* Research Brief no. 7, 2004-2005, http://www.aph.gov.au/library/Pubs/rb/2004-05/05rb07.htm

Peter Thompson, *Implications of Corporate Manslaughter Bill,* The Faculty of Finance and Management, http://www.icaew.com/en/technical/legal-and-regulatory/business-crime-and-misconduct/the-corporate-manslaughter-and-corporate-homicide-act-2007/fm128-legal-implications-of-the-corporate-manslaughter-bill, Visited on: 20-06-2014

Philip Mattera, *Dow Chemical: Corporate Rap Sheet*, Corporate Research Project, http://www.corp-research.org/dowchemical, Visited on: 16-06-2014

Prafulla Das, *POSCO Land Acquisition: Police Arrest Agitating Villagers,* The Hindu, 3 February 2013, http://www.thehindu.com/news/national/other-states/posco-land-acquisition-police-arrest-agitating-villagers/article4374896.ece, Visited on: 17-06-2014

Product Regulation: Sulfanilamide Disaster http://www.fda.gov/aboutfda/whatwedo/history/productregulation/sulfanilamidedisaster/default.htm, visited on: 26-06-2014

Radha Venkatesan, *Is India a global trash can?;* The Times of India, 24th of April, 2010, http://timesofindia.indiatimes.com/india/Is-India-a-global-trash-can/articleshow/5851954.cms, Visited on: 09-07-2014

Rebecca Samervel, *Record Rs.6 crore payout for lift accident in Delhi,* The Times of India, 28 January 2014, http://timesofindia.indiatimes.com/city/mumbai/Record-Rs-6cr-payout-for-lift-accident-in-Delhi/articleshow/29460794.cms, Visited on: 18-06-2014

Richard, *Manslaughter Charges Filed in Vedanta Chimney Case*, 14 January 2010, http://londonminingnetwork.org/2010/01/manslaughter-charges-filed-in-vedanta-chimney-case/, Visited on: 16-06-2014

Rick Sarre, *Sentencing those convicted of industrial manslaughter,* National Judicial College of Australia, The Australian National University, http://njca.anu.edu.au/Professional%20Development/programs%20

by%20year/2010/Sentencing%202010/Papers/SARRE.pdf, Visited on: 29-06-2014

SabreTech charged with murder in ValuJet crash, 13 July 1999, http://www.cnn.com/US/9907/13/valujet.indictments.03/, Visited on: 17-06-2014

SC Dismisses CBI petition, Rejects Harsher Punishment for Bhopal Gas Tragedy Accused, The Times of India, 11th of May, 2011, http://archive.today/76k4, Visited on: 07-07-2014

South Korea indicts four crew members of ferry for manslaughter, The Times of India, 15 May 2014, http://timesofindia.indiatimes.com/world/rest-of-world/South-Korea-indicts-four-crew-members-of-ferry-for-manslaughter/articleshow/35142602.cms, Visited on: 14-06-2014

Stop Vedanta, The Killer Corporate; http://www.southasiasolidarity.org/2011/08/04/foil-vedanta-stop-the-killer-corporate/, Visited on: 18-05-2014

Suchandana Gupta, *Bhopal Gas Case Verdict: Justice Delayed, Denied*, The Times of India, 8th of June, 2010, http://timesofindia.indiatimes.com/india/Bhopal-gas-case-verdict-Justice-delayed-denied/articleshow/6021821.cms, Visited on: 06-07-2014

Sulfanilamide Disaster, http://www.fda.gov/aboutfda/whatwedo/history/productregulation/sulfanilamidedisaster/default.htm, visited on: 23-06-2014

Supreme Court Sore Over Delay in Bhopal Gas Tragedy Case, The Hindu, 8th of August, 2010, www.hindu.com/2010/08/08/stories/2010080859750400.htm, Visited on: 06-07-2014

Szu Ping Chan, *History of Corporate Manslaughter: Five Key Cases*, The Telegraph, 18 February 2011, http://www.telegraph.co.uk/finance/yourbusiness/8330905/History-of-corporate-manslaughter-five-key-cases.html, Visited on: 20-05-2014

The Ajkia Timfoldgyar Plant, *The BBC*, http://www.bbc.com/news/world-europe-11481740, Visited on: 03-06-2014

The B.P. Oil Spill, *The Guardian*, http://www.theguardian.com/environment/bp-oil-spill, Visited on: 02-06-2014

The Corporate Crime Reporter, http://www.corporatecrimereporter.com/top100.html, Visited on: 09-06-2014

The Corporate Manslaughter Act, New Bill in Indiana, 18 January 2006, http://www.unbossed.com/index.php?itemid=590, Visited on: 20-06-2014

The Environment Green Crimes, http://www.historylearningsite.co.uk/environmental_green_crimes.htm, Visited on: 05-06-2014

The Report of the Royal Commission on the Pike River Coal Mine Tragedy, Volume 1, http://pikeriver.royalcommission.govt.nz/vwluResources/Final-Report-Volume-One/$file/ReportVol1-whole.pdf, Visited on: 25-06-2014; Also see: The Report of the Royal Commission on the Pike River Coal Mine Tragedy, Volume 2, http://pikeriver.royalcommission.govt.nz/vwluResources/Final-Report-Vol2-Part1-only/$file/Report-Vol2-Part1-only.pdf, Visited on: 25-06-2014

The Statement of Joan Claybrook on "Firestone Tire Defect & Ford Explorer Rollovers", United States Senate Committee on Commerce, Science and Transportation, Washington D.C., 12 September 2000, http://www.citizen.org/autosafety/article_redirect.cfm?ID=5414, Visited on: 17-06-2014

Unilever: Corporate Crimes, Corporate Watch, http://www.corporatewatch.org.uk/content/unilever-corporate-crimes, Visited on: 09-07-2014

www.ingramcontent.com/pod-product-compliance
Lightning Source LLC
Chambersburg PA
CBHW032002170526
45157CB00002B/516

9781482846836